Information

A
**SCIENTIFIC
AMERICAN**
Book

Information

W. H. FREEMAN AND COMPANY
SAN FRANCISCO

The twelve chapters in this book originally
appeared as articles in the September 1966 issue
of *Scientific American.*

Library of Congress Catalogue Card Number
66-29386

International Standard Book Number O-7167-0966-X

Printed in the United States of America

9 8 7 6 5

Introduction

"They are called computers simply because computation is the only significant job that has so far been given to them." With these words, the physicist Louis N. Ridenour, writing in the September, 1952, issue of *Scientific American,* raised a question that deserves still closer consideration today. "The name has somewhat obscured the fact that they are capable of much greater generality. . . . To describe its potentialities the computer needs a new name. Perhaps as good a name as any is 'information machine.' "

In this book, a scant 15 years later, the information machine appears in all its portentous generality. The computer proper has become the "central processor," housed in an anonymous cabinet surrounded by cabinets full of the "peripheral" gear that gives access to the enormous capacity of its logic and memory circuits. Its cubic bulk has diminished over the years as its capacity has increased. The vacuum tube of the early 1950's has been replaced by solid-state triodes and diodes; these in turn are being replaced by "integrated circuits" which incorporate the elements necessary to a given logical operation into a single microscopic chip of semiconductor material, and even these are being replaced by "microelectronic networks" in which whole banks of integrated circuits are interconnected microelectronically and fused into a single tiny chip. The design and fabrication of the computer memory has followed the same trend toward evanescence. In its physical embodiment the computer is approaching thought itself.

Freed of the inertia of hardware, the authors of this book are concerned with the uses of information technology. They are members of the second generation of information scientists whose forte is "programming," and they are responsible for much of the work reported in these pages. Programming, as Christopher

Strachey shows in his chapter on that subject, deals with the question of "how to get a computer to do what you want." A major step in promoting this subjection of the machine to man was taken by Ivan E. Sutherland, author of the chapter on input-output technique. The computer's response to a casual inquiry may issue in the form of typewritten columns of numbers running down yards of print-out paper. But the computer may now also present the same information instantaneously in the form of a picture on a cathode-ray tube. Equipped with a "light pencil," the user may thereupon make instantaneous amendments to what the picture shows. The cathode-ray tube and the light pencil are, of course, remarkable artifacts of electronic technology. But it was Sutherland's program, called Sketchpad, that made this system work.

As long ago as 1959, Christopher Strachey saw how to capitalize on the enormous difference between the computing speeds of man and machine. He proposed that not one but many input-output systems be plugged into the high-capacity central processors then under development; these would give as many users access to the computer at the same time. In such a "time-sharing" system, the central processor responds sequentially to the demands of its users, but so rapidly that each has the sensation he has the machine to himself. Again it is the programming, by Strachey, R. M. Fano, F. J. Corbató and by others, that has made time-sharing a reality. By 1961 progress on this line had inspired John McCarthy's vision of the "public utility" information system interacting with computer consoles in home, schoolroom and office.

Within a few years many readers of this book will be programming and operating information systems routinely in facilitation of their work, study or entertainment. The ways in which people will find their individual capacities amplified are suggested by the chapters on the uses of the computer in science, technology, administration and education. At one and the same time—by time-sharing—the same system can serve as a microscope that inspects the structure of large molecules, a master tool and die maker, a working model of the economy and an insistent but understanding tutor. What use will the reader find for his information system?

The authors of this book are equally concerned with the anticipated impact of these developments upon human dignity and welfare. They have been exploring these issues as they have pushed forward the work that raises them. They conclude that there is nothing inherent in the computer—not even its efficiency —that commits social evolution in the direction of the brave new world. On the contrary, they find, the computer capacitates the individual to resist the conformist pressures set up by the preceding phases of the scientific-industrial revolution. They are even willing to conjure with a future in which man may find himself instructed by the presence in the world of intellectually superior beings.

The chapters in this book were first published as articles in the September, 1966, issue of *Scientific American*. This was the 17th in the series of single-topic issues published annually by the magazine. The editors herewith express appreciation to their colleagues at W. H. Freeman and Company, the textbook affiliate of *Scientific American*, for the journalistic enterprise that has made the contents of this issue so speedily available in book form.

September, 1966

THE EDITORS*

* BOARD OF EDITORS: Gerard Piel (Publisher), Dennis Flanagan (Editor), Francis Bello (Associate Editor), John Purcell, James T. Rogers, Armand Schwab, Jr., C. L. Stong, Joseph Wisnovsky, Jerome Snyder (Art Director), Samuel L. Howard (Assistant Art Director)

Contents

Plates

following page 116

JOHN MCCARTHY

Information

Presenting a study of its processing by computers.
The moral of this introductory chapter: computers,
far from robbing man of his individuality, enable
technology to adapt to human diversity.

The computer gives signs of becoming the contemporary counterpart of the steam engine that brought on the industrial revolution.
The computer is an information machine. Information is a com-
modity no less intangible than energy; if anything, it is more
pervasive in human affairs. The command of information made
possible by the computer should also make it possible to reverse
the trends toward mass-produced uniformity started by the industrial revolution. Taking advantage of this opportunity may
present the most urgent engineering, social and political questions of the next generation.

A computer, as hardware, consists of input and output devices,
arithmetic and control circuits and a memory. Equally essential
to the complete portrait is the program of instructions—the
"software"—that puts the system to work. The computer accepts
information from its environment through its input devices; it
combines this information, according to the rules of the program
stored in its memory, with information that is also stored in its
memory, and it sends information back to its environment through
its output devices.

The human brain also accepts inputs of information, combines it with information stored somehow within and returns outputs of information to its environment. Social institutions—such as the legislature, the law, science, education, business organizations and the communication system—receive, process and put out information in much the same way. Accordingly, in common with the computer, the human brain and social institutions may be regarded as information-processing systems, at least with respect to some crucial functions. The study of these entities as such has led to new understanding of their structures.

The installation of computers in certain organizations has already greatly increased the efficiency of some of the organizations. In the 15 or 20 years that computers have been in use, however, it has become clear that they do not merely bring an increase in efficiency. They induce basic transformation of the institutions and enterprises in which they are installed.

In the first place, computers are a million to a billion times faster than humans in performing computing operations. This follows from the fact that their working parts now change state in a few millionths or billionths of a second. Why should this quantitative change in speed produce a qualitative change in human activities that are facilitated by a computer? It might seem that there is no way to use such speeds outside of the missile business and other exotic undertakings. The answer is that the increase in speed has meant the building of computers with the capacity to handle information on a correspondingly larger scale. The interaction of high-speed, high-capacity computers with their environment is often continuous, with many input and output devices operating simultaneously with the ongoing internal computation.

The computer is, furthermore, a universal information-processing machine. Any calculation that can be done by any machine can be done by a computer, provided that the computer has a program describing the calculation. This was proved as a general proposition by the British mathematician A. M. Turing as early as 1936. It applies to the most rudimentary theoretical system as well as to the big general-purpose machines of today that make it possible, in practice, to write new programs instead of having to build new machines.

The speed, capacity and universality of computers make them

machines that can be used to foster diversity and individuality in our industrial civilization, as opposed to the uniformity and conformity that have hitherto been the order of the day. Decisions that now have to be made in the mass can in the future be made separately, case by case. To take a practical example, it can be decided whether or not it is safe for an automobile to go through an intersection each time the matter comes up, instead of subjecting the flow of automobiles to regulation by traffic lights. A piece of furniture, a household appliance or an automobile can be designed to the specifications of each user. The decision whether to go on to the next topic or review the last one can be made in accordance with the interests of the child rather than for the class as a whole. In other words, computers can make it possible for people to be treated as individuals in many situations where they are now lumped in the aggregate.

The quality of such individual response and attention is another matter. It will depend on the quality of the programs. The special attention of a stupid program may not be worth much. But then the individual can write his own program.

The future that is contemplated here has come into view quite abruptly during the past few years. According to a report published by the American Federation of Information Processing Societies (AFIPS), there were only 10 or 15 computers at work in the U.S. in 1950. Today there are 35,200, and by 1975 there will be 85,000. Investment in computers will rise from $8 billion to more than $30 billion by 1975. Present installations include 2,100 large systems costing about $1 million each; in 1975 there will be 4,000 of these. Even the medium and small systems that are in use today have a capacity equal to or exceeding that of the 1950 generation.

A scientific problem that took an hour on a big 1950 machine at 1,000 operations per second can be run on the fastest contemporary computers in less than half a second. Allowing another 3.5 seconds to transfer the yield to an external storage memory for later printing, it can be said that program running time has been reduced from an hour to three or four seconds. This reflects the impressive recent progress in the design and manufacture of computer hardware.

Big computers are currently equipped with internal memories

—the memory actively engaged in the computation under way—
that usually contain 10 or 12 million minute ring-shaped ferrite
"cores" in three-dimensional crystalline arrays. Each core is capable of storing one "bit," or unit, of information. Along with the
replacement of the vacuum tube by the transistor and now the
replacement of the transistor by the microelectronic circuit there
has come a steep increase in the speed of arithmetic and control
circuits over the past 10 years. The miniaturization of these
circuits (from hundreds of circuits per cubic foot with vacuum-
tube technology to hundreds of thousands and prospectively
millions of circuits per cubic foot with solid-state technology)
has speeded up operations by reducing the distance an impulse
has to travel from point to point inside the computer [see Plate 3].

As increases in speed and capacity have realized the inherent
universality of the computer, expenditures for programming have
been absorbing an increasing percentage of total installation
costs. The U.S. Government, with a dozen or so big systems serving its military and space establishments, is spending more than
half of its 1966 outlay of $844 million on software. Without doubt
the professions in this field—those of system analyst and programmer—are the fastest-growing occupations in the U.S. labor
force. From about 200,000 in 1966 it is estimated that their
numbers will increase to 500,000 or 750,000 by 1970. Courses in
programming are now offered in many universities and even in
some high schools. In a liberal education an exposure to programming is held to be as bracing as an elementary course in mathematics or logic.

Calculating devices have a history that goes back to the ancient
Greeks. The first mechanical digital calculators were made by
Blaise Pascal in the 17th century. In the mid-19th century Charles
Babbage proposed and partially constructed an automatic machine that would carry out long sequences of calculations without
human intervention. Babbage did not succeed in making his
machine actually work—although he might have, had he used
binary instead of decimal notation and enjoyed better financial
and technical support.

In the late 1930's Howard H. Aiken of Harvard University
and George R. Stibitz of the Bell Telephone Laboratories developed automatic calculators using relays; during World War

II, J. Presper Eckert and John W. Mauchly of the University of Pennsylvania developed ENIAC, an electronic calculator. As early as 1943 a British group had an electronic computer working on a war-time assignment.

Strictly speaking, however, the term "computer" now designates a universal machine capable of carrying out any arbitrary calculation, as propounded by Turing in 1936. The possibility of such a machine was apparently guessed by Babbage; his collaborator Lady Lovelace, daughter of the poet Lord Byron, may have been the first to propose a changeable program to be stored in the machine. Curiously, it does not seem that the work of either Turing or Babbage played any direct role in the labors of the men who made the computer a reality. The first practical proposal for universal computers that stored their programs in their memory came from Eckert and Mauchly during the war. Their proposal was developed by John von Neumann and his collaborators in a series of influential reports in 1945 and 1946. The first working stored-program computers were demonstrated in 1949 almost simultaneously in several laboratories in Britain and the U.S. The first commercial computer was the Eckert-Mauchly UNIVAC, put on the market in 1950.

Since that time progress in the electronic technology of computer circuits, the art of programming and programming languages and the development of computer operating systems has been rapid. No small part in this development has been played by the U.S. Government, which is always in the market for the latest and biggest systems available. It is not too much to say that the systems designed for the industry's biggest customer have been the prototypes for each major advance in computer hardware. The creation of the high-speed computer has been as central to the contemporary revolution in the technology of war as the intercontinental missile and the thermonuclear warhead.

The basic unit of information with which these machines work is the bit. Any device that can be in either of two states, such as a ferrite core or a transistor, can store a single bit. Two such devices can store two bits, three can store three bits, and so on. Consider a five-bit register made of five one-bit devices. Since each device has two states, represented, say, by 0 and 1, the five together have 2^5, or 32, states. The combinations from 00000 to

11111 can be taken to represent the binary numbers from 0 to 31. They can also be used to encode the 26 letters of the alphabet, with six combinations left over to represent word spaces and punctuation. This would permit representation of words and sentences by strings of five-bit groups. (Actually, to accommodate uppercase and lowercase letters, the full assortment of punctuation marks, the decimal digits and so on it is now customary to use seven bits.)

For many purposes, however, it is better not to be specific about how the information is coded into bits. More important is the task of describing the kinds of information to be dealt with, the basic operations to be carried out on them and the basic tests to be performed on the information in order to decide what to do next. For bits the basic operations are the logical operations $\cdot$, $+$ and $-$ (the last usually placed above a symbol, as $\bar{A}$), which are read "and," "or" and "not" respectively. Operations are defined by giving all the cases. Thus $\cdot$ is defined by the equations $0 \cdot 0 = 0$, $1 \cdot 0 = 0$, $0 \cdot 1 = 0$, and $1 \cdot 1 = 1$. The basic decision concerning a bit is whether it is 0 or 1. Designers of computers do much of their work at the level of bits. They have systematic procedures, as the following chapter by David C. Evans shows, for translating logical equations into transistor circuits that carry out the functions of these equations.

At the next level above bits come numbers. On numbers the basic operations are addition, subtraction, multiplication and division [see illustrations on pages 7 and 9 and on pages 20 and 21]. The basic tests are whether two numbers are equal and whether a number is greater than zero. Programmers are generally able to work with numbers because computer designers build the basic operations on numbers out of the logical operations on bits in the design of the circuits in the machine.

Another kind of information is a string of characters, such as A or ABA or ONION. It is well to include also the null string with no characters. A basic operation on characters may be taken to be concatenation, denoted by the symbol $*$. Thus ABC$*$ACA = ABCACA. The other basic operations are "first" and "rest." Thus first(ABC) = A and rest(ABC) = BC. The basic tests on strings are whether the string is null and whether two individual characters are equal.

LOGIC

	YES		NO	
	1		0	

NUMERATION

	YES		NO	
0	0		0	0
1	1		1	1
2	10		2	10
4	100		3	2 1 11
8	1000		4	100
16	10000		5	4 1 101
32	100000		6	4 2 110
64	1000000		7	4 2 1 111
128	10000000		8	1000
256	100000000		9	8 1 1001

SEVEN-BIT CODE

					COLUMNS							
	BITS		$b_7 b_6 b_5$		$0\ 0\ 0$	$0\ 0\ 1$	$0\ 1\ 0$	$0\ 1\ 1$	$1\ 0\ 0$	$1\ 0\ 1$	$1\ 1\ 0$	$1\ 1\ 1$
b_4	b_3	b_2	b_1		0	1	2	3	4	5	6	7
0	0	0	0	0	NUL	DLE	SP	0	\	P	@	;
0	0	0	1	1	SOH	DC1	!	1	A	Q	a	
0	0	1	0	2	STX	DC2	"	2	B	R	Ͱ	r
0	0	1	1	3	ETX	DC3	#	3	C	S	c	s
0	1	0	0	4	EOT	DC4	$	4	D	T	d	t
0	1	0	1	5	ENQ	NAK	%	5	E	U	e	u
0	1	1	0	6	ACK	SYN	&	6	F	V	f	v
0	1	1	1	7	BEL	ETB	'	7	G	W	g	w
1	0	0	0	8	BS	CAN	(	8	H	X	h	x
1	0	0	1	9	HT	EM	)	9	I	Y	i	y
1	0	1	0	10	LF	SS	*	:	J	Z	j	z
1	0	1	1	11	VT	ESC	+	;	K	Γ	k	{
1	1	0	0	12	FF	FS	,	<	L	~	l	⌐
1	1	0	1	13	CR	GS	−	=	M	]	m	}
1	1	1	0	14	SO	RS	.	>	N	∧	n	l
1	1	1	1	15	SI	US	/	?	O	−	o	DEL

Binary numbers serve computers in logic, arithmetic and coding functions. The array of binary numbers at top left under "Numeration" shows that the system, which is based on 2, represents each new power of 2 by adding a 0. The same arrangement reappears at top right in the binary version of the numbers 1 through 9; it shows, for example, that 111, representing 7, can be read from the left as "one 4, one 2 and one 1." The seven-bit code (bottom) is widely used to accomplish the printing done by computers in issuing results and communicating with operators. On receiving pulses representing 1011001, for example, the computer would print Y. Columns 0 and 1 contain control characters; BS, for example, means "back space," and is coded 0001000.

Out of one kind of information, then, more elaborate kinds of information can be built; numbers and characters are built out of bits, and strings are built out of characters. Similarly, the operations and tests for the higher forms of information are built up out of the operations and tests for the lower forms. One can represent a chessboard, for example, as a table of numbers giving for each square the kind of piece, if any, that occupies it. For chess positions a basic operation gives the list of legal moves from that position. A picture may be similarly represented by an array of numbers expressing the gray-scale value of each point in the picture. The *Mariner IV* pictures of Mars were so represented during transmission to the earth, and this representation was used in the memory of the computer by the program that removed noise and enhanced contrast. Christopher Strachey shows in this chapter how programmers put together the basic operations and tests for a given class of information in designing a program to treat such information [see "System Analysis and Programming," by Christopher Strachey, page 56].

What computers can do depends on the state of the art and science of the programming as well as on speed and memory capacity. At present it is straightforward to keep track of the seats available on each plane of an airline, to compute the trajectory of a space vehicle under the gravitational attraction of the sun and planets or to generate a circuit diagram from the specifications of circuit elements. It is difficult to predict the weather or to play a fair game of chess. It is currently not clear how to make a computer play an expert game of chess or discover significant mathematical theorems, although investigators have ideas about how these things might be done [see "Artificial Intelligence," by Marvin L. Minsky, page 193].

Input and output devices also play a significant part in making the capacity of a computer effective. For the engineering computations and the bookkeeping tasks first assigned to computers it seemed sufficient to provide them with punched-card-readers for input and line-printers for output, together with magnetic tapes for storing large quantities of data. To fly an airplane or a missile or to control a steel mill or a chemical plant, however, a computer must receive inputs from such sensory organs as radars, flowmeters and thermometers and must deliver its outputs

ADDITION

```
 1 11
  111            7
   11          + 3
 ----          ----
 1010           10
```

```
11   1
110101          53
 11001        + 25
-------        ----
1001110         78
64  8 4 2
```

SUBTRACTION

```
 11
1101            13
 111          - 7
----          ----
 110             6
```

```
11
110101          53
 11001        - 25
------        ----
 11100          28
16 8 4
```

MULTIPLICATION

```
1001             9
 101           × 5
----          ----
1001
1001
------
101101          45
32 8 4  1
```

DIVISION

$$11000 \div 110 \qquad 24 \div 6$$

```
         100
110) 11000          4
```

Binary arithmetic involves only the manipulation of 0 and 1 and hence is the basis of the extremely rapid calculating done by computers. The small superscript numerals represent carries; small subscript numerals show how binary numbers are read decimally.

directly to such effector organs as motors and radio transmitters. Still other input and output devices are demanded by the increasing speed and capacity of the computers themselves. To keep them fully employed they must be allowed to interact simultaneously with large numbers of people, most of them necessarily at remote stations. This requires telephone lines, teletypewriters and cathode-ray-tube devices. For many purposes a picture on the cathode ray tube is more useful than the half-ton of print-out paper that would deliver the underlying numerical information. Simultaneous access to the computer for many users also calls for new sophistication in programming to establish the time-sharing arrangements described in the article by R. M. Fano and F. J. Corbató [see "Time-sharing on Computers," by R. M. Fano and F. J. Corbató, page 76].

It is possible to describe at greater length the perfection and promise of the new technology of information. This discussion must go on to certain pressing questions. To put the questions negatively: Will the computer condemn us to live in an increasingly depersonalized and bureaucratized society? Will the crucial decisions of life turn on a hole punched in Column 17 of a card? Will "automation" put most of us out of work?

Experience with the computerized systems most people have so far encountered in governmental, business and educational institutions has not tended to dispel the anxiety that underlies such questions. One can ascribe the bureaucratic ways of these systems to their computers or to the greed, stupidity and other vices of the people who run them. I would argue three more direct causes: one economic, one technical and one cultural.

In the first place, computers are expensive. When a computer is first installed in an organization, the impulse of the authorities is to use the new machine to cut corners, to do the old job in the old way but more cheaply, to achieve internal economies even at the expense of external relations with citizens, customers and students. Secondly, the external memories that store the data for most large organizations are inherently inflexible. Between runs through a magnetic-tape file, for example, there is no possibility of access to the account that generates today's complaint. Finally, most practitioners in the expanding software professions were beginners; it was all they could do to get the systems going at all.

In my opinion the opportunity to cure these faults is improving steadily. Computers are cheaper, and competition between systems should soon compel more attention to the customers. (The effect is not yet noticeable at my bank.) Secondly, high-speed memory devices such as magnetic-disk files, now used as internal memories, are taking up service in external data-storage. They make access to any record possible at any time. Finally, although there are a lot of young fogies who know how things are done now and expect to see them done that way until they retire in 1996, programmers are acquiring greater confidence and virtuosity.

All of this should encourage the development of systems that serve the customer better without offending either his intelligence or his convenience. In particular, organizations such as schools should not have to ask people questions the answers to which are already on file.

The computer will not make its revolutionary impact, however, by doing the old bookkeeping tasks more efficiently. It is finding its way into new applications that will increase human freedom of action. No stretching of the demonstrated technology is required to envision computer consoles installed in every home and connected to public-utility computers through the telephone system. The console might consist of a typewriter keyboard and a television screen that can display text and pictures. Each subscriber will have his private file space in the computer that he can consult and alter at any time. Given the availability of such equipment, it is impossible to recite more than a small fraction of the uses to which enterprising consumers will put it. I undertake here only to sample the range of possibilities.

Everyone will have better access to the Library of Congress than the librarian himself now has. Any page will be immediately accessible, although Ben-Ami Lipetz holds that this may come later rather than sooner [see "Information Storage and Retrieval," by Ben-Ami Lipetz, page 175]. Because payment will depend on usage, all levels and kinds of taste can be provided for.

The system will serve as each person's external memory, with his messages in and out kept nicely filed and reminders displayed at designated times.

Full reports on current events, whether baseball scores, the smog index in Los Angeles or the minutes of the 178th meeting of the Korean Truce Commission, will be available for the asking.

Income tax returns will be automatically prepared on the basis of continuous, cumulative annual records of income, deductions, contributions and expenses.

With the requisite sensors and effectors installed in the household the public-utility information system will shut the windows when it rains.

The reader can write his own list of assignments. He can do so with the assurance that various entrepreneurs will try to think up new services and will advertise them. In this connection the Antitrust Division of the Department of Justice should see to it that companies set up to operate the computers are kept separate from companies that provide programs. Competition among the programmers will intensify and diversify demand on the public-utility systems. Anyone who has a new program he thinks he can sell should be free to put it in any computer in which he is willing to rent file space and to sell its services to anyone who wants to use it.

As for the conformities currently imposed by mass production, consider how the computer might facilitate the purchase of some piece of household equipment. In the first place, the computer could be asked to search the catalogues and list the alternatives available, together with appraisals from such institutions as Consumers Union. If the consumer knows how to use an automatic design system such as that described by Steven Anson Coons [see "The Uses of Computers in Technology," by Steven Anson Coons, page 131], he might design the desired equipment himself. The system will deliver not only drawings but also the findings of a simulation study that will show how well the equipment works. The consumer could also consult a designer, who will be able to render his service through the computer at less cost, together with firm estimates from prospective suppliers. With more or less elaboration, the procedures sketched here could do the paper work for the building of an entire house.

Apart from the physical construction of the public-utility information system, the full realization of these possibilities will require new advances in programming. No application illustrates the virtues and limitations of present-day programming so well as do efforts to use computers to aid teaching in elementary and secondary schools. In principle, one computer can give simultaneous individual attention to hundreds of students, each at his own console, each at a different place in the course or each concentrating on a different topic. The treatment of the student can be quite individual because the computer can remember the student's performance in every preceding session of instruction. The pace and the range of study can be entirely determined by the student's progress.

The teaching programs that have been written so far, however, put the student in a passive role. They are extremely pedantic. They have no understanding of the student's state of mind; they decide what to do next only in accordance with rather stereotyped sets of rules. As Patrick Suppes concludes, these programs do not compare too unfavorably with the performance of a teacher who has a large class [see "The Uses of Computers in Education," by Patrick Suppes, page 157]. Particularly where practice and repetition are the dominant ways of learning, the computer may even prove superior. The present programs fail in subjects that ought to cultivate the student's capacity for generating new ideas.

For the future it would be well, perhaps, to think of computers as study aids rather than teachers. The aim of the program should be to place the system under the control of the learner. He should be able to select from a list of topics the one he wants to work on; he should decide whether he prefers to read an exposition or to try to solve a problem. Best of all, he should be able to use the computer as a tool for testing his own ideas.

Reflection on the power of computer systems inevitably excites fear for the safety and integrity of the individual. In many minds the computer is the ultimate threat. It makes possible, for instance, a single national information file containing all tax, legal, security, credit, educational, medical and employment information about each and every citizen. Certainly such a file would be the source of great abuses. The files that exist today are abused. Security files, for example, have provided material for politically motivated persecutions. Credit files, to which access is wide open in the business community, have been used for purposes irrelevant to credit decisions. Accordingly it can be expected that more centralized files will facilitate even greater abuses.

On the other hand, citizens could seize the creation of centralized files as the occasion to cure existing abuses and to establish for each individual certain rights with respect to these files. Such a "bill of rights" might specify the following:

No organization, governmental or private, is allowed to maintain files that cover large numbers of people outside of the general system.

The rules governing access to the files are definite and well publicized, and the programs that enforce these rules are open to any interested party, including, for example, the American Civil Liberties Union.

An individual has the right to read his own file, to challenge certain kinds of entries in his file and to impose certain restrictions on access to his file.

Every time someone consults an individual's file this event is recorded, together with the authorization for the access.

If an organization or an individual obtains access to certain information in a file by deceit, this is a crime and a civil wrong. The injured individual may sue for invasion of privacy and be awarded damages.

At present an organization that claims to be considering extending credit to a person can learn a lot about his financial condition. In the new system no such information will be available without authorization from the person concerned. The normal form of authorization will allow no more than a yes-or-no answer to the question of whether he meets a particular definite credit criterion—whether he meets credit condition $C1$, for example, and can be expected to manage the installment purchase of a television set.

To establish such rights people must revise their ideas about the source and nature of their freedom. Most individual rights now recognized are based on the claim that the individual always had them; the safeguards of the law are said to be designed to prevent their infringement. Technology is advancing too fast, however, to allow such benevolent frauds to work in the future.

The right to keep people from keeping files on us must first be invented, then legislated and actively enforced.

It may be supposed that, as happened with television and then color television, the enthusiasts and the well-to-do will be the first to install computer consoles in their homes. Eventually, however, everyone will consider them to be essential household equipment. People will soon become discontented with the "canned" programs available; they will want to write their own. The ability to write a computer program will become as widespread as the ability to drive a car.

Not knowing how to program will be like living in a house full of servants and not speaking their language. Each of the canned programs will be separately useful. It will be up to the individual, however, to coordinate them for his own fullest benefit. People will find, in fact, that console control of a process leads directly to the writing of one's own programs.

At first the computer says in effect: I can do the following things for you, which do you want? You reply. Then it says: In order to do this I need the following information. You respond and the dialogue continues. After you get used to using a particular facility, the computer's questions become annoying. You know in advance what they will be and you want to give the answers without waiting for the questions. Next you want to be able to give the entire sequence of actions a name and bring forth the sequence by typing only the name. As you become bolder you will want to make a later action conditional on the results of earlier actions and to provide for the repetition of actions until a criterion is reached. You are then already programming in full generality, albeit awkwardly.

As a skill, computer programming is probably more difficult than driving a car but probably less difficult than flying an airplane. It is more difficult than arithmetic but less difficult than writing good English. It does not require long study. Many people can write simple programs after an hour or two of instruction. Some success ordinarily comes quickly, and this reward reinforces further effort. Programming is far easier to learn than a foreign language or algebra.

Success in writing a program to do a particular task depends more on understanding the task and less on mastery of programming technique. To program the trajectory of a rocket, for example, requires a few weeks' study of programming and a few years' study of physics.

Writing a program to carry out some activity requires that an individual make explicit what he wants. The public-utility computer will do exactly what it is told to do within limitations imposed to protect other people's interests. A person who has experienced the unexpected and sometimes unpleasant consequences of the faithful execution of his wishes is usually ready to reexamine his preferences and premises. Fortunately programs can be readily changed. As people acquire greater control over their environment by explicit programming they will discover greater self-understanding and self-reliance. Some people will enjoy this experience more than others.

DAVID C. EVANS

Computer Logic and Memory

A large modern computer can contain nearly half a
million switching elements and 10 million high-speed
memory elements. They operate with the simplest
of all logics: the binary logic based on 0 and 1.

Electronic digital computers are made of two basic kinds of
components: logic elements (often called switching elements)
and memory elements. In virtually all modern computers these
elements are binary, that is, the logic elements have two alternative pathways and the memory elements have two states. Accordingly all the information handled by such computers is coded
in binary form. In short, the information is represented by binary
symbols, stored in sets of binary memory elements and processed
by binary switching elements.

To make a digital computer it is necessary to have memory
elements and a set of logic elements that is functionally complete.
A set of logic elements is functionally complete if a logic circuit
capable of performing any arbitrary logical function can be
synthesized from elements of the set. Let us examine one such
functionally complete set that contains three distinct types of
circuit designated *and, or* and *not*. Such circuits can be depicted
with input signals at the left and output signals at the right
[see illustrations on pages 20 and 21].

Since the logic elements are binary, each input and output is
a binary variable that can have the value 0 or 1. In an electrical

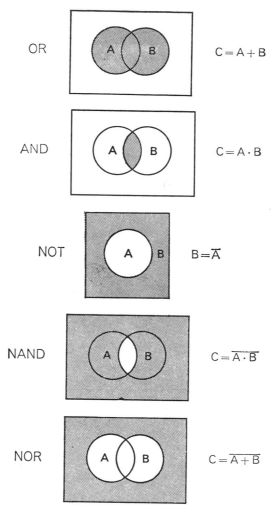

Venn diagrams use circles to symbolize various logic concepts and relations. Circles represent statements that can be either true or false; they are placed in a universe, or field, that represents all other statements. The logical relation and is represented by the shaded area where two circles overlap. This area, C, is "true" only if both circles, A and B, are true; it is "false" if either A or B or both are false. The logical relation or (the "inclusive or") is represented by shading the entire area within both circles. This area, C, is true when either A or B or both are true. Not is represented by a circle, A, surrounded by a universe, B, which is not A. The equations at right are Boolean statements. The dot in the and statement stands for "and." The plus sign in the or statement stands for "or." The Ā in the not statement signifies "not A." Nand and nor stand respectively for "not and" and "not or," as is made clear in the shading of their Venn diagrams. Such diagrams are named for John Venn, a 19th-century English logician.

circuit the logical value 0 corresponds to a particular voltage or current and the logical value 1 to another voltage or current. For each symbolic circuit one can construct a "truth table," in which are listed all possible input states and the corresponding output states. Each truth table, in turn, can be represented by a Boolean statement (named for the 19th-century logician George Boole) that expresses the output of the circuit as a function of the input. In the case of the *and* circuit the output variable C has the value 1 if, and only if, the input variables A and B both have the value 1. In the Boolean statement the operation *and* is designated by the dot; it reads "C is equal to A *and* B." In the *or* circuit C has the value 1 if at least one of the input variables has the value 1. The Boolean statement is read "C is equal to A *or* B." The *not* circuit has for its output the logical complement of the input. Its Boolean statement is read "B is equal to *not* A." The *and* and *or* circuits described have only two input variables. Circuits that have a larger number of input variables are normally used.

There are a number of other functionally complete sets of logic elements. Two sets are particularly interesting because each contains only one element, in one case called *nand* (meaning "not and") and in the other case called *nor* (meaning "not or"). A two-input *nand* circuit, together with its truth table, is shown in the upper illustration on page 21.

Although a practical *nand* circuit is designed as an entity, it is evident that it can be realized by an *and* and a *not* circuit. The reader can easily devise *and, or* and *not* circuits from *nand* circuits to demonstrate to himself that the *nand* circuit is also functionally complete.

With *and* and *not* circuits it is not difficult to construct a decoding circuit that will translate binary digits into decimal digits. Such a circuit and its truth table are shown in the illustration on page 25.

The decimal digits are each represented by a four-digit binary code (A_0, A_1, A_2, A_3). In the decoding circuit, which yields the first four decimal digits, the input signals A_0, A_1, A_2, A_3 are applied. The signal at each of the numbered outputs is 0 unless the input code is the code for one of the numbered outputs, in which case the signal at that output is 1.

The circuits that store information in a computer can be

divided into two classes: registers and memory circuits. Registers are combined with logic circuits to build up the arithmetic, control and other information-processing parts of the computer. The information stored in registers represents the instantaneous state of the processing part of the computing system. The term "memory" is commonly reserved for those parts of a computer that make possible the general storage of information, such as the instructions of a program, the information fed into the program and the results of computations. Memory devices for such storage purposes will be discussed later in this chapter.

Registers are usually made up of one-bit storage circuits called flip-flops. A typical flip-flop circuit, called a set-reset flip-flop, has four terminals [see illustration on page 27].

It is convenient to refer to such a flip-flop by giving it the name of the variable it happens to store; thus a flip-flop for storing the variable A will be named A. If the inputs to the terminals S and R are 0, the flip-flop will be in one of two states. If A has the value 1, it is in the set state; if it has the value 0, it is in the reset state. It can be switched to the set state by applying a 1 signal to the S terminal and switched to the reset state by applying a 1 to the R terminal. The application of 1's to the S and R terminals at the same time will not yield a predictable result. The flip-flop can therefore be regarded as remembering the most recent input state.

Memories for general storage could be made up of logic circuits and flip-flops, but for practical reasons this is not done. A memory so constructed would be large and expensive and would require much power; moreover, the stored information would be lost if the power were turned off.

We are now ready to consider how logic circuits and registers can be combined to perform elementary arithmetical operations. A circuit for one-digit binary addition, together with its truth table, is shown in the illustration on page 29.

The inputs to the adder are the binary digits X and Y, together with the "input carry" C_{i-1}. The outputs are the sum digit S and the "carry out" C_i. Also illustrated is an implementation of the binary adder using *and, or* and *not* logic elements. A logic circuit such as this binary adder, which contains only switching elements and no storage circuits, is called a combinatorial circuit.

NAND

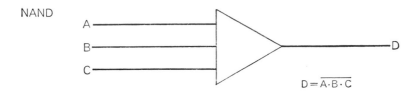

$$D = \overline{A \cdot B \cdot C}$$

NAND CIRCUIT

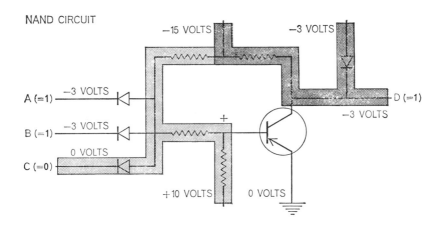

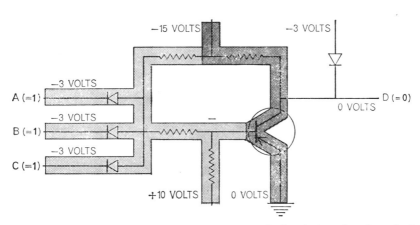

Electronic embodiment of nand *circuit contains four diodes (triangular shapes), four resistors (zigzags) and one transistor (inside circle). The symbol for this three-input* nand *circuit and its Boolean statement appear at the top. In the circuit the dark shading represents the flow of large current that is switched to produce the output, 0 or 1, depending on the flow of small current (light shading), which is controlled by the input voltages. Current flow is shown for two different inputs: 1, 1, 0 and 1, 1, 1. By reversing the choice of voltage the* nand *circuit shown here acts as a* nor *circuit. Such circuits can be designed in many ways.*

In a computer employing binary arithmetic the arithmetic unit may have to process numbers consisting of 60 or more digits in order to produce results with the desired precision. (A computer able to handle 60-digit numbers is said to have 60 bits of precision.) Numbers of such length can be added in two general ways. One way is to use an adder for each digit; the other is to use a single "serial" adder and process the digits sequentially. When an adder is used for each digit, the assembly is called a parallel adder. A four-digit parallel adder is shown in the illustration on page 31.

The inputs for this adder are two four-digit binary numbers: $X_3 X_2 X_1 X_0$ and $Y_3 Y_2 Y_1 Y_0$. The adder produces the five binary-digit sum $S_4 S_3 S_2 S_1 S_0$. This four-digit adder is also a combinatorial circuit. The X and Y inputs to the parallel adder can be provided by two four-bit registers of four flip-flops each. The inputs are all provided at the same time. The sum can be stored in a five-bit register that has previously had all its stages reset to 0.

For the serial adder we need a means of delivering the digits of the inputs to the adder in sequence and of storing the sum digits in sequence. To implement these requirements special registers that have the ability to shift information from one stage to the next are employed; such a register is called a shift register. Each of the three shift registers of a serial binary adder has an input from the terminal called SHIFT [see illustration on page 32].

Normally the SHIFT signal has the value 0, but when it is desired to shift the three registers, the SHIFT signal is given the value 1 for a brief period, causing the registers to shift their contents one bit to the right. As in the case of the parallel adder, the serial adder can add one group of binary digits (such as $X_3 X_2 X_1 X_0$) to another group (such as $Y_3 Y_2 Y_1 Y_0$). At the first command to shift, the serial adder stores the sum of the first pair of digits (X_0 and Y_0); at the second command to shift, it stores the sum of the second pair of digits (X_1 and Y_1), and so on. The carry-out (C_i) of each addition is passed along at each command to shift.

Registers are needed for both serial and parallel adders. For the serial adder the registers must be shift registers and only a

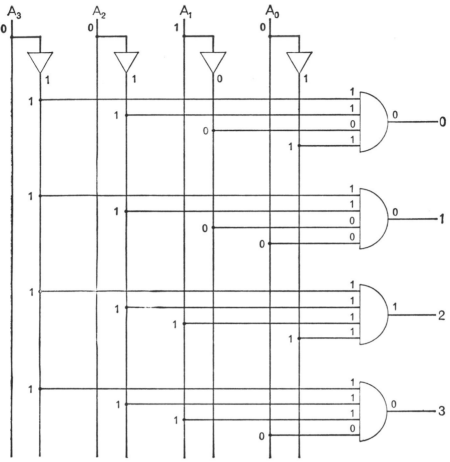

DECIMAL		BINARY		
	A_3	A_2	A_1	A_0
0	0	0	0	0
1	0	0	0	1
o 2	0	0	1	0
3	0	0	1	1
4	0	1	0	0
5	0	1	0	1
6	0	1	1	0
7	0	1	1	1
8	1	0	0	0
9	1	0	0	1

Conversion of binary to decimal digits is accomplished by this circuit, made up of four not circuits and four and circuits. The truth table at left shows the binary equivalent for the decimal digits from 0 to 9. To show the principle involved in decoding binary digits, the circuit carries the decoding only as far as decimal digit 3. The signal at each of the numbered outputs is 0 unless all the inputs are 1. In the example this is true for the third and circuit from the top, labeled 2. Thus the binary digits 0010 are decoded to yield the decimal digit 2.

one-digit binary adder is required. For the parallel adder a binary adder is required for each bit of precision, that is, for each pair of X and Y inputs. The parallel adder is simply a large combinatorial circuit. The serial adder includes the binary adder, a flip-flop (known in this case as the C flip-flop) and associated circuitry. It is not a combinatorial circuit because its output (S) is not merely a function of the immediate inputs (X and Y); it is also a function of the internal state as represented by the value stored in the C flip-flop. Circuits in which the output is not only a function of the immediate inputs but also a function of the circuit's history as represented by its internal state are called sequential circuits. Such circuits are fundamental to the design of computers. Multiplication, for example, is usually implemented by a sequential circuit that repetitively uses an adder circuit.

For most of the period during which computers have evolved, the limiting factor in their design and cost has been memory. The speed of computers has been restricted by the time required to store and retrieve information. The cost of computers has been determined by the information-storage capacity of the memory. As a result much effort has been devoted to the development and improvement of memory devices.

A typical memory, which I have previously described as an array of registers of uniform size, is characterized by word length, storage capacity and access time. Each register in a memory is called a word; its size is expressed in bits and typically is in the range of 12 to 72 bits. The total storage capacity of a memory can be expressed in bits but is more often expressed in words; depending on various factors, which will be examined below, the storage capacity can vary from 100 words to billions of words. The time required to store (write) or retrieve (read) a specified word of information is called the access time; it can range from a fraction of a microsecond to several seconds or minutes.

Access to a particular word in a memory is achieved by means of an addressing scheme. There are two classes of addressing schemes: "structure-addressing" and "content-addressing." In the first, which is the more common, each word is given a number by which it is identified; this number is called its address. Access to a particular word of a memory is achieved by specifying the

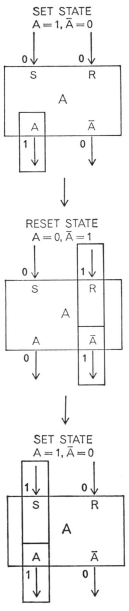

Typical one-bit storage element is represented by a "set-reset flip-flop." The one shown here is given the name A because it stores the variable A. A flip-flop "remembers" the most recent input state. If A has the value 1, it is in the set state; if A has the value 0, it is in the reset state. Applying a 1 to the S terminal yields the set state; applying a 1 to the R terminal yields the reset state. Flip-flops act as transient memories in computers.

address as a binary-coded number. In content-addressing, access is determined by the content of the word being sought. For example, each word of a content-addressed memory might contain a person's name and certain information about him (such as his bank balance or his airline reservation); access to that information would be achieved by presenting the person's name to the memory. The internal logic of the memory would locate the word containing the specified name and deliver the name and the associated information as an output. Since most memories are structurally addressed, no further consideration will be given to content-addressing.

Among the various memory designs there is a wide range of compromises among cost, capacity and access time. Most memories fall into one of three access categories: random, periodic or sequential. In random-access memories the access time is independent of the sequence in which words are entered or extracted. Memories with short random-access times are the most desirable but also the most costly per bit of storage capacity. Magnetic-core devices are the most widely used random-access memories. An example of a memory device that provides periodic access is the magnetic drum, in which information is recorded on the circumference of a cylinder that rotates at a constant rate. Sequentially located words may be read at a high rate as they pass the sensing position. The maximum access time is one revolution of the drum, and the average access time to randomly selected words is half a drum revolution. The most common sequential memories—used when neither random nor periodic access is required—are provided by reels of magnetic tape. To run a typical 2,400-foot reel of tape containing 50 million bits of information past a reading head can take several minutes [see illustration on page 33].

Since magnetic materials, in one form or another, supply the principal storage medium in computers, I shall describe magnetic memories somewhat more fully. The high-speed random-access memory in a typical computer is generally provided by a three-dimensional array of about a million tiny magnetic cores, or rings, each of which can store one bit of information. The cores are threaded on a network of fine wires that provide the means for changing the magnetic polarity of the cores; the polarity

C_{i-1}	X	Y	C_i	S
0	0	0	0	0
0	0	1	0	1
0	1	0	0	1
0	1	1	1	0
1	0	0	0	1
1	0	1	1	0
1	1	0	1	0
1	1	1	1	1

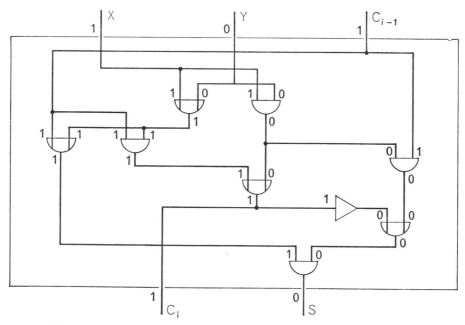

Binary adder circuit (bottom) can add two one-digit binary numbers. It is made up of *and, or* and *not logic elements. Because the adder will usually be one of several linked in parallel* (see illustration on page 31), *it must also be able to accept a digit known as the input carry* (C_{i-1}) *produced by an adder immediately to its right. The truth table* (top) *shows the "carry-out"* (C_i) *and the sum digit* (S) *for all combinations of three inputs. In the example the inputs are 1, 0 and 1. This is a combinatorial circuit.*

determines whether a particular core stores a 1 or a 0 [see illustration on page 36].

The cores are made of ferrite, a ferromagnetic ceramic. Highly
automatic methods have been devised for forming, firing, testing
and assembling the cores into memory arrrays. In early magnetic-
core memories the cores had an outside diameter of about a
twelfth of an inch and cost about $1 per bit of storage capacity.
The cycle time of these memories (the minimum time from the
beginning of one access cycle to the beginning of the next) was
in the range of 10 to 20 microseconds.

As the art has developed, the size of the cores has decreased,
the cycle time has decreased and the maximum capacity has increased. The cores in most contemporary computers have a
diameter of a twentieth of an inch; cycle times are between .75
microsecond and two microseconds. The fastest core memories
have cores less than a fiftieth of an inch in diameter and cycle
times of less than 500 nanoseconds (half a microsecond).

The essential requirement of a material for a random-access
magnetic memory is a particular magnetic characteristic that
allows a single element of a large array of elements of the material
to be stably magnetized in either of two directions. Early in the
1950's it was discovered that certain thin metallic films also have
this characteristic [see illustration on page 37]. The constant
dream of computer designers since this discovery was made has
been the development of a practical large-capacity memory that
can be constructed directly from bulk materials without fabrication, test or assembly of discrete components for individual bits.
Many geometries for thin-film memories, including flat films and
films deposited on wires or glass rods, have been devised. Some
film memories are in service and many more will be used in the
future. It is anticipated that there will be dramatic reductions in
the cost of random-access memories over the next few years.

In another widely used memory technology a thin film of
magnetic material is deposited on some surface such as a plastic
tape or card, or a metallic drum or disk. This magnetic surface
is moved with respect to a head that can produce or detect
patterns of magnetization in the magnetic film; the patterns are
of course coded to represent the binary digits 1 and 0. The film for
magnetic recording usually consists of finely ground iron oxides

DECIMAL 4

X_3	X_2	X_1	X_0
0	1	0	0

DECIMAL 11

Y_3	Y_2	Y_1	Y_0
1	0	1	1

DECIMAL 15

S_3	S_2	S_1	S_0
1	1	1	1

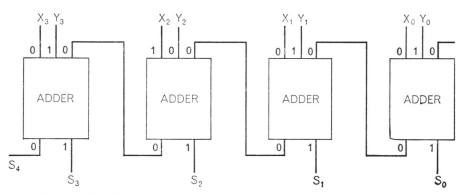

Four-digit parallel adder consists of four one-digit binary adders like the one shown on page 29. In a computer, registers (not shown) would be needed to supply the input signals and to store the output signals. In the example illustrated here the binary number 0100 (decimal 4) is being added to 1011 (decimal 11). The sum is the binary number 1111 (decimal 15).

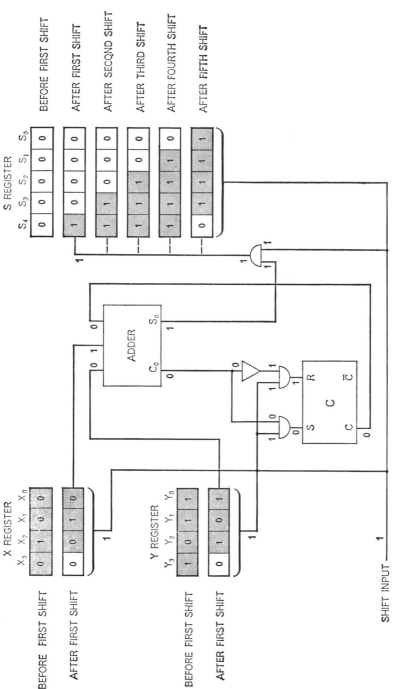

Four-digit serial adder uses only one adder like the one shown on page 29 but requires three shift registers and a flip-flop to pass along the carry-out of each addition. Each register has an input from the terminal called SHIFT. At the shift signal each register shifts its contents one bit to the right. Simultaneously the digits shifted out of the X and Y registers enter the adder, together with the input-carry from the C flip-flop. Five shift signals are needed to add two four-digit binary numbers.

TYPE OF MEMORY	RANDOM ACCESS TIME (MICROSECONDS)	INFORMATION TRANSFER RATE (BITS PER SECOND)	CAPACITY (BITS)	COST (DOLLARS PER BIT)
INTEGRATED CIRCUIT	$10^{-2}-10^{-1}$	10^9-10^{10}	10^3-10^4	10
TYPICAL CORE OR FILM	1	10^8	10^6	10^{-1}
LARGE SLOW CORE	10	10^7	10^7	10^{-2}
MAGNETIC DRUM	10^4	10^7	10^7	10^{-3}
TAPE LOOP OR CARD	10^6	10^6	10^9	10^{-4}
PHOTOGRAPHIC	10^7	10^6	10^{12}	10^{-6}

Comparison of memory systems shows a range of roughly a billion to one in access time and capacity and about 10 million to one in cost per bit. The spread in the rate of information transfer is smaller: about 10,000 to one from the fastest memories to the slowest. Integrated circuit memories (similar to logic circuits) and photo memories (for digital storage) are just appearing.

bonded together and to the surface by a small amount of organic binder. For magnetic drums and disks the magnetic medium often consists of a metallic film of a nickel-cobalt alloy.

Magnetic tape about a thousandth of an inch thick, half an inch wide and up to 2,400 feet long per reel has provided the main bulk information store for many years. Tape systems have reached a high state of development: they are able to transport the tape past the head at a rate of more than 100 inches per second and to start or stop the tape in a few milliseconds. Six or eight bits are usually written across the width of the tape; it is common for 800 of these six-bit or eight-bit groups to be written per inch along the tape. A current trend in information-processing systems is toward using tape for dead storage or for transporting data from one location to another. Magnetic recording devices with shorter random-access times are taking over the function of active file storage.

Storage devices with a capacity of a few hundred million words and an access time of a few seconds or less are just beginning to be delivered. These devices employ a number of magnetic cards or tape loops handled by various ingenious mechanisms.

In memory systems that use magnetic drums and disks rotating at high speed, the heads for reading and writing information are spaced a fraction of a thousandth of an inch from the surface. The surface velocity is about 1,000 or 2,000 inches per second. In early drum systems severe mechanical and thermal problems were encountered in maintaining the spacing between the heads and the recording surface. In recent years a spectacular improvement in performance and reliability has been achieved by the use of flying heads, which maintain their spacing from the magnetic surface by "flying" on the boundary layer of air that rotates with the surface of the drum or disk. One modern drum memory has a capacity of 262,000 words and rotates at 7,200 revolutions per minute; it has a random-access time of about four milliseconds and an information-transfer rate of 11.2 million bits per second.

Magnetic information storage is meeting competition from other memory technologies in two areas: where fairly small stores of information must be accessible in the shortest possible time and where ultralarge stores must be accessible in a matter of seconds. For the first task, which today is usually performed by magnetic cores and thin films, one can now obtain memories fabricated by the same techniques used to produce monolithic integrated circuits. Such circuits, resembling flip-flops, can be built up from tiny transistors and resistors; scores of such elements can be packed into an area no more than a tenth of an inch square. A memory of this kind can store 100 words and have a random-access time of 100 nanoseconds. Although the present cost of such memories is a few dollars per bit, the cost will probably decline to a few cents per bit by 1970. Integrated-circuit memories have the drawback that power is continuously dissipated by each element (unlike magnetic elements) whether it is actively being read (or altered) or not.

For very-high-volume storage and moderately fast access time, magnetic devices are being challenged by high-resolution photography. In these systems bits are recorded as densely packed dots on transparent cards or short strips of photographic film. During the next year or so several such systems will go into service; each will have a capacity of 10^{11} or 10^{12} bits and a maximum access time of a few seconds.

To combine rapid average access time and large storage capacity at a minimum cost to the user, computer designers have recently introduced the concept of the "virtual memory." Such a memory simulates a single large, fast random-access memory by providing a hierarchy of memories with a control mechanism that moves information up and down in the hierarchy, using a strategy designed to minimize average access time.

The logic and main memory of a very large modern computer contains nearly half a million transistors and a somewhat larger number of resistors and other electrical components, in addition to 10 million magnetic cores. In such a machine—or even in a smaller one with a tenth or a hundredth of this number of components—the matters of packaging, interconnection and reliability present very serious design problems.

The active circuit elements in early electronic computers were vacuum tubes. These computers encountered three major problems. First, the rate at which tubes failed was so high that in large computers the ratio of nonproductive time was nearly prohibitive. Second, power consumed by vacuum tubes was so large that adequate cooling was extremely difficult to achieve. Third,

1 STORE

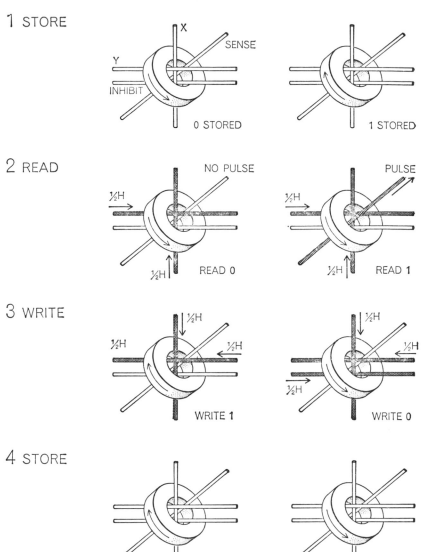

2 READ

3 WRITE

4 STORE

Operation of magnetic-core memory involves switching the direction of magnetization, or polarity, of a ferrite core between two positions 180 degrees apart. One position is selected to represent 0, the other to represent 1. "Reading" and "writing" signals are carried on two wires (X and Y), each of which carries only half of the current ($\frac{1}{2}$H) needed to change the core's direction of polarization. During the reading cycle the direction of current flow is selected so that the pulses reverse the polarity of a core that is storing a 1, with the result that a voltage pulse signifying 1 is created in the "sense" wire. No pulse emanates from a core that is storing a 0. During the writing cycle the flow in the X and Y wires is reversed. This reverses the polarity of the core and writes 1 unless an opposing current is coincidentally passed through an "inhibit" wire, in which case the core polarity remains in the 0 position. Typical memories have a million cores.

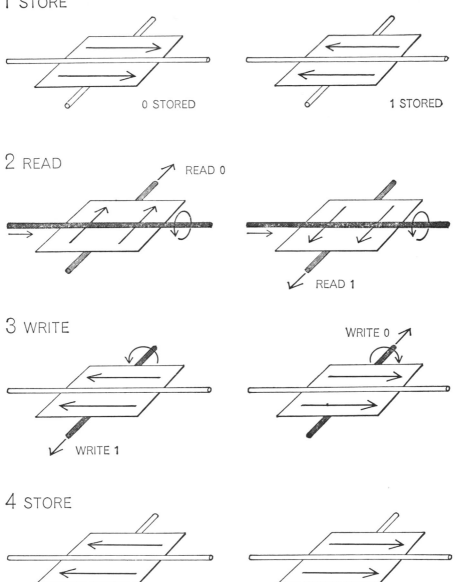

Operation of thin-film memory differs from that of a magnetic-core memory, illustrated on the facing page. One difference is that the read-out for a 0 or 1 is determined by the polarity of the voltage pulse in the sense wire rather than by the presence or absence of a voltage. Also, in the thin-film memory reading and writing are performed by passing current through different wires. Finally, the change in direction of magnetization that induces a read-out pulse involves a rotation of only 90 degrees rather than 180 degrees.

the components were so large that the distances over which signals had to travel would have limited computer speeds to levels that today would be regarded as slow.

In 1948 the point-contact transistor was invented. It was small and used little power, but it was too unstable a device to replace the vacuum tube in large-scale computers. A few years later the junction transistor was developed, but it was too slow. In 1957 the planar silicon transistor was invented. It provided high-speed transistors that were reliable and made possible the design of the present high-speed computers. Further development of the planar technology led to the monolithic integrated circuit, in which scores of components are created and linked together in a single tiny "chip" of silicon. A variation of this technique is used to create the integrated-circuit memories.

The integrated logic circuit, which is just beginning to make its way into large-scale use for computers, contributes substantially to the solution of the three problems that beset the vacuum-tube computer and that were only partially solved by discrete transistors. An integrated circuit on one chip of silicon can have the logic capacity of several of the logic circuits described earlier. It occupies far less space and consumes less power than an equivalent transistor circuit. Its small size makes possible systems with higher speeds because the interconnections of the circuits are shorter. Reliability is increased because the interconnections are themselves reliable. Indeed, the reliability of an entire integrated circuit is expected to approach that of an individual transistor. The latest integrated circuits have a signal delay of only a few nanoseconds, and still faster circuits are being developed. However, the physical size of a computer's components, together with their interconnections, remains a fundamental limitation on the complexity of the computer: an electrical signal can travel along a wire at the rate of only about eight inches per nanosecond (two-thirds the speed of light).

Computer technology has a way of confounding those who would predict its future. The thin-film memory, for example, has been "just around the corner" for more than 10 years, but the ferrite core is still the main element of random-access memories. Nevertheless, one can try to make certain predictions based on the situation at present. It now seems clear that integrated-circuit technology will soon produce circuits of great complexity at very low cost. These circuits will include high-speed memory circuits as well as logic circuits. Already one can get commercial delivery of a 100-bit register on a single chip of silicon that is a tenth of an inch in its largest dimension. It is my personal opinion that computer designers will be hard-pressed to develop concepts adequate to exploit the rapid advances in components.

Because computers built with integrated components promise to be much cheaper than present machines, one can expect significant changes in the comparative costs of information processing and information transmission. This in turn will influence the rate of growth of data-transmission facilities. Low-cost computers will also change the cost factors that help in deciding whether it is cheaper to do a job with human labor or to turn it over to a machine.

IVAN E. SUTHERLAND

Computer Inputs and Outputs

The input-output system of a computer consists of the
programs and devices that allow the machine and
its user to communicate. Recently graphical devices
for this purpose have evolved rapidly.

If a computer is to be useful, it must obviously be able to communicate with the outside world. Data and programs have to be
put into the machine before it can do any work. The computer
must record and store for later reference information it has processed. Answers must come out of the computer in some usable
form. The programs, mechanical devices and electronic circuits
that perform these essential tasks of communication constitute
what is called the input-output system of the computer.

A fact easily lost from view as a computer performs its prodigies
of calculation is that a man is the reason for it all. He gives the
computer data and programs and uses the results. Hence an input-
output system has to cater to human needs as well as those of the
computer. The total process from human recognition of a need
than can be met by a computer to human use of the computer's
answer consists of four parts. First, the data required must be put
into a form the computer can use. Second, someone must tell the
computer what to do. Third, the computer must read the data,
process them and write the answers. Fourth, the computer's answers must be put into a form people can use. Input-output

equipment must be designed to make each of these steps as easy as possible.

Improvements in input-output technique can lead to improved performance in all four parts of the computing process. For the input of data it is obvious that new kinds of input equipment make it possible for computers to accept directly a wider variety of information. A case in point is the recent development of stylus devices, such as the "Rand Tablet," that enable the computer to interpret human sketching. These devices make it possible to put diagrams and sketches into the computer without the time-consuming process of reducing them manually to numerical coordinates.

Secondly, and less obviously, the ability of the computer to accept a wider variety of input forms opens new ways of using such forms to specify what the computer is to do. For example, programming languages based on pictures rather than typed instructions may be much more convenient for specifying some processes of calculation to be carried out by the computer. Thirdly, improvements in the speed and organization of input-output systems can reduce computing costs. The "interrupt" systems I shall describe can reduce computing delays by allowing several input and output operations to proceed while computation is being done. Finally, new kinds of output equipment enable computers to produce output in more directly usable forms. A graph is often much more useful than a column of numbers.

Until fairly recently nearly all input-output systems in general use were designed to economize on the computer's time at the expense of some inconvenience to the user. The reason was the costliness of delaying computation, which was considered to be the computer's prime function, just to get data in and out. As a result of many years of work we have learned how to make input-output equipment operate efficiently from the computer's point of view.

Although care is still taken to operate computers efficiently, much more attention is now being paid to human convenience. Recent developments such as time-sharing [see "Time-sharing on Computers," by R. M. Fano and F. J. Corbató, page 76] and reductions in the cost of computing, console and display devices have given us an unprecedented freedom in designing input-output equipment. New devices and programs, some of which will be discussed later in this article, are changing computers from hard-to-use consultants into ready tools to aid human thought. For the time being, however, these programs and devices are mainly experimental. First it would be well to consider input-output as it is generally practiced today.

Different computer installations have quite different collections of input-output devices, even though the installations may have the same type of computer. The particular complement of input-output equipment depends on the purpose of the installation and is a strong factor in determining its price. A typical computer installation might have a card-reader, several magnetic-tape units, a typewriter and a high-speed printer. Information prepared on punched cards is entered into the computer through the card-reader. The magnetic-tape units provide the computer with storage for intermediate results. They can also provide for long-term storage of information and, by the transfer of tapes, for communication with other computers. The typewriter can be used for the output of short messages, such as one instructing the operator to mount a particular reel of tape. It can also be used by the operator to signal when computations should start, for instance when he has finished mounting the tape. The printer provides for the output of results.

The typical pattern of card-reader, magnetic tapes, typewriter and printer varies when there are special needs. Many installations have card-punches in addition to card-readers. Some low-cost computing systems use punched paper tape instead of cards, substituting tape-readers and tape-punches for card equipment. An array of magnetic disks, usually called a file, is sometimes used with or instead of magnetic tapes.

Switches and lights are often used at the console instead of a typewriter for control by the operator. Some computers drive more than one printer. Others operate entirely without printers, depending on auxiliary computers to print from magnetic-tape output produced by the master computer.

All the input-output devices connected to computers have been designed to run as fast as possible. They seem, when running, to consume or produce information at a prodigious rate. A fast card-reader reads about 1,000 cards per minute; it seems to speed through the pile of cards like a power saw cutting through wood. Similarly, printed pages come out of an output printer much faster than one can read them. Even a computer typewriter, one of the slowest of the input-output devices, types far faster and more accurately than a skilled human typist.

Nonetheless, the speed of such input-output devices is slow compared with that of a modern electronic computer. To see just how slow their operations are from the computer's point of view, let us imagine slowing down an entire computer system a million-fold. Instead of performing a million operations per second, our slowed-down computer will perform at a more human pace: one operation per second. In the slowed-down model a computer typewriter that normally types 10 characters per second would type about one character per day! To put it another way, a computer receiving input from a fast typist is much like a man getting one new character of a telegram each morning.

Most input-output devices are faster than typewriters, but because nearly all of them have mechanical parts they cannot approach the speed of the electronic computer. A computer printer that can print 1,500 lines per minute, each with 132 characters, would accept a new character every five minutes in our millionth-speed model. Magnetic tape that accepts about 100,000 characters per second would accept a new character every 10 seconds. Since it takes about two milliseconds to start or stop a tape in ordinary computer operation, however, it would take the tape unit in the slowed-down model half an hour to deliver its first character. On the other hand, some input-output devices (microsecond clocks, very-high-speed magnetic drums, cathode-ray-tube displays and converters that change data such as voltages into digits) can work as fast as electronic computers. Thus the difficulty of coordinating input-output processes with computing is not only that some input-output devices are extraordinarily slow compared with the speed of computers but also that the range of input-output speeds is very large.

Another difficulty is that the computer must be able to accept information from input devices and deliver information to output devices promptly on demand. Promptness is required because many input-output devices, once they are started, cannot be stopped quickly. For example, once a magnetic tape has started moving, new characters will come from it at regular intervals whether or not the computer accepts them. The inertia of the tape is too great to permit starting and stopping for each character. If the computer fails to accept a character before the next one arrives, information will be lost.

Although the computer must be able to handle each piece of information promptly, it can hardly afford to stand by idly. Modern computers are very costly, and each second they wait for input or output equipment to function corresponds to hundreds of thousands of irretrievably lost computations. Much of the complexity of modern computing systems arises from the desire of the designers to avoid unnecessary waiting for input and output. A well-designed modern computer can operate half a dozen or so input-output devices concurrently and do useful computation in the time left over. This is a juggling act of colossal proportions. Developing the computer hardware and programs to realize it has been a major task.

Most of the early computers lacked the hardware that makes efficient input and output feasible. A typical input-output system consisted of a few special instructions. They enabled a program to select and activate an input-output unit, transfer data to or from it and determine if it was ready for another transfer of data. With only these simple instructions it was easy to write a crude input-output program but nearly impossible to write an efficient one. The input-output programs in common use wasted the time between successive transfers of data in a "waiting loop," a set of instructions in which the computer asked repeatedly if the input-output unit was yet ready for another transfer of data. An efficient input-output program would have provided for useful computation in the time between data transfers.

In the early computers computation between inputs or outputs of information could be done only if the instructions for input-output and those for computation were carefully interwoven. The programmer faced a dilemma. To obtain maximum efficiency he had to provide for as much computation as possible between transfers of data. If he allowed too much computation, however, input-output data would be lost. Writing an efficient program required a detailed knowledge of the timing of both the input-output operations and the computation. Since each new computation program presented its own special timing problems, every program required its own careful interweaving of input-output and computation. It was impossible to write, once and for all, an independent program to accomplish efficient input and output. The only independent input-output programs possible were the crude, time-wasting kind. Programmers either used inefficient input-output routines or faced the long, irksome task of interweaving input-output and computation.

The beauty of today's input-output systems is that they not only enhance efficiency but also provide for a clean separation of input-output programs from computation programs. It is this separation that enables programmers to use the full capacity of the modern computer.

The basic hardware required for efficient use of input-output equipment is the system of devices called the "program-interrupt." This hardware serves the computer as a kind of doorbell that signals the arrival of any important piece of information. When an input-output unit is ready to transfer data, it sends a signal to the interrupt hardware, which causes the computer to suspend whatever it was doing and execute instead a totally independent input-output program located somewhere else in its memory. The input-output program transfers the data and then returns the computer to its former activity.

Program-interrupt hardware provides many advantages. Because it can interrupt a computation at any time, demands for input and output receive the prompt response they require. The input-output program runs efficiently because it is activated only when it is actually needed. Most important of all, efficient handling of input-output transfers no longer requires any complicated interweaving of computation and input-output instructions. Computation programs can now be written without regard for the input-output activities that may be under way simultaneously.

If several input-output units are connected to a computer, many interrupt signals can be generated at once. The priority to be given to these demands for service is usually designed into the interrupt hardware. Faster input-output equipment is generally given a higher priority. Units that operate at irregular intervals may get a lower priority if they can be made to wait; in this way they do not break the pace of synchronous units. Computation itself is given the lowest priority because it can nearly always wait. Computation takes place only when no interrupts are being processed, which usually turns out to be most of the time.

Most input-output interrupts result in the transfer of just one piece of information to or from the memory. Such an operation is described as one memory cycle. Often additional memory cycles are required to control the transfer. Some computers contain special hardware that processes each of the frequent but simple transfers of data in only one memory cycle. Such a unit, called a "data channel" or "memory-snatch" system, takes a single memory cycle away from calculation whenever an input-output device is ready. A data channel or memory-snatch incorporates a pointer that is changed after each transfer, so that successive data are put into or taken from successive locations in the memory. It also contains a counter, so that only a specified number of transactions can take place automatically. Data channels are useful for very-high-speed tape and disk units that transfer new information every few memory cycles.

Although different types of computers use different kinds of interrupt systems, nearly every computer now being manufactured has some form of program-interrupt. Larger systems with fast input-output equipment usually include at least one data channel. Since it is uneconomical to interrupt the largest computing machines even momentarily for input-output, they are often directly coupled to a smaller computer that does their input and output for them. Since input-output operations rarely require sophisticated arithmetic, this separation of calculation and input-output is becoming more common.

Most computers are delivered with a tape containing a comprehensive program (called an "operating system" or "executive") to do their input-output operations. The operating system should take care of all details of timing, running several input-output programs at the same time and dealing with correctable failure in the input-output equipment. Viewed through a well-designed operating system, input-output equipment is fast, accurate, economical of computer time and easy to use.

In addition to using the program-interrupt hardware to handle input-output operations efficiently, the operating system provides for the scheduling of jobs and the allocation of input-output and memory resources. Without an effective operating system a modern large computer is almost useless. In fact, operating systems are so important that they are usually covered in the specifications for a computer; failure of a manufacturer to deliver a suitable operating system on time usually results in a heavy financial penalty. The task of preparing a good operating system is substantial. Writing a new operating system is roughly equivalent in complexity to designing a new computer.

The operating system enables relatively unskilled programmers to utilize the parts of the computer they need without concern for details of timing, interference from other users or malfunctioning of equipment. For example, a user's program that requires the printing of data can call on a part of the operating system to perform the output. When asked to print, the operating system will accept responsibility for the data to be printed and will return control to the user program. If the printer is free, the operating system may begin to print the data at once. The user's computation program will proceed, interrupted from time to time when the printer actually requires transfers of data. If the printer is not free, the operating system may choose to put the data on magnetic tape for later printing. In this case too the user's computation will proceed, interrupted from time to time for data transfers. The operating system may check the information written on tape for accuracy. Should an error be found, the operating system will rewrite the information correctly.

All the complex activities of the operating system are accomplished by processing interrupts. The user for whom these processes are carried out has no need to be concerned with the details of the processing; indeed, he is quite unaware of them. Needless to say, the highly skilled system programmers who write operating systems must have an intimate knowledge of the input-output equipment and program-interrupt hardware involved.

Although the input-output programs and hardware described here solve the timing problems of using input-output equipment, they do little to assist in specifying the format of the information transferred. The format in which information appears outside the computer is usually very different from that of the information inside. Humans want to see decimal numbers; computers normally use binary numbers. Humans want dollar signs, decimal points, separately printed units and separately printed exponents; computers just deal with numbers. Specifying the desired format for input-output information is an important part of any programming job. Converting information to and from the specified format is an essential function of the computer.

The specification and conversion of format are well understood for ordinary scientific and business computation. Formats consisting of columns of numbers with headings, convenient spacing and suitable units are easily specified through the "compilers" that most programmers use to help tell the computer what to do. Simple statements enable the programmer to describe each line he wants printed. For example, a format statement such as FORMAT (1H1,4F10.3,5H FEET) would be interpreted by the computer as follows: 1H1, start a new page; 4F, print four numbers in decimal notation; 10.3, use 10 columns for each number and give three places after the decimal point; 5H, put the unit designation "feet" at the end of the line. Most compilers make it easy to print numbers as integers, as decimal fractions with a specified number of places before and after the decimal point or in scientific notation, such as 11.73×10^6 (which comes out 11.73 E6 in computers that cannot print superscript). In addition the computer can print comments, units and titles either from internal data or by copying part of the format statement.

Fairly simple formats serve for the large bulk of computer inputs and outputs. They are well matched to the limited capacity of the common output printers. Since most printers can print only capital letters, numbers and a few punctuation symbols, no great complexity of format is required. Most users of computers have become accustomed to receiving columns of numbers as the output from their computations. Research now under way, however, has shown that less common input-output devices and more complicated format-control tools for them can make much more useful forms of input and output possible.

We are beginning to recognize that it is not enough for a computer to calculate and print an answer. The answer is useful only when it leads to new human understanding. Diagrams, drawings, graphs and sketches are essential tools for human understanding in many scientific and technical fields. All too often users of computers have been forced to convert pictures into numerical co-ordinates before giving them to a computer and to convert columns of numerical answers back into a picture or graph before understanding the answer. The time it takes a man to do the conversion keeps him from trying many examples; in some cases it may even cause him to lose sight of what it was he wanted. If the computer can accept information in the form most natural for the man and produce answers in the form he can most readily understand, it can be much more useful to him. The difference is readily apparent if one considers that a single straight line flashed on a display tube in one or two milliseconds might require 15 minutes of typed output to give the coordinates of the 1,000 or so points making up the line.

During the past few years several experimental systems have been built that rely on diagrams rather than printed or typed numbers as a medium of communication between a computer and its user. These systems have shown that proper use of graphical input-output equipment can produce a substantial increase in a computer's ability to aid human understanding of complex phenomena. In one such system, developed by Cyrus Levinthal at the Massachusetts Institute of Technology, protein molecules are shown in perspective. The effects of various assumptions on the shape of the molecule can be observed directly. In another system, devised by E. E. Zajac of the Bell Telephone Laboratories, the tumbling motion of a simulated satellite was recorded on motion-picture film. Engineers viewing the film were able to decide why the actual satellite's stabilizing system failed to work. Such demonstrations have hastened the development and application of computer systems that can accept and give graphical information.

The basic hardware for graphical output is the cathode-ray-tube display, known around computer installations as the CRT display. Such a display contains a cathode ray tube and some electronic devices that enable a computer to control it. When given a set of coordinates by the computer program, a simple cathode-ray-tube display will flash the corresponding spot on its face. Complete pictures including lines, curves and letters can be made up out of thousands of individual spots. Because the display is entirely electronic, it can work very fast; a single spot may take only a few microseconds to show.

The process has its limitations. The more elaborate the picture, the longer it takes the computer to compute the coordinates of all the thousands of spots in the picture. For this reason some displays have circuits that can paint straight lines on the display face automatically, thus eliminating the need for a program to compute coordinates for all the spots on each line. Since computer output usually contains some letters and numbers, many displays contain character-generating hardware that will cause a letter or number to appear on the display screen automatically. The character is formed either by passing the cathode ray through a letter-shaped mask or by electronically manipulating the beam to paint the letter. Display hardware for generating various conic sections automatically is now being developed.

Making good use of cathode-ray-tube display equipment often requires quite complex programs. The few installations that now make extensive use of such displays have built up libraries of programs for producing a variety of display formats. Programs for producing bar graphs, contour plots, scatter diagrams and a wide variety of other useful formats are separately available. If the format desired does not fit one of the available forms, careful individual programming of the new format is required. It is fairly easy to program simple formats such as graphs, but it is considerably more difficult to get all the labels, scales and notes in the right places.

Some output formats are quite difficult to achieve. An adequate view of a solid object, for example, must have hidden lines removed. It is easy to write a program that can compute the apparent position of each part of an object from the shape of the object and the desired viewing angle. It is very much harder to write a program that can decide which parts to omit to make the object look solid; moreover, the task of elimination takes much more time than the simple transformation of coordinates. Similarly, it is difficult to program a computer to place the parts of a drawing wisely so that its topology will be clear. For these reasons output plots of family trees, simplified circuit diagrams, organization interaction diagrams and the like are rare.

With suitable attachments a cathode-ray-tube display can also be used as an input device. Since the parts of a picture displayed on a cathode ray tube are "painted" on the tube face one after another, a photocell placed where light from a part of the tube can fall on it will respond when it detects light. The computer can tell what the photocell saw by noting when it responded.

In one arrangement the photocell and cathode ray tube are used as a scanner: the photocell is placed behind an exposed film on which is recorded some data such as the tracks of nuclear particles. The computer can then read the data from the film by noting which displayed points are hidden from the photocell by opaque parts of the intervening film. Scanners of this type are now manufactured commercially for converting data from photographic to digital form, so that the computer can make the desired calculations. These scanners are proving to be a boon to physicists who need to scan hundreds of thousands of frames from a bubble chamber to find a single significant event.

Picture input through scanners requires more complicated programs than picture output. Although a cathode-ray-tube scanner can tell a computer which parts of a photograph are opaque, a complicated program and a good deal of computer time are necessary to convert that information into a simple usable fact. Lawrence G. Roberts of the Lincoln Laboratory of M.I.T. wrote such a program for recognizing solid objects from photographs. Roberts' program demonstrated its ability to recognize simple plane-faced objects by drawing additional views of them. Although the computer required only a few seconds to read prerecorded picture data from tape, it took several minutes (an enormous amount of computing time) for the computer to make sense of the data. Pattern-recognition programs such as Roberts' and those used in analyzing the tracks of nuclear particles must be written on an individual basis. Because of this exacting requirement picture-scanning input is economical only experimentally or where there are large bodies of data to process.

The stylus-photocell arrangement called the light pen can be used to make the cathode-ray-tube display serve for the manual input of sketches and diagrams. For this purpose the photocell is placed in a small hand-held tube. Since the photocell responds only when light from some part of the cathode-ray-tube drawing falls within its limited field of view, it can tell the computer which part of a drawing its user is pointing at. With an appropriate feedback program a light pen can also be used to enter position information into the computer [see illustration on the facing page].

Other stylus input devices that detect the position of the stylus through electric and magnetic-field effects can serve a similar function. Some of these, such as the Rand Tablet (developed by Thomas O. Ellis of the Rand Corporation), provide the computer not only with position but also with a "pencil down" indication; that is, the device signifies to the computer not only the position of the stylus but also whether or not the user is pressing it down. The "pressing down" signal can be used to signify lines that are to be retained in the computer.

In a drawing system based on input from a stylus the computer interprets motions of the stylus and instructions given by the operator through push buttons or a typewriter keyboard; from these data the computer constructs a drawing in its memory. The program displays the growing drawing on a cathode-ray-tube display. Unlike an ordinary pencil, the stylus itself does not make any direct mark on the display. The computer is placed, in effect, between the "point of the pencil" and the "paper." Because the drawing is built directly in the computer's memory, no complicated pattern-recognition programs are required. A stylus-input device therefore provides a convenient method for getting diagrams, circuits, geometric shapes, chemical symbols and other pictorial data into a computer.

Such a drawing system is very different from ordinary drawing with pencil and paper. Because the computer is placed between the "point of the pencil" and the "paper" it can assist in every step of drawing. For example, the computer can display lines as straight even though they were sketched badly. It can join lines at mathematically precise corners in spite of slight human errors. It will erase without any trace, or temporarily if you prefer, any unwanted line you point to. It can quickly copy any part of the drawing. It can stretch parts of the drawing to make them fit with other parts. It can move lines you have already drawn. It can refuse to draw lines that are meaningless in the context of the work in hand.

Most computer drawing systems use push buttons as input devices to signal what action is desired. An experimental system at the Rand Corporation, however, uses motions of a stylus as

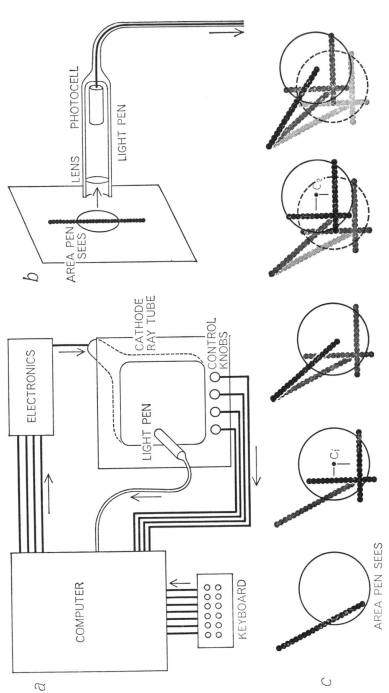

Two uses of a light pen are pointing and drawing. Pointing ("a" and "b") tells a computer which parts of a drawing to erase or move. Drawing (c) is done with a tracking program. Here, to move the end of a line, the operator points at the end and pushes a "move" button; the computer follows the pen by displaying cross-like arrays of spots 100 times a second. Each time, the computer "senses" outer vertical and horizontal spots seen by pen, computes position of pen's center and redisplays line to end there,

the exclusive control. Since the Rand program is intended for drawing block diagrams, it recognizes crudely sketched blocks and substitutes neat ones for them. It also recognizes lines drawn between boxes as logical connections between them. No matter how you draw the connection, it will appear as a series of straight-line segments. It will have an arrowhead at one end. The Rand program also recognizes printed characters. It substitutes its own highly precise printing for your letters. It is impossible to leave bad printing on your drawing. You can insert letters by making a caret, whereupon the program will push existing letters aside to make room for your addition. You can erase boxes, lines and letters by making a score-out mark over them. With these facilities you can quickly and easily sketch out or modify a diagram.

The topology of a drawing sketched into a computer with a stylus-input device is available explicitly in the computer's memory. If the drawing represents a circuit, for example, the electrical connections shown in the drawing will be represented in the memory in a form suitable for use in a circuit-simulator. The computer will "know" that two terminals are connected because it will have "watched" while the connecting wire was drawn. There are many computer applications for which specification of topology is important. Stylus input is beginning to be used to state topology for circuit simulation, analysis of communication networks, digital simulation of analogue systems and diagramming the flow of digital-computer programs.

The geometry of shapes is also stated easily with a stylus-input device. The stylus serves to sketch the part. If exact dimensions are important, they can be entered through a keyboard. In one case the parts specified by this technique are cut out by computer-controlled machine tools. In another case the computer does engineering computations on the shapes as an aid to the design of mechanical devices.

Stylus input to computers opens up new vistas for the application of computers. We are just beginning to explore these vistas. The ability to specify topology, for example, will make possible a new generation of computer-programming languages based on pictures rather than on written words. The ability to specify geometry will bring computers into use as aids to mechanical design. The ability to specify graphical-output formats will make possible ever clearer presentations of computed results. Perfection of the techniques for drawing with a stylus will make a stylus and computer easier to use than pencil and paper.

Although the full potential of graphical input and output is still unknown, there is a growing belief that important new insights will be gained through its use. Today graphical capability is unknown at most computer installations, even major scientific ones. Widespread recognition of its potential, however, is a strong motivating force that will bring graphics to the computers in most scientific research programs. It is my conviction that the widespread use of graphical inputs and outputs with computers will bring about a major increase in scientific, engineering and educational productivity.

CHRISTOPHER STRACHEY

System Analysis and Programming

The process of stating a problem in a language that is
acceptable to a computer is primarily intuitive rather than
formal. A specific example of the process is given.

*It is a profoundly erroneous truism, repeated by all copy-books
and by eminent people when they are making speeches, that we
should cultivate the habit of thinking of what we are doing. The
precise opposite is the case. Civilization advances by extending
the number of important operations which we can perform without thinking about them. Operations of thought are like cavalry
charges in a battle—they are strictly limited in number, they require fresh horses, and must only be made at decisive moments.*
—ALFRED NORTH WHITEHEAD

This chapter is about how to get a computer to do what you
want, and why it almost always takes longer than you expect.
What follows is not a detailed report on the state of the art of
programming but an attempt to show how to set about writing a
program. The process of writing a program is primarily intuitive
rather than formal; hence we shall be more concerned with the
guiding principles that underlie programming than with the particular language in which the program is to be presented to the
machine.

We shall start with a specific example of a programming problem that is decidedly nontrivial and yet sufficiently simple to be understood without any previous knowledge of programming. I have chosen an unorthodox approach to the problem, one that will look strange to many professional programmers. This approach enables us to tackle an example that would be much too elaborate to explain otherwise.

Our problem is to program a computer to play checkers. How should we set about it? There are two main aspects to the problem. To equip the computer to deal with the game at all we must find a way to represent the board and positions on it and furnish the computer with a program for identifying legal moves and making them. This is a programming problem. Secondly, we must provide the machine with a method of selecting a suitable move from the ones available. This is mainly a problem in game-playing. Arthur L. Samuel of the International Business Machines Corporation has studied this game-playing aspect extensively and with considerable success [see "Artificial Intelligence," by Marvin L. Minsky, page 193]. Here, however, since we are concerned with programming rather than game-playing, we shall content ourselves with a simple general strategy and leave most of the details unsettled.

The usual approach to writing a program, particularly for a complex problem, divides the process into two stages. The first of these is called system analysis. It involves analyzing the task to decide exactly what needs to be done and adopting an overall plan [see illustration on page 58].

Once the general outline of the work to be performed has been decided on, the second stage is to write the required operations in a form suitable for the computer. This involves a large number of more detailed decisions (for example how information is to be represented in the machine and how the representations are to be stored). The detailed form of the program will depend on the particular computer to be used [see illustration on page 59].

Confusion has developed about the naming of these two stages. Some programmers reserve the term "programming" for the second stage; others call the first stage "programming" and the second stage "coding"; still others use the term "programming" for the entire process—stages one and two. My own view is that the distinction between system analysis and programming is not a

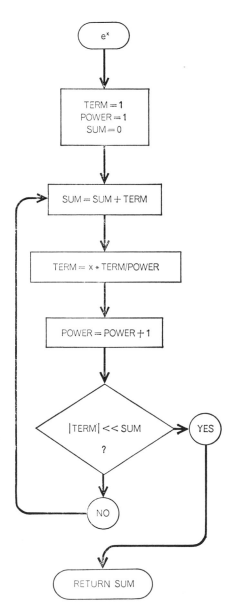

Orthodox approach to the problem of writing a computer program is illustrated here. The problem in this example is comparatively simple: to find the function e^x by summing the series $1 + x + x^2/2! + x^3/3! + \ldots$ until the terms become negligible. The process of writing a program to solve such a problem is usually divided into two stages. The first stage, sometimes called system analysis, involves analyzing the task to decide exactly what needs to be done and adopting an overall plan; this stage is represented by the block diagram at left. The second stage, called programming by some programmers and coding by others, involves writing the required operations in a form suitable for the computer. The problem in question is expressed in three different programming languages at right. The diamond-shaped box in the block diagram contains a "decision function"; the straight vertical lines before and after the word "term" signify "absolute value of," and the symbol $<<$ means that "$|term|$" is negligible compared with "sum." In CPL (Combined Programming Language) the expression "value of" governs the immediately following statement; "repeat" governs the immediately preceding statement, and the symbols § and § act as statement brackets. In both CPL and ALGOL the operator ":=" stands for assignment: the quantities on the right of this operator are evaluated and simultaneously assigned to the variables on the left. The symbol * in FORTRAN is a multiplication sign.

a

CPL

```
let Exp [x] = value of
    § let t, r, s = 1, 1, 0
       t, r, s := xt/r, r+l, s+t
       repeat until t << s
       result is s §.
```

b

ALGOL

```
real procedure Exp (x);
value x; real x;
begin real term, power, sum, q;
   term: = power: = q: = 1;
   sum = 0;
   for sum = sum + term while q >₁₀ − 12 do ·
      begin term: = x × term/power;
         power: = power + 1;
         q: = abs (term/sum) end;
   Exp: = sum;
end
```

c

FORTRAN IV

```
     FUNCTION   EXP (X)
     TERM = 1.
     POWER = 1.
     SUM = 0.
  10 SUM = SUM + TERM
     TERM = X * TERM/POWER
     POWER = POWER + 1.
     IF (ABS (TERM/SUM).GT. 10E − 12) GO TO 10
     EXP = SUM
     RETURN
     END
```

very useful one. If the system analysis were carried through to a description of the program outline in a slightly more rigorous language than is used at present, it should be possible to relegate the whole of the remaining process of producing a detailed program in machine language to the computer itself.

Let us get on to the problem of programming a computer to play checkers against an opponent. How shall we represent the relevant features of the game, and what kind of operations do we want to be able to perform on them? A good working rule is to start with the operations and allow them to determine what it is you need to represent in the machine. In this case we clearly require, to begin with, representations of positions and moves and of the values associated with them.

We can approach the kind of precision the computer requires and still avoid getting bogged down in premature detail by using a functional notation. We let P stand for a position and agree to include in P not only the number and arrangement of the pieces on the board but also various other important facts such as which player is to move. The value of a position can be expressed by a function PositionValue(P). The value of any move (say M) obviously depends on the position from which it is made; therefore we must specify the position in writing the function MoveValue(M,P). Next, in order to be able to look ahead and examine the possible consequences of moves, the computer will need a third function: MakeMove(M,P), with P representing the position from which the move is made. The result of this function is the new position produced by the move. Finally, the program needs a fourth function to find all the legal moves that can be made from a given position: LegalMovesFrom(P). This function has as its result a list of moves.

These four functions, together with the two types of object (P and M), are sufficient to specify the kernel of our checkers program. There are two players in a game of checkers (in our case the machine and its opponent), and a position that is good for one will be bad for the other. We must therefore make our idea of the value of a position more precise by saying that PositionValue(P) gives the value of the position P to the player who has to move from it. We can plausibly assume that the value of the position P to the other player is the negative of this; that is, if

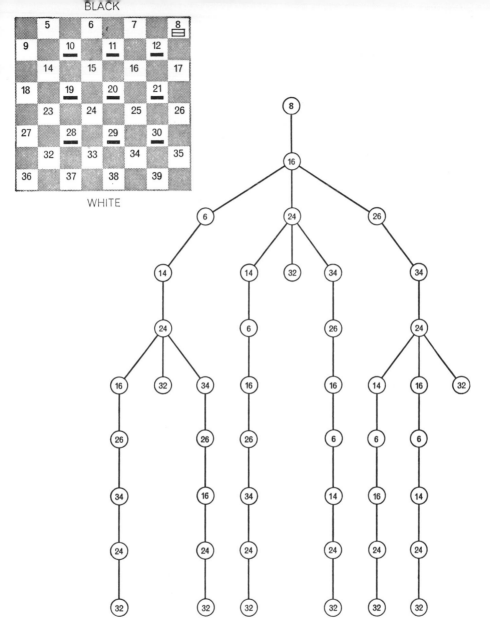

Capture "tree" depicts all the possible "partial capture moves" for a given piece after the first such move. In checkers a move is not complete until no more captures can be made. A maximum of nine captures in a single move is possible, as shown in this example. Capture-move situation, like that in the main game, can be programmed by using "recursive" functions, that is, functions that are defined in a circular manner in terms of other functions. Program for this situation is incorporated in the complete checkers program on page 68.

the value of a position to one player is v, its value to the other will be $-v$. (This assumption is expressed in the terms of game theory by saying that checkers is a zero-sum game.)

Next we can define the value of a move to the player who makes it as the value *to him* of the resulting position. Suppose the result of making the move M from the position P is the position P'. Remembering that it is the opponent who has to make the move from P', we can see that the value of the move M to the player who makes it will be $-$PositionValue(P'). Thus in our notation we can define the value of a move as follows: MoveValue$(M,P) = $ $-$PositionValue[MakeMove(M,P)]. This formal statement could be paraphrased by saying that to value a move for yourself you make it, find the value of the resulting position to your opponent and change its sign.

How shall we find the value of a position? The basic procedure of the game is to explore all your possible moves and all possible replies by the opponent to some depth and evaluate the resulting positions. Let us call these "terminal" positions and say that their values are produced by the function TerminalValue(P). This function makes an immediate assessment of a position (in terms, perhaps, of such factors as the number of pieces still in play, their mobility, the command of the center of the board and so forth) without any further look-ahead. We can now say that if P is a terminal position, its value is TerminalValue(P), and that if it is not, its value is that of the best legal move that could be made from it. Note that the question of whether a position is terminal or not may depend not only on the position itself but also on what depth (d) the look-ahead has reached. This is necessary in order to put some limit on how far the machine looks ahead.

The definitions we have been writing are in fact circular (for example, the definition of PositionValue involves the use of MoveValue and vice versa), and the functions are called recursive, because each is defined in terms of the others. This circularity is no disadvantage; indeed, it makes it possible to start right in the middle of things, to set up a number of functions whose purpose is only intuitively understood at the beginning and to define each of them in terms of the others. This recursive, or hierarchical, approach to programming is by far the simplest method of handling complicated operations, since it allows them to be broken up into smaller units that can be considered separately.

We have now constructed a general game-playing scheme without having decided on either the details of the strategy or the structure of the game itself. We can complete the outline of our program by deciding on the representation of positions and moves and defining four functions. The functions LegalMovesFrom(P) and MakeMove(M,P), together with the form of P and M, will determine the nature of the game, and the functions Terminal (P,d) and TerminalValue(P) between them will determine the strategy.

The selection of ways to represent objects in the computer is an art, and there is little we can do in a systematic fashion to decide the best way. The main requirements are that the representation should be as compact as possible and yet as easy as possible to manipulate.

For representing the various positions on a checkerboard we have two distinct possibilities. To describe a particular position we could either specify whether each of the 32 available squares on the board is or is not occupied, and if it is, by what, or we could merely give the locations of the pieces still in play. The first of these alternatives is more convenient from the standpoint of finding the legal moves, because it makes it easier to discover which squares are unoccupied [see illustration on page 64].

When we come to a detailed consideration of the representation of moves, we find that the numbering of squares on the ordinary board is inconvenient because there are two kinds of squares (on alternate rows) that need different rules. Samuel devised a neat method of avoiding this difficulty. By extending the board with rows and columns that are not used and renumbering the squares, he produced a scheme in which the possible moves were similar for all squares on that part of the board which is actually used [see illustration on page 65].

All the possible moves (other than those in which pieces are captured) fall into four types, each of which can be represented by a word (consisting of 45 bits, or binary digits) that can specify any move of its type. Within the framework of the scheme of notation we have been using it is also a simple matter to represent

A

BLACK

WHITE

B BLACK MEN ON 11, 20, 21
   WHITE MEN ON 19, 22, 30, 32
   BLACK KING ON 29

C BLACK MEN = ...1. ....1 1... .... 1...
   WHITE MEN = ...1. .1.. .... .1.1
   KINGS = ... 1...

Positions on a checkerboard can be represented in a computer in two different ways. To describe a particular position one has the choice of specifying either what is on each square (A) or where the pieces that are still in play are located (B). An equivalent alternative to A is given in C, which uses only binary numbers. Three binary digits, or "bits," are needed to specify each square: one to show the presence of a black man or king, another to show the presence of a white man or king and a third to show the presence of kings of either color.

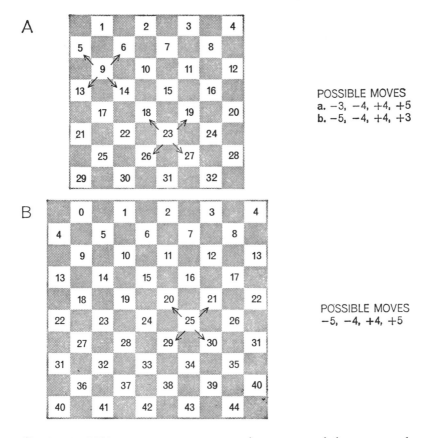

A

POSSIBLE MOVES
a. −3, −4, +4, +5
b. −5, −4, +4, +3

B

POSSIBLE MOVES
−5, −4, +4, +5

C BLACK MEN = ...1. ....1 1... . .... 1... . ....
WHITE MEN = ...1. .1.. . .... .1.1 . ....
KINGS = ... 1... . ....
EMPTY SQUARES = ... 1111 1111 . 11.1 1111 . 11.. ..11 . 1111 ..1. . ....

Moves on a checkerboard can be represented using the numbering scheme of an ordinary checkerboard (A), but this is inconvenient, as there are two kinds of squares (on alternate rows), which need different rules. Arthur L. Samuel of the International Business Machines Corporation devised a neat method of avoiding this difficulty. By extending the board with rows and columns that are not used and renumbering the squares, he produced a scheme in which the possible moves are similar for all squares on that part of the board which is actually used (B). The position shown at the top of this page is represented in this new scheme of notation in C. Empty squares are indicated by 1's for all the squares on the board proper.

capture moves and the promotion of men to kings. The capture-move situation, for example, can be visualized in the graphical form of a "capture tree" [see illustration on page 61].

It would go beyond the scope of this article to discuss all the details of a working checkers program. The main outlines of the process of writing such a program should, however, be apparent by now. The first step is to have a vague idea of how to solve the problem. The second step is to specify the operations needed to carry out this initial plan, formalizing it by giving names to the objects on which these operations are to act. The third step is to clarify the definitions of the objects and to settle on a representation for each of them. These representations should be determined primarily by the operations to be performed on the objects. Once the representations have been decided on, the component operations can be defined more precisely in terms of them. One can then go on to refine the program, correcting errors or deficiencies that may show up in the representations and adjusting the operations accordingly.

At this stage the major intellectual work of the program seems to be finished. We have specified precisely what we want the computer to do. The rest—converting the program into instructions for the computer—should be merely routine. Unfortunately it does not quite work out that way, and anyone who has not had the experience of using a computer will be unpleasantly surprised by the amount of time and effort that is still needed.

In the first place, the computer is unable to accept directly the rather sophisticated kind of instructions we should like to give it. It is almost certain that we shall have made use of operations that are too much for any computer. To get around the inability of the machine to do directly what we want, we can write our program in a standard programming language and make the machine translate this into its own much simpler code. This seems an excellent use of a computer to do the donkey work for us, but unfortunately it does not get rid of all the labor. We have to do a good deal of apparently irrelevant and *ad hoc* work to force the program into a form suitable for existing programming languages.

There are now a considerable number of these programming languages: FORTRAN, ALGOL and MAD (used primarily for scientific problems); JOVIAL (for military applications); CO-BOL; SIMSCRIPT; LISP; PL/I; CPL, and others. To give an indication of the varying styles of the languages, three samples are given: a simple program (to find the mathematical function e^x) is written in CPL, in ALGOL and in FORTRAN [see illustration on page 59].

The advent of programming languages of this kind some nine years ago vastly enriched the art of programming. Before then a program containing 5,000 instructions was considered quite large, and only the most experienced or foolhardy programmers would attempt one. Today an individual can tackle programs about 10 times larger; a team by cooperative effort may produce a program still larger by a factor of five to 10.

By far the most important of the new programming languages was FORTRAN; until recently, it has been estimated, more than 90 percent of all scientific and engineering programs were written in it. In the past few years it has gradually become clear that current programming languages are by no means perfect and that the great success of FORTRAN was due to its relative merits rather than its absolute ones. Other programming languages such as ALGOL and LISP have shown that there are easier ways to do at least some things on computers.

To get back to our checkers program: I have written the complete program (except for certain details, including the input and output arrangements) in an informal and somewhat extended version of CPL (which stands for "Combined Programming Language"). The program is not by any means in final form; it has not been run on a machine and therefore, in accordance with the views expressed below, probably still contains some errors. Interested readers may like to look for them. The program in symbolic form, together with a list of the terms used and their definitions, is shown on pages 68 and 69.

In the early days of computer programming—say 15 years ago —mathematicians used to think that by taking sufficient care they would be able to write programs that were correct. Greatly to their surprise and chagrin, they found that this was not the case and that with rare exceptions the programs as written contained numerous errors. The process of discovering, locating and

ChosenPosition(P) = **value of**
§ **let** L = LegalPositionsFrom(P)
if Null(L) **then** Resign
let (p,v) = BestPosition(NIL,− ∞,L,0)
result is p §

BestPosition(P,V,L,d) = Null(L)→(P,V), **value of**
§ **let** (p,l) = Next (L)
let v = − PositionValue(p.d + 1)
result is (v > V) → BestPosition(p,v,l,d),
BestPosition(P,V,l,d) §

PositionValue(P,d) = Terminal(P,d) → TerminalValue(P), **value of**
§ **let** L = LegalPositionsFrom(P)
let (p,v) = BestPosition(NIL,− ∞,L,d)
result is v §

LegalPositionsFrom(P) = **value of**
§ **let** L = RemainingPositionList(P,Capture,5)
result is Null(L)→RemainingPosition List(P,NonCapture,5),L §

RemainingPositionList(P,C,s) =
PartialPositionList(P,C,s,FindMoveList(P,C,s))

PartialPositionList(P,C,s,L) =
Null(L)→((s = −5)→NIL,
RemainingPositionList(P,C,NextMoveDirection(s)),
value of
§ **let** φ = SingleDigitFrom(L)
let lp = MakeMove(P,C,s,φ)
let l = (C = Capture)→CaptureTree(lp),
FinalPosition(lp)
result is Join (l,PartialPositionList(P,C,s,L − φ))§

NextMoveDirection(s) = (s = 5)→4, ((s = 4) → − 4,− 5)

FindMoveList(P,C,s) = **value of**
§ **let** (X,Y,K,σ) = P
let Empty = ∼X ∧ ∼Y∧ Board
let ψ = (C = Capture) → (Shift(Empty,σs)∧Y),Empty
let φ = Shift(ψ,σs)∧ X
result is (s > 0) → φ,φ ∧ K §

MakeMove(P,C,s,φ) = **value of**
§ **let** (X,Y,K,σ) = P
let ψ = (C = Capture) → Shift(φ,− σs),NIL
let θ = (C = Capture) → Shift(ψ,− σs),
Shift(φ,− σs)
let Xk = Null(φ ∧ K) → (θ ∧ LastRows),(θ − φ)
result is ((X − φ + θ),(Y − ψ),(K − ψ ∧ K + Xk),σ,θ).§

FinalPosition(lp) = **value of**
§ **let** (X,Y,K,σ,φ) = lp
result is (Y,X,K,− σ) §

CaptureTree(lp) = **value of**
§ **let** L = PartialCapturePositionList(lp)
result is Null(L) → (FinalPosition(lp)),
CombineCaptureTrees(L) §

PartialCapturePositionList(lp) = **value of**
§ **let** (X,Y,K,σ) = lp
let P = (X,Y,K,σ)
result is MinList(PCP(P,φ,5),PCP(P,φ,4),
PCP(P,φ ∧ K,− 4),PCP(P,φ ∧ K,− 5))§

PCP(P,φ,s) = **value of**
§ **let** (X,Y,K,σ) = P
let ψ = Shift(φ,− σs) ∧Y
let Empty = ∼ X ∧ ∼Y∧ Board
let θ = Shift(ψ,− σs) ∧ Empty
let Xk = Null(φ ∧ K) → (θ ∧ LastRows),(θ − φ)
result is Null(θ) → NIL,
((X − φ + θ),(Y − ψ),(K − ψ ∧ K + Xk),σ,θ) §

CombineCaptureTrees(L) = Null(L) → NIL, **value of**
§ **let** (lp,l) = Next (L)
result is Join (CaptureTree(lp),CombineCaptureTrees(l)) §

Checkers program, expressing author's hierarchical approach, is shown above. The language used in the program is an informal and somewhat extended version of CPL. *The names of the logical functions that are specific to this particular program ("ChosenPosition" and so on) were selected to be suggestive of the operations they govern. A list of the primitive, or generalized, functions and the specific data structures used in the program is provided on the facing page. The chief omissions from the program are the input and output arrangements and the functions that define the game-playing strategy* [Terminal(P,d) *and* TerminalValue(P)]. *The program has not been debugged on a machine and so, in accordance with the views expressed in the article, probably still contains some errors; interested readers may like to look for them. The general notation "Condition → A,B" is a conditional expression whose value is* A *if the condition is satisfied (that is, if it is true) and* B *otherwise. The section that deals with capture moves is shown in the right-hand column above.*

PRIMITIVE FUNCTIONS

a LIST FUNCTIONS

L	LIST
Null(L)	TRUE IF L IS THE EMPTY LIST (NIL), FALSE OTHERWISE
Head(L)	FIRST MEMBER OF L
Tail(L)	WHAT REMAINS OF L AFTER Head(L) IS REMOVED
Next(L)	LIST WHOSE MEMBERS ARE Head(L) AND Tail(L)
$Join(L_1,L_2)$	A SINGLE LIST FORMED FROM THE MEMBERS OF L_1 AND L_2
$MinList(L_1,L_2..)$	A SINGLE LIST FORMED FROM THE MEMBERS OF SEVERAL LISTS; ALSO LEAVES OUT NULL LISTS AND REPETITIONS

b BIT-STRING FUNCTIONS

~	NOT
∧	AND
∨	INCLUSIVE OR
$x + y$	SAME AS $x ∨ y$
$x - y$	SAME AS $x ∧ (\sim y)$
SingleDigitFrom(x)	A BIT-STRING OF THE SAME LENGTH AS x WITH A SINGLE 1 IN A POSITION CORRESPONDING TO ONE OF THE 1'S IN BIT-STRING x
Shift(x,n)	THE BIT-STRING x SHIFTED n PLACES TO THE RIGHT. IF $n < 0$, THE SHIFT WILL BE TO THE LEFT. DIGITS THAT ARE SHIFTED OFF THE END OF THE BOARD ARE LOST. DIGITS SHIFTED ONTO THE BOARD ARE 0'S.

c STRATEGY FUNCTIONS

Terminal(P,d)	TRUE IF P IS TERMINAL, FALSE OTHERWISE
TerminalValue(P)	VALUE OF P (COMPUTED WHEN LOOK-AHEAD BEYOND P IS UNDESIRABLE)

DATA STRUCTURES

a 45-BIT STRINGS

X	PLAYER'S MEN AND KINGS
Y	OPPONENT'S MEN AND KINGS
K	KINGS ON BOTH SIDES
φ	SQUARE MOVED FROM
ψ	CAPTURED PIECE (IF ANY)
θ	SQUARE MOVED TO
Board	1'S ON BOARD SQUARES, 0'S ELSEWHERE
LastRows	1'S ON SQUARES NUMBERED 5, 6, 7, 8, 36, 37, 38, 39

b POSITIONS

σ	NEXT PLAY
	$σ = +1$: BLACK TO PLAY
	$σ = -1$: WHITE TO PLAY
P,p	ORDINARY POSITIONS WITH COMPONENTS X, Y, K, σ
Ip	INTERMEDIATE POSITIONS WITH COMPONENTS X, Y, K,σ,φ, WHERE φ INDICATES THE PIECE THAT CAN MOVE

c MISCELLANEOUS

C	CAPTURE OR NONCAPTURE
s	DIRECTION OF MOVE
	$s = 5$: FORWARD, LEFT
	$s = 4$: FORWARD, RIGHT
	$s = -4$: BACKWARD, LEFT
	$s = -5$: BACKWARD, RIGHT
l,v	POSITION VALUE
d	DEPTH OF LOOK-AHEAD

correcting these errors proved to be one of major difficulty, often taking considerably longer than writing the program in the first place and using a great deal of machine time.

Although programming techniques have improved immensely since the early days, the process of finding and correcting errors in programs—known, graphically if inelegantly, as "debugging"— still remains a most difficult, confused and unsatisfactory operation. The chief impact of this state of affairs is psychological. Although we are all happy to pay lip service to the adage that to err is human, most of us like to make a small private reservation about our own performance on special occasions when we really try. It is somewhat deflating to be shown publicly and incontrovertibly by a machine that even when we do try, we in fact make just as many mistakes as other people. If your pride cannot recover from this blow, you will never make a programmer.

It is not, in fact, in the nature of human beings to be perfectly accurate, and it is unrealistic to believe they ever will be. The only reasonable way to get a program right is to assume that it will at first contain errors and take steps to discover these and correct them. This attitude is quite familiar to anyone who has been in contact with the planning of any large-scale operation, but it is completely strange to most people who have not.

The trouble, I think, is that so many educational processes put a high premium on getting the correct answer the first time. If you give the wrong answer to an examination question, you lose your mark and that is the end of the matter. If you make a mistake in writing your program—or, indeed, in many other situations in life outside a classroom—it is by no means a catastrophe; you do, however, have to find your error and put it right. Maybe it would be better if more academic teaching adopted this attitude also.

It is when we first come to grips with a computer and actually try to run a program, either to test it or to obtain some useful results, that we really begin to get frustrated. In spite of the much vaunted speed of the machine itself, it is normally several hours and sometimes several days before one can actually get back the answer to even the shortest program. When this delay is added to the fact that computers and their programming languages and compilers are often most unhelpful, so that the only information you receive at the end of a day's wait may be that your program is still wrong, it is easy to understand why so many people get the impression that using a computer is more a matter of fighting the machine and the system than it is one of cooperation.

The reason for this curious situation is the desire to keep the computer, which is a very expensive machine, fully occupied for as much of the time as possible. The organization outside the computer, which frequently employs quite a large human operating staff, accounts for almost all the "turn-around time" and a fair proportion of the frustration. The introduction of time-sharing systems should remove this source of frustration, at the cost of greatly increasing the size and complexity of the operating programs [see "Time-sharing on Computers," by R. M. Fano and F. J. Corbató, page 76].

A large part of the work involved in actually getting a program running can be done by the computer itself. Operations such as translating the programming language into detailed machine code, allocating storage space inside the computer, keeping records to assist in the diagnosis of program errors, organizing the scheduling and accounting for a sequence of short jobs from various users and the like are precisely the kind of high-grade routine clerical work a computer can handle, and it is therefore only rational to expect the machine to do it.

The programs to make the machine carry out these operations are of the greatest importance. Most users of the computer will have far more contact with them than they do with the computer itself, and for this reason the operating programs are known as the software of the system (as opposed to the computer itself, which is known as the hardware). In actuality the performance of a system is as much dependent on its software as on its hardware, and the planning and writing of software systems is rapidly becoming a major problem for computer manufacturers. The entire set of these programs, known as the software package, can easily cost the machine manufacturer as much to produce and debug as the machine itself. As a result there is strong pressure not to change either the programming language or the operating system, in spite of the fact that in many respects they are seriously inadequate.

Why is the road from the conception of a program to its execution by the machine so long and tiresome? Why are the operating systems today—the software—so costly and unsatisfactory? Are we perhaps reaching the limit of human ability to write complicated programs, and is the present software crisis really the result of attempting the humanly impossible? Anyone who deals with the large computer systems today knows how close the whole thing is to collapsing under the weight of its own complexity.

There is no doubt that with the current techniques we have nearly reached our limit in programming. Could we not, however, improve the techniques? The checkers example we have considered in this article gives a strong hint that a simplified approach and improvement of the programming language would make things a great deal easier. If a suitable programming language existed, it should clearly be possible to write the entire checkers program in the way outlined above and leave nearly all the remaining stages to be performed by the computer. As a matter of fact, that can almost be done now, and it would probably not be too difficult to construct a language in which it was possible.

The only reasonable way to set up a large and complicated program is to use a hierarchical method. Since there is a limit to the size and complexity of a problem we can hold in our head at one time, it appears that the best way to extend our capability is to treat relatively large and complex operations as single units and combine these units hierarchically. This strategy I have demonstrated in the design of the checkers program [see illustration on facing page]. The present programming languages all pay at least lip service to this idea, but many do not allow for a genuine and unlimited hierarchy—only for two or three levels of operation (such as "local" and "global") the programmer has to consider simultaneously. Those languages that do allow a truly hierarchical treatment of a problem have only a limited ability to deal with representations.

The present-day computer is itself a stumbling block to the use of programs that are written hierarchically (or recursively). Because the computers are unsuitable for this kind of organization, the running of such a program is much slower than it is for a program written and coded in the conventional way. I am convinced, however, that the advantages of this kind of programming will far outweigh any increase of machine time that may be re-

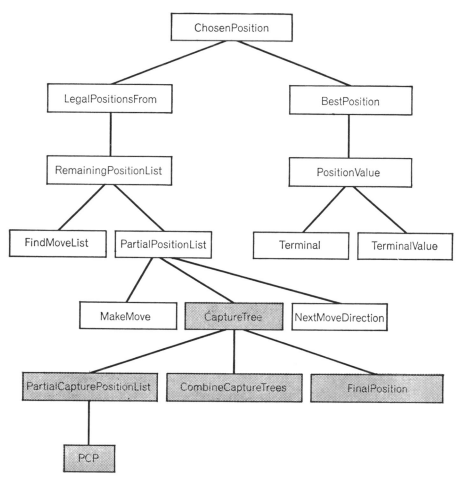

Hierarchical structure of the author's checkers program is evident in this diagram. Since there is a limit to the size and complexity of a problem one can keep in mind at one time, it appears that the best way to deal with large and complicated problems is to treat fairly sizable operations as separate units and then combine them hierarchically. The logical function "ChosenPosition" is defined recursively in terms of two other functions: "LegalPositionsFrom" and "BestPosition." The function "LegalPositionsFrom" deals with the problem of finding legal positions on the checkerboard at a given point in the game; all the functions that branch out from "LegalPositionsFrom" treat various aspects of this problem. The gray tint identifies, for example, the capture moves that branch from this major function. The function "BestPosition" and all the functions that branch out from it deal with the problem of choosing the best position from the list supplied by "LegalPositionsFrom."

quired. The advantages are so great that I believe the hierarchical method will eventually be adopted universally. After all, the chief purpose of any machine is to save human beings trouble; therefore we should not be unduly alarmed about giving the computer more of man's work. In addition, there is good reason to expect that it will be possible to design computers that will deal much more naturally and efficiently with deeply hierarchical programs. These machines will probably be slightly more complex than present ones, but the difference in cost will be well worthwhile.

I have left to the end what seems to me to be the most difficult, but also the most interesting and potentially rewarding, problem concerning programming languages. This is to lay a firm mathematical foundation for the construction of hierarchical systems of programs and to develop a calculus for manipulating them.

The difficulty arises basically from the fact that programming presents us with certain new questions that are not present, or at least not important, in any other branch of mathematics. The mathematical problem has two aspects. The first is how to deal explicitly and in a detailed way with complicated structures (involving representations of data) when not only the structure as a whole but also its component parts must be given names and have values assigned to them. The second aspect of the difficulty is that the use of imperatives (or commands) in programming introduces variables, and mathematics in general does not recognize the existence of variables in this sense, that is, values varying over a period of time. In its traditional branches mathematics deals only with static situations. Even the calculus, which is concerned with the approaches of objects to a limit, deals with the subject in terms of a series of fixed values. In general the things mathematicians call variables are either constants whose values are not yet known or nonexistent quantities (such as "nobody") that are introduced for purposes of logical syntax. In programming, on the other hand, we deal with time-varying variables by the very nature of the process; a program is essentially a schedule of changes.

An experienced programmer reading this chapter will have been struck by the fact that in the formulation of the checkers program I have used no commands, and in particular by the fact that the program contains no assignment statements (statements assigning values to names or objects). The reason for this is that we know how to combine recursively defined functions into hierarchical structures only in the absence of assignment statements. There is still no satisfactory way of doing the same thing if they are included.

Investigation of the mathematical problems I have discussed has now begun. It is clear at the start that the field to be explored is almost entirely new, without established guidelines such as exist in most other areas of mathematical research. It is also evident that the first and most difficult task is to clarify what we mean, in a programming context, by terms such as "name" and "value." The chief trouble is that the introduction of assignments (changes of value with changes in circumstances) makes the meaning of the terms ambiguous from the standpoint of the way they are ordinarily used in mathematics, so that it seems probable we shall need to generate new concepts in order to get a firm grasp of the situation.

Much of the theoretical work now being done in the field of programming languages is concerned with language syntax. In essence this means the research is concerned not with *what* the language says but with *how* it says it. This approach seems to put almost insuperable barriers in the way of forming new concepts—at least as far as language *meaning* is concerned. I believe the way to progress for programmers lies along the path of research on meaning rather than syntax. It is primarily through the study of meaning that we shall develop the concepts required to build up hierarchical structures.

R. M. FANO AND F. J. CORBATÓ

Time-sharing on Computers

This technique, whereby a computer serves a large
number of people at once, does more than save
time and money. It sets up a dialogue between user and
machine and allows communication among users.

The history of the modern computer has been characterized by a series of quantum leaps in our view of the machine's possibilities. To mention only two of the crucial advances, the application of electronics, vastly increasing the computer's speed of operation, and later the invention of special languages, facilitating communication with the machine, each in its turn opened new vistas on the computer's potentialities. Within the past few years the technique called time-sharing has again stimulated the imagination. It has created an unexpected new order of uses for the computer.

At first thought time-sharing seems simply a convenience: a means of allowing fuller use of the machine by more people and of saving time for the users. In practice, however, experiments with the technique have demonstrated a wide range of more interesting possibilities. It enables the user to conduct a continuous dialogue with the machine and in effect makes the computer his intellectual assistant. Further, the system makes it possible for the users to carry on a discourse with one another through the machine, drawing on its large store of knowledge and its computing speed as they do so. The time-sharing computer system can unite a group of investigators in a cooperative search for the solution to a common problem, or it can serve as a community pool of knowledge and skill on which anyone can draw according to his needs. Projecting the concept on a large scale, one can conceive of such a facility as an extraordinarily powerful library serving an entire community—in short, an intellectual public utility.

It was Christopher Strachey, the author of the chapter on system analysis and programming in this book, who first proposed (in 1959) a time-sharing system. The large, expensive computing machines had become far removed from their users, both in time and in distance. An applicant in effect had to deliver his problem or program to a receptionist and then wait hours or sometimes days for an answer that might take the machine only seconds or even less time to produce. The computer, working on one program at a time, kept a queue of users waiting for their turn. If, as commonly happens, a submitted program contained a minor error that invalidated the results, the user often had to wait several hours for resubmission of his corrected program. Strachey suggested that the rapidity of a computer's operations made all this waiting unnecessary. By segregating the central processing operations from the time-consuming interactions with the human programmers, the computer could in effect work on a number of programs simultaneously. Giving only a few seconds or often less than a second at a time to each program or task, the machine could deal with many users at once, as if each had the machine to himself. The execution of various programs would be interspersed without their interfering with one another and without detectable delays in the responses to the individual users.

The Computation Center at the Massachusetts Institute of Technology quickly took up Strachey's suggestion. By November, 1961, the center had implemented and demonstrated a first model of the Compatible Time-Sharing System, using an International Business Machines Corporation 709 computer. Two years later an improved version of this system was operating on two IBM 7094 computers, one at the Computation Center and another at M.I.T.'s Project MAC (an acronym that has been variously translated as standing for multiple-access computer, machine-aided cognition or man and computer). By that time three other time-sharing systems had been developed: at Bolt, Beranek and Newman, Inc., at M.I.T.'s Research Laboratory of Electronics and at the System Development Corporation, and several more have since been developed at other research institutions.

Inherent in the time-sharing concept is a system of multiple direct connections to the computer from many points, near and far. At M.I.T. there are now 160 such stations, each with a teletypewriter that enables the user to enter his message directly in the computer's input and to receive its replies. These stations are installed in various offices and laboratories on the M.I.T. campus and in the homes of some of the research staff and faculty members. Through a private branch exchange each station can by dialing reach either the Project MAC computer or the one in the Computation Center. Moreover, the Project MAC installation is connected to the teletype networks of the Bell System and Western Union, so that access to the computer can be had from thousands of terminals in the U.S. and abroad. Thus the two computer systems at M.I.T. are being used daily by a large and varied community, with each of them providing prompt response for up to 30 simultaneous users. The systems constitute an operating model of the information utility that John McCarthy, the author of the first chapter of this book, described in 1961 in an address picturing computer services of the future.

For professional programmers the time-sharing system has come to mean a great deal more than mere ease of access to the computer. Provided with the opportunity to run a program in continuous dialogue with the machine, editing, "debugging" and modifying the program as they proceed, they have gained immeasurably in the ability to experiment. They can readily investigate new programming techniques and new approaches to problems. The bolder exercise of the imagination encouraged by the new system has resulted not only in more flexibility in attacks on problems but also in the undertaking of important new researches in a variety of areas.

Let us now examine the operation of a time-sharing system. Taking the M.I.T. Compatible Time-Sharing System (CTSS) as our model, we shall first present a sample of what it can do, using a program dialogue for illustration, and then describe the anatomy and machinery of the system in schematic terms.

To begin with, the system contains a large store of information—supervisory and utility programs, language-translating facilities, a library of subroutines and so on—adding up to nearly a million computer words, which is equivalent to about 2,000 book pages crowded with nonredundant symbols. The basic content of the system is a set of some 100 programs, each of which is called into play by a specific command issued through a teletypewriter. They have to do with the ordinary operations of the system and involve communication, control of its various processes, the use and translation of computer languages and so forth. In addition to these 100 basic programs the system contains a great variety of special programs that are also available for general use. To all this "public" information there is added a large amount of material consisting of individual users' private files of programs and information.

Consider, then, an illustrative dialogue between a user and the computer as shown in the actual "print-outs" from the MAC system reproduced on pages 81–84.

The user introduces himself by giving the command "login" and stating the project he wants to work on and his name. The machine responds by printing the time of day (to the hour, minute and tenth of a minute), and the user is now called on to give his password. This has been found to be a highly important requirement: it is necessary to guard the privacy of each personal set of files and protect the information and programs from accidental or malicious alteration by someone else. (Experience has shown that some people are unable to resist the temptation to commit mischievous vandalism of that kind.) The printer is disconnected while the password is being typed so that no record of it appears on the print-out.

If the given password does not check with the person's name and problem number, or if he has exhausted his monthly allowance of time on the computer, or if the machine is already being used to capacity (the maximum number of people who can use the computer at one time in our present system is 30), the machine prints a message stating that access is not available. If access can be granted, the user is allowed to proceed with further commands. Before beginning his work he may ask for an accounting of the amount of time and storage space he has used up from his allotted quotas (as one illustration shows). After this housekeeping query the user goes to work on his problem. Here, in our simple illustration, he writes, translates and executes a program to compute the arithmetic mean and the geometric mean of two given numbers. A command signified by "ed" (for "editing") brings into play a subsystem in the computer that accepts various editing instructions, so that the user can call on it to write his program in a particular language (here it is the language called Michigan Algorithmic Decoder, or MAD) and make alterations, corrections or other manipulations of the program text as directed. Typing errors have been introduced deliberately in our example to illustrate some of these editing functions. The corrections are carried out through a dialogue between the user and the computer. Finally the program is translated and tested on a pair of numbers. The user presses an "interrupt" button at that point to end the computation and the computer prints out "QUIT" in acknowledgment. The user then gives the command "save demo," which instructs the machine to file the program in what becomes a new private file named "demo saved." This file is stored permanently in the system's mass memory.

The owner can command the system to print out the list of files in his file directory by giving the instruction "listf." He may also give a command authorizing the system to allow other named users access to one of his files, and conversely may gain access to other private or public files he is permitted to use. Although a person given access to someone else's file is not usually allowed to change that file, he can copy its contents, file the information separately under his own name and then modify the data or program for his own use. This technique is employed by a second person to use the program for computing the arithmetic and geometric means of a pair of numbers. Another convenient feature of the time-sharing system that is illustrated allows the depositing of messages from one user to another in the computer. On logging into the computer a user may be informed by the machine that there is a message in his "mail box," and the computer will then print the message on command.

To illustrate the editing capabilities of the system we have added a sample print-out of a paper delivered at a conference, to-

```
login t193 fano
W 2237.7
Password
T0193  2859 LOGGED IN  05/27/66    2237.8 FROM 2000N
CTSS BEING USED IS      MAC5A4
LAST LOGOUT WAS  05/27/66  2237.0
R 2.833+.900

ttpeek
W 2238.2

5/27  2238.2 TUSED =  .1

SHIFT    MINUTES
      ALLOTTED  USED
  1      60       3.8
  2      20       1.0
  3      30        .3

DEVICE  STORAGE
        QUOTA   USED
DISK    100      4

R 1.950+.350

ed mad
W 2238.8
INPUT: read and print data
start an"mean = (x+y)/2.
      gmean = (x? gmean = sqrt. (x*y)
      print results "amean, gmen
      transfer to start
      end of program

EDIT:
top
print 10

START    READ AND PRINT DATA
         AMEAN = (X+Y)/2.
         GMEAN = SQRT./(X*Y)
         PRINT RESULTS AMEAN, GMEN
         TRANSFER TO START
         END OF PROGRAM

END OF FILE REACHED BY:
file demo
R 3.983+2.550
```

```
mad demo
W 2242.7
THE FOLLOWING NAMES HAVE OCCURRED ONLY ONCE IN THIS PROGRAM.
   COMPILATION WILL CONTINUE.
   GMEAN
   GMEN
LENGTH 00066.  TV SIZE 00005.  ENTRY 00017

ed demo mad
W 2243.3
EDIT:
locate gmen
change /gmen/gmean/
print           PRINT RESULTS AMEAN, GMEAN
top
change /amean/armean/ 10
END OF FILE REACHED BY:
CHANGE /AMEAN/ARMEAN/ 10
file
R 3.800+1.300

mad demo
W 2244.7
LENGTH 00063   TV SIZE 00005.  ENTRY 00016
R 1.466+.416

loadgo demo
W 2245.0
EXECUTION.
x = 123.456, y = 234.567 *
x = 123.456, y = 234.567 *

         ARMEAN = 179.011499,        GMEAN =  170.172569

   QUIT,
R 5.483+1.283

save demo
W 2245.9
R .866+.283
```

Running dialogue between man and machine is demonstrated by a computer print-out. The user (lowercase letters) announces himself; the computer (uppercase) gives the time. The user gives his password (which, to preserve privacy, is not printed) and the machine logs him in and reports the number of seconds used by the central processor in the exchange. In response to the command "ttpeek" the machine summarizes Fano's time and memory-space account. With "ed mad" Fano writes and edits a program in MAD language for computing the arithmetic and geometric means of any two numbers. (The symbols " and ? erase the preceding character or all the preceding characters in the line respectively.) The program is filed under the name "demo." The machine queries a typing error ("GMEN" for "GMEAN"), which is corrected, and "AMEAN" is changed to "ARMEAN." The program is translated and executed. After a test computation the user ends the execution by pressing an "interrupt" button. The computer acknowledges the interruption ("QUIT") and is thereupon instructed to "save" the program.

```
listf
W 2246.0

     6 FILES    24 RECORDS
   NAME1   NAME2 MOD NOREC   USED
   DEMO    SAVED 000    18 05/27/66
  (MOVIE  TABLE) 001     1
   DEMO      BSS 000     1
   DEMO      MAD 000     1
  PERMIT   FILE 120      1
   FJCC   (MEMO) 000     3 05/19/66

    28 LINKS
   NAME1   NAME2 MOD PROBN. PROGN. LNAME1 LNAME2
   BASIS   SAVED 104  T0173     44
   CIRKIT  SAVED 000  T0113 CMFL04
   CONVOL  SAVED 104  T0173     44
   CONVT     BSS 104
   DATA    SAVED 104
   DATTOC (MEMO) 104  T0254   3212
   DOCTOR  SAVED 144  T0109   2531
    GETF   SAVED 104  T0173     44
   GRPS1    DGET 144  T0263    32
  - QUIT.
  R 1.666+.300




permit demo saved 4 t100 385
W 2248.4
R .816+.266

edl permit mills
W 2248.9
 FILE PERMIT MILLS NOT FOUND.
Input
t 19?t193 2859 per "mits file demo saved to t100 385 mills

Edit
top

print 2

T193 2859 PERMITS FILE DEMO SAVED TO T100 385 MILLS
file
R 4.400+1.500

mail permit mills t100 385
W 2254.7
R 1.366+.433
```

Directory of Fano's personal files is printed out in response to the command "listf." It includes three files associated with the new "DEMO" program as well as "LINKS" to public and private files that Fano may use. Fano goes on to give permission for another user named Mills to use the new program and sends a message to Mills telling him so.

```
login t100 mills
W 2255.4
Password
YOU HAVE      MAIL   BOX
T0100    385 LOGGED IN  05/27/66     2255.7 FROM 20000A

CTSS BEING USED IS     MAC5A4
LAST LOGOUT WAS 05/27/66    1555.3
R 2.766+.716

print mail box
W 2256.2

   MAIL    BOX      05/27 2256.3

FROM   T0193  2859 05/27 2254.7
T193 2859 PERMITS FILE DEMO SAVED TO T100 385 MILLS
R .683+.516

link demo saved t193 2859
W 2257.9
R 1.266+.433

resume demo
W 2258.0
x = 345.678, y = 456.789 *
X = 345.678, Y = 456.789 *


        ARMEAN =    401.233498,          GMEAN =    397.368725
   QUIT,
   R .133+1.450

logout
W 2259.2
T0100    385 LOGGED OUT 05/27/66    2259.3 FROM 20000A
TOTAL TIME USED=     .1 MIN.
```

User Mills, logging in, is told that there is a message in his "MAIL BOX." After reading the message he asks that a link be established to the "demo saved" program that has been permitted to him. When this has been done, he asks the computer to "resume" the program, applying it to two new numbers he provides. The machine does so.

```
resume who
W 2300.6

MAC5A4 STARTED AT 1451.1 05/27

   BACKGROUND USED 142.6.     PERCENTAGE =    0
   17  USERS AT  2300.9 05/27

LINE   USER      NAME   GRP UNIT   TUSED TIMEON
 1 C0056 99995 FIBMON  0 (FIB)      .1 2217.9
 2 C0056 99999 DAEMON  0 DAEMON   37.6 1451.2
 4 T0269  8048 ENNING  3 200007    2.0 2115.9
 5 T0143   799    LIU  1 20000+    7.8 1923.7
 6 T0281  3712 MAURER  1 20000+    8.8 1805.0
 7 T0113  4619  WYLIE -1 600040     .8 2250.0
 8 T0193  2859   FANO  2 20000N     .7 2237.8
 9 T0269  8031 SSANNA  3 20000.    3.6 2044.0
10 T0234  1122 GARMAN  1 700168    1.4 2211.7
11 T0186  4288 INTOSH 15 20000+    5.9 2128.2
12 T0109  2531 ENBAUM  1 20000W    4.5 2125.9
13 T0145  3667 HITMAN  1 600038    1.8 2218.7
14 T0312  3047 NICHEL  1 20000Y    1.9 2222.5
15 T0335  4655 ULIANO -1 20000+     .1 2258.2
16 T0113  3556 EPHUIS  1 200000    3.3 2139.8
17 T0186  3187 MORRIS -1 100035     .4 2223.9
19 T0234  3308 WIDRIG  1 100001    1.4 2227.8

R 1.850+2.133
```

Through a link to the system's public file, Fano asks for and receives a print-out of the system's current users, when they logged in and the amount of time they have used.

```
typset fjcc
W 2303.3
Edit
top
print  20

.page
.header SOCIAL IMPLICATIONS OF ACCESSIBLE COMPUTING
.center
SOME THOUGHTS ABOUT THE SOCIAL
.center
IMPLICATIONS OF ACCESSIBLE COMPUTING
.space
.center
by
.space
.center
E. E. David, Jr.
.center
Bell Telephone Laboratories
.space
.center
R. M. Fano
.center
Massachusetts Institute of Technology
file
R 5.733+.916


runoff fjcc
W 2305.8
Load paper, hit return



                SOME THOUGHTS ABOUT THE SOCIAL
                IMPLICATIONS OF ACCESSIBLE COMPUTING

                              by

                        E. E. David, Jr.
                    Bell Telephone Laboratories

                         R. M. Fano
                Massachusetts Institute of Technology


                           ABSTRACT

        The pattern of our  business  and  private  lives  has  been
        shaped by many important technological developments such  as
        automobiles, electric power and telephones.   The  influence
        of these products of technology was felt  when  they  became
        available to a large segment of the population.  We are  now
        at that stage with computers.

        As   with   previous   products  of  technology,  accessible
        computing will undoubtedly benefit  society  but  will  also
        face us  with  new  problems  and  new  frustrations.    The
        underlying issues are very complex and they  deserve  prompt
        and thoughtful consideration on the part of all of us.



        logout
        W 2307.9
          TO193  2859 LOGGED OUT 05/27/66    2308.0 FROM 20000N
          TOTAL TIME USED=    .9 MIN.
```

Editing capability of the system is illustrated by the machine's reproduction of the beginning of an article. The command "typset" calls up the program for editing and printing the text. Commands prefaced by a period, such as "center" and "space," are instructions on format. The command "runoff" produces a print-out in the specified format. Logging out, Fano learns that his demonstration of a dialogue between man and machine, which lasted 30.3 minutes, used .9 minute of computer time.

gether with the commands that enabled the computer to present it in the desired typographical form. The system includes a special facility for editing English text, and this facility has been used in the preparation of technical reports and other publications [see illustration on the facing page].

Not the least useful feature of the Compatible Time-Sharing System is the fact that it carries its own set of instructions to its users. Stored in its mass memory is the manual describing the system; this is indexed by a table of contents listing the various services and sections in the reverse chronological order of their addition to the system; that is, the latest are listed first. Thus a user can readily check at any time to see whether or not his copy of the manual is up to date and can then obtain a print-out of any new or modified sections.

To explain the workings of the system we have focused on the dialogue carried on between the user and the computer through the medium of printed commands and responses. The Project MAC system also includes two display stations with facilities for light-pen drawing on a cathode ray tube and for viewing the projection of continuously rotating three-dimensional objects. This equipment has been used by Cyrus Levinthal of M.I.T. for studying the structure of biological molecules.

Of the anatomy and internal operations of the M.I.T. time-sharing system we can only give a schematic outline. It employs a very large and complex installation, built around an IBM 7094 computer and containing in addition a number of special units [see illustration on page 86].

The heart of the system is a complex of programs called "the supervisor." It coordinates the operation of the various units, allocates the time and services of the computer to users and controls their access to the system. The allocation function includes scheduling of users' requests, transferring control of the central processor from one user to another, moving programs in and out of the core memory and managing the users' private files. Obviously the time allowance for each program-run must be closely regulated. If a program runs too long without interruption, other users will be kept waiting unduly; on the other hand, if the execution of a program is interrupted many times, the repeated movement of the program in and out of the core memory

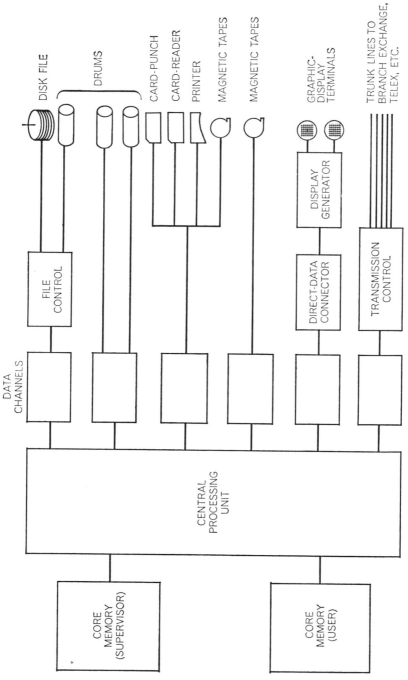

DISK FILE

DRUMS

CARD-PUNCH

CARD-READER

PRINTER

MAGNETIC TAPES

MAGNETIC TAPES

GRAPHIC-DISPLAY TERMINALS

TRUNK LINES TO BRANCH EXCHANGE, TELEX, ETC.

FILE CONTROL

DISPLAY GENERATOR

DIRECT-DATA CONNECTOR

TRANSMISSION CONTROL

DATA CHANNELS

CENTRAL PROCESSING UNIT

CORE MEMORY (SUPERVISOR)

CORE MEMORY (USER)

Principal elements of the M.I.T. time-sharing computer installation are shown in a simplified schematic diagram. One of the two core memories is occupied by the supervisor program, which runs the system; the other is available to users. Files are moved into the core memory as needed from the disk and drum memories. The transmission control is actually a special-purpose computer.

will entail a waste of time. We have adopted a time-allowance scheme based on task priorities that in turn are determined initially by the amount of information that must be transferred into the core memory. The smaller the amount of information, the higher the initial priority the task is given. The time allowance is at least two seconds and doubles with each level of decreasing priority. If a task is not completed in its allotted time—or if a higher-priority task is waiting—it is interrupted and enough of the program moved out to a storage drum to make room in the core memory for the next task awaiting the processor's services. If the allotted time has been exhausted, the task's priority is lowered and a correspondingly doubled allocation of time is made. The interrupted task is then continued when its turn comes up again [see illustrations on pages 88 and 89].

The user need not remain in communication with the system while his program is being run. He may write a program in collaboration with the machine, test it and, after he is satisfied that it is correct, instruct the internal supervisor to run the program for him and store the results in a file from which he can retrieve them later at his convenience. This arrangement, called FIB (for "Foreground-initiated Background"), is designed particularly for programs involving lengthy computations that do not require human intervention. The present system also allows, in effect, for the concurrent running of programs on a "batch" basis (that is, not time-sharing), but this facility is now largely superseded by FIB.

This, then, in sketchy outline, is the compatible time-sharing system we have been working with so far at M.I.T. It is only a precursor, of course, of systems that will be developed in the future. What improvements or advances are needed to create an installation that will serve a large community as a general public utility?

One obvious necessity is that the system provide continuous and reliable service. A public utility must be available to the community 24 hours a day and seven days a week without interruption. It should not shut down for accidents, repairs, maintenance, modifications or additions to the system. This implies, among other things, that the system should not depend completely on any one unit. It suggests that every part of the

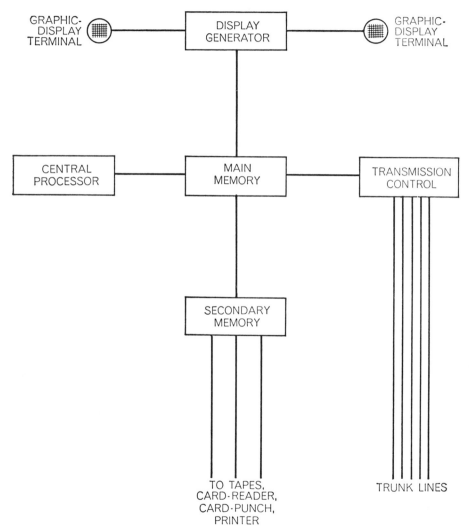

GRAPHIC-
DISPLAY
TERMINAL

DISPLAY
GENERATOR

GRAPHIC-
DISPLAY
TERMINAL

CENTRAL
PROCESSOR

MAIN
MEMORY

TRANSMISSION
CONTROL

SECONDARY
MEMORY

TO TAPES,
CARD-READER,
CARD-PUNCH,
PRINTER

TRUNK LINES

Supervisor has the effect of reducing the equipment layout diagrammed on page 86 to the functional arrangement illustrated here. The main (core) memory, rather than the central processing unit, is in effect the central unit with which other units communicate; the various mass storage devices are in effect a single secondary memory.

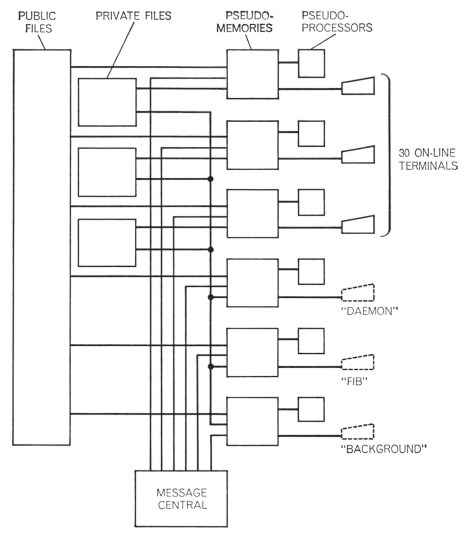

PUBLIC FILES

PRIVATE FILES

PSEUDO-MEMORIES

PSEUDO-PROCESSORS

30 ON-LINE TERMINALS

"DAEMON"

"FIB"

"BACKGROUND"

MESSAGE CENTRAL

"User's view" presents still another system diagram different from that on page 86. Each of the 30 on-line users has available, for all practical purposes, his own processor and memory. Each memory has in effect a capacity of 32,768 words and has access to public files as well as the user's own files. Messages can be exchanged through the message central. Three special pseudo-processors are available to the supervisor. "Daemon" copies files on tape. "FIB" executes programs for users who do not need to wait for lengthy answers. "Background" operates as a conventional computer, batch-processing large tasks that have been fed into the central computer.

system should consist of a pool of functionally identical units (memories, processors and so on) that can operate independently and can be used interchangeably or simultaneously at all times. In such a system any unit could be taken out of service for repair or maintenance during a period when the system load was low, and the supervisor would distribute the load among the remaining units. It would also be a simple matter to add units, without interrupting service, as the use of the system grew. Moreover, the availability of duplicate units would simplify the problem of queuing and the allocation of time and space to users [see illustration on the facing page].

A second need is more efficient use of the computer's time. In the Compatible Time-Sharing System, as in most conventional batch-processing systems, the central processor is idle for about 40 percent of the time because it must wait while programs and data are being transferred in and out of the core memory and while necessary information is being fetched from or written into the users' files. One way to reduce the processor's idle time would be to have at all times in the core memory several executable programs (instead of only one), so that as soon as the processor finishes a task or transmission of more data is required, it would find another task available. The computer art now presents a technique for producing this desirable situation without having to waste too much core memory to store entire programs waiting to be executed. A program can be divided into pages, each containing, say, only 1,024 words, and the core memory can be divided into logical blocks of the same size. Pages are transferred into core memory only when needed, if at all, so that tasks can be initiated with minimal use of precious memory space.

Another new technique, called program segmentation, has been advocated by Jack B. Dennis of M.I.T. to increase the ease and flexibility with which subprograms may be linked to form large programs. The process followed by a computer in executing a large program is similar to that followed by the reader of an article that refers to a section of another article that in turn refers to a chapter of a book, and so on. The traditional technique for linking subprograms is equivalent to having a clerk in the library make copies of all articles and books to be read, assemble them into a single volume, and translate all

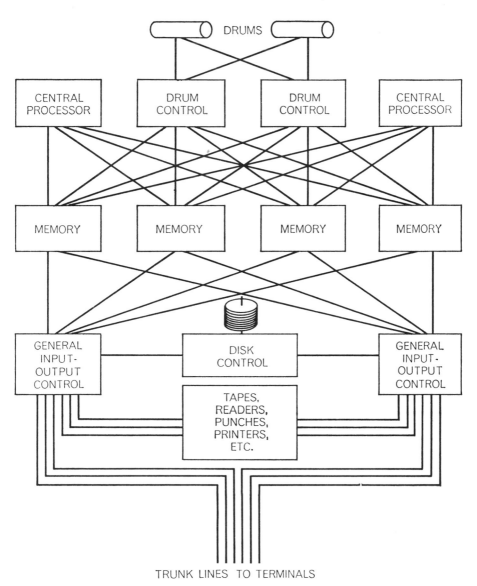

DRUMS

CENTRAL PROCESSOR

DRUM CONTROL

DRUM CONTROL

CENTRAL PROCESSOR

MEMORY

MEMORY

MEMORY

MEMORY

GENERAL INPUT-OUTPUT CONTROL

DISK CONTROL

GENERAL INPUT-OUTPUT CONTROL

TAPES, READERS, PUNCHES, PRINTERS, ETC.

TRUNK LINES TO TERMINALS

Proposed design for a time-sharing computer would provide more dependability and flexibility than present systems. There would be several elements of each kind, so that no one unit would be critical. The main memories would be central physically as well as functionally. And the supervisor would assign each task to available units as required.

references into references to specific page numbers of the volume. This technique has the disadvantage that popular subprograms have to be copied and stored many times as parts of different programs. Moreover, programs, unlike articles and books, are often changed and new subprograms have to be incorporated. This is particularly true in a time-sharing system. With the technique of program segmentation the segments, or subprograms, retain their individual identity at all times. They are retrieved from mass storage only when the computer finds a reference to them during the execution of some other segment. Speed of retrieval, and particularly speed of access to individual words of a segment after the segment has been retrieved, is essential. For this purpose the computer must include special equipment features, and appropriate directories of all segments must be maintained. The position of the computer is then analogous to that of a user of an ideal automatic library who finds in his reading a reference to some article or book. He gives the name or names identifying the article or book and the page or line number in which he is interested, and the desired text is quickly displayed for him so that his reading can continue without appreciable interruption. The technique of program segmentation appears to have many other advantages beyond those suggested here, and these are currently being explored in a number of research laboratories. Segmentation makes it possible for several central processors to combine in working on a program involving much computation and improves intercommunication within the system [see illustration on the facing page].

Finally, in this catalogue of improvements needed to develop time-sharing computers into general intellectual utilities we must mention a bottleneck for which a practicable solution is not yet in sight. The output devices still leave a great deal to be desired. The teletypewriter is a frustratingly slow means of communication—and it cannot draw a picture. The graphical display devices that are currently available are expensive and require elaborate communication facilities. Inasmuch as, from the standpoint of convenience and of economics, efficient communication between the time-sharing system and its users will become at least as important as the operation of the system itself, this problem presents a crucial challenge to designers.

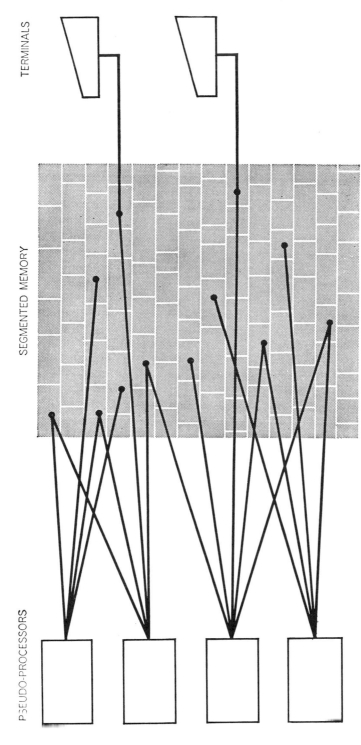

TERMINALS

SEGMENTED MEMORY

PSEUDO-PROCESSORS

Segmentation of programs adds to the flexibility of a time-sharing system. Each public and private file becomes an independent segment stored in the main memory, each with its own list of authorized users. There are no pseudo-memories, since each pseudo-processor can communicate with a number of segments, some of which are shared with other processors.

Three years of experience with the Compatible Time-Sharing System at M.I.T. have been a revelation in many ways. In a sense the system and its users have developed like a growing organism. Most striking is the way the users have built on one another's work and become dependent on the machine. More than half of the commands now written into the system were developed by the users rather than by the professionals charged with programming and developing the system. The users have very generally chosen to link up with one another's private files and the public files. Whereas in conventional computer installations one hardly ever makes use of a program developed by another user, because of the difficulty of exchanging programs and data, here the ease of exchange has encouraged investigators to design their programs with an eye to possible use by other people. They have acted essentially as if they were writing papers to be published in technical journals. Indeed, the analogy is not farfetched: an editorial board representing the community of users acts as a referee to pass on all new commands that are to be introduced into the system and on all information that is to be stored in the public files.

All in all, the mass memories of our machines are becoming more and more like a community library. The users are beginning to complain about the difficulty of finding out just what the library contains and locating the items that may be of interest to them. The facility actually goes beyond a library's usual services. It already has a rudimentary mechanism whereby one person can communicate with another through a program in real time, that is, while both are using the same program at the same time. There have been cases in which a member of the faculty, sitting at a teletypewriter at home, has worked with a student stationed at a terminal on the campus. It is easy now to envision the use of the system for education or for real-time collaboration between the members of a research team. And it does not take a long stretch of the imagination to envision an entire business organization making and executing all its major decisions with the aid of a time-shared computing system. In such a system the mass memory at all times would contain an up-to-date description of the state of the business.

Looking into the future, we can foresee that computer utilities are likely to play an increasingly large part in human affairs. Communities will design systems to perform various functions— intellectual, economic and social—and the systems in turn undoubtedly will have profound effects in shaping the patterns of human life. The coupling between such a utility and the community it serves is so strong that the community is actually a part of the system itself. Together the computer systems and the human users will create new services, new institutions, a new environment and new problems. It is already apparent that, because such a system binds the members of a community more closely together, many of the problems will be ethical ones. The current problem of wiretapping suggests the seriousness with which one must consider the security of a system that may hold in its mass memory detailed information on individuals and organizations. How will access to the utility be controlled? Who will regulate its use? To what ends will the system be devoted, and what safeguards can be devised to prevent its misuse? It is easy to see that the progress of this new technique will raise many social questions as well as technical ones.

J O H N   R .   P I E R C E

The Transmission of Computer Data

Computer users are sending an increasing volume
of digital data over the nation's electrical communication
network. To transmit such data efficiently
at high speed, the network is being modified.

Electrical communication is an adaptation of science and technology to the service of man. Computers too are servants of men. Computers can respond to and interact with man directly and immediately, as an automatic telephone switching system or an airline reservation system does. Or computers can do assigned chores and report back to man intermittently, as they do in inventory control or the making up of payrolls. In either case computers and the data they manufacture must somehow enter into the pattern of man's telecommunication.

Modern electrical communication had its origin in two apparently distinct inventions of the 19th century. One of these was the telegraph, which transmitted information by means of on-off signals that produced audible clicks. The receiving operator interpreted these clicks as letters and words of a message; he transcribed the message on a piece of paper or, in some instances, spoke it to an expectant recipient. The other early invention was the telephone, which transmitted, over a limited distance and faintly, the sound of the human voice.

I think we should add to these two inventions another two that are crucial to human uses of electrical communication. These are automatic telephone switching, which first brought man into large-scale contact with complicated logical machines, and the teletypewriter. These inventions enabled men who had no special training (such as the training of telegraph operators) to communicate electrically by dialing or by typing letters and numbers.

As we look back on the early telegraph and the early telephone, we see that they were as specialized as they were simply because of the limitations of the electrical art of their time. Even then, however, they were not entirely separate. Alexander Graham Bell discovered the telephone while working toward a harmonic telegraph, in which different signals would be simultaneously conveyed over the same pair of wires by electrical tones of different frequency. Still, for a long time there seemed to be some sort of intellectual or electrical distinction made between the kinds of signals employed for telegraphy and telephony [see illustration on page 98].

This distinction gradually became less clear as telegraph signals were multiplexed—transmitted many at a time—over telephone lines in much the way Bell had envisioned in his work on the harmonic telegraph. Recently it has been shown that telephone signals can be transmitted by on-off impulses, using the method known as pulse-code modulation (PCM). In this method the varying amplitude of the telephone signal is sampled at frequent intervals and coded in numerical values, which are then converted into binary digits for transmission. At the receiving end of the line the operation is reversed [see illustration on page 99].

Thus we have begun to see in electrical communication something of the universality of man's behavior and man's nervous system. We all use a mixture of reading and writing, listening and speaking and even gesturing in everyday life. In the human nervous system we find no distinction among the signals associated with different human senses and activities. The nerve impulses that travel from our fingers to our brain in the operation of the sense of touch, the nerve impulses that travel from the eyes to the brain in vision and the nerve impulses from the ear to the brain in hearing are all the same spikelike electrical signals. There is a uniform medium through which all our senses serve us. The same spikelike pulses control the muscles

a TELEGRAPH SIGNAL (MORSE CODE)

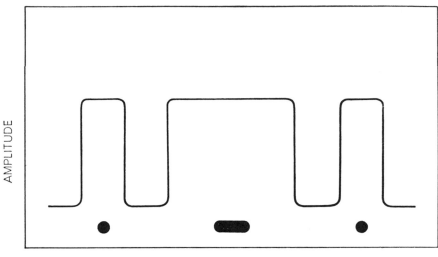

AMPLITUDE

TIME

b TELEPHONE SIGNAL (ANALOGUE FORM)

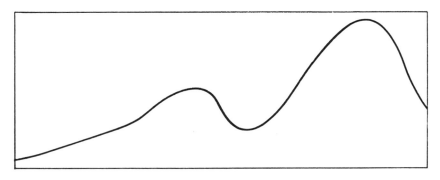

Signal-coding takes two basic forms: digital and analogue. A digital signal carries information in the form of pulses. Morse code (a) is an early example of a digital code in which the pulses vary in duration but not in amplitude. An analogue signal, such as a telephone signal (b), varies continuously in amplitude. An analogue signal can be converted to digital form by sampling its amplitude at regular intervals and assigning a numerical value to each sample (c). The numerical values of the samples can be converted to binary digits and transmitted as a sequence of 0's and 1's (d). This signaling method is called pulse-code modulation. At the receiving end of the line the binary numbers can be converted to smoothed pulses whose amplitude is proportional to the size of the number (e). The sum of these pulses regenerates the original analogue signal.

c CONVERSION TO DIGITAL FORM

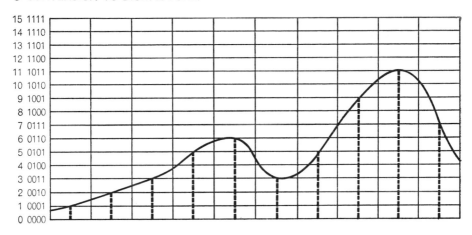

d TRANSMITTED DIGITAL SIGNAL (PULSE CODE MODULATION)

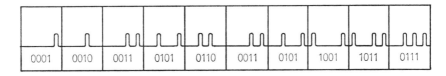

| 0001 | 0010 | 0011 | 0101 | 0110 | 0011 | 0101 | 1001 | 1011 | 0111 |

e RECONVERSION TO ANALOGUE FORM

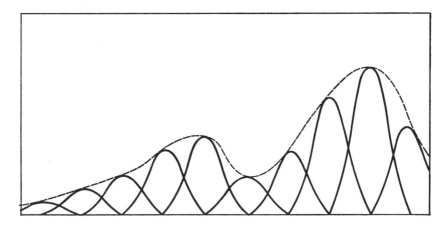

we use in writing and those we use in speaking. The human body employs a common communication system for both sensory and motor activities. The differences among such activities lie in the differences among the various sensors and effectors and in the functioning of the central nervous system.

In 1948, quite late in the evolution of communication technology, a logical framework was developed that is capable of describing, unifying, and quantifying the process of communication and control. Claude E. Shannon, then a young mathematician working for the Bell Telephone Laboratories, inquired: What are we really trying to do in the process of communication? This process, he said, begins with a source of information, which generates information at some particular rate. Information from the source is encoded and then transmitted over a communication channel. At the far end the message is decoded and a replica of the information at the source arrives at a destination.

In order to talk sense about the process Shannon had to have a measure of the information rate of the source and a measure of the information capacity of the communication channel. He defined a universal measure and a universal unit of information: the bit (binary digit). A bit is the choice between plus or minus; it is the amount of information needed to remove the uncertainty between yes or no. It is a distinct choice, and hence it reminds us of the on-off character of the telegraph signal, but it is a universal choice. It applies equally well to the information rates and channel capacities of telegraph signals, voice signals, picture signals, and the signals that circulate through modern electronic digital computers and telephone switching systems. Through Shannon's work our conception of communication has come to fit the actual nature of electrical communication systems: circuits that can be used interchangeably for telegraph, voice and picture signals.

Shannon's equations demonstrated for the first time just how wasteful most communication channels are. He showed, for example, that a letter of English text contains only about one bit of information, if due allowance is made for letter frequencies in English words and the predictable constraints that exist in all written languages. In order words, with an efficient coding scheme one should be able to transmit ordinary English text with an expenditure of one bit per letter. Thus the information contained in a typical 300-word page of typewritten text is only some 1,800 bits. To transmit 300 words with ordinary data-transmission coding techniques, however, requires the expenditure of about 12,600 bits (a seven-bit code group for each letter). To transmit a page of text by facsimile requires about a million bits. In this case, of course, the entire page is transmitted as a picture, which is mostly white space. If the page were read aloud over a pulse-code-modulation telephone channel, one would need more than 11 million bits to transmit it. Finally, if the same page were transmitted by television for the time needed to read it aloud (say three minutes), more than 10 billion bits would be required. An obvious way to reduce the number of bits transmitted in this case would be to send the picture once, which would take only a thirtieth of a second, and then send a few bits of information containing the message: "Hold picture on screen for three minutes." Something analogous does happen, in fact, when a few lines of input to a computer result in many pages of print-out. In Shannon's sense there is no more information in the print-out than in the input that gave rise to it. Accordingly any message that can be generated at the terminal of a communication channel contains no information beyond the local input needed to produce it and therefore need not be transmitted.

This brief excursion into information theory is relevant because the users of computers are increasingly concerned about whether to install a computer at the site where computer problems exist or to transmit the problems to a computer at a remote site. By adopting the latter course one may be able to justify the installation of a large computer that can handle many inputs by the technique of time-sharing [see "Time-sharing on Computers," by R. M. Fano and F. J. Corbató, page 76]. Information theory makes it clear, however, that the "information" transmitted from the computer back to one of the time-sharing stations is not truly information. One can therefore afford to transmit it only as long as communication channels are cheaper than the computing machinery needed to generate it. The debate about when it is cheaper to transmit and when it is cheaper to compute has been agitating the computer industry for several years and will doubtless continue to do so as economic advantages swing one way and then another.

Still, it takes little imagination to foresee that in a world filled with computers as well as people the communication mix will be vastly different from what it is today. The trend is already foreshadowed in the use being made of the long-lines circuits of the Bell System. For the past 10 years "special service" circuits have been growing much faster than "message" circuits. The latter are used for ordinary switched telephone calls. The former are circuits, usually of the same nature, that are not used as part of the switched telephone plant but are used rather for the transmission of data, television, radio programs or the voice part of the television signal, facsimile, nonswitched private-line telephony or some other special service. The growth of special-service circuits reflects several areas of use: data transmission, closed-circuit television for educational and other purposes, and networks of circuits rented to large companies, sometimes for a highly mixed usage [see illustration on facing page].

It is important to realize that, although the distinction between messages and special services is an important one, it is not a distinction between data and voice. Some of the most promising prospects of data transmission involve the telephone-message network. In Wilmington, Del., a person with an account at the Bank of Delaware can pay for a purchase at the nearby Stroms department stores even if he has left his wallet home and has no credit account at Stroms. After a purchase the salesclerk simply "dials" the number of the bank on a push-button ("Touch-Tone") telephone, enters a code that identifies the customer and then enters the amount of the purchase. Other banks that are pioneering in similar services include the Mercantile Trust Company N.A. of St. Louis, the Wells Fargo Bank of San Francisco and the Manufacturers Bank of Detroit.

The interaction of men and computers is not limited to "data" signals; it can involve voice or visual signals. Moreover, unlike the pulses produced by a telephone dial, the signals produced by push-button signaling resemble musical notes; they can be transmitted over any voice circuit and hence can be used to interrogate remote computers. How can the computer answer? In a system

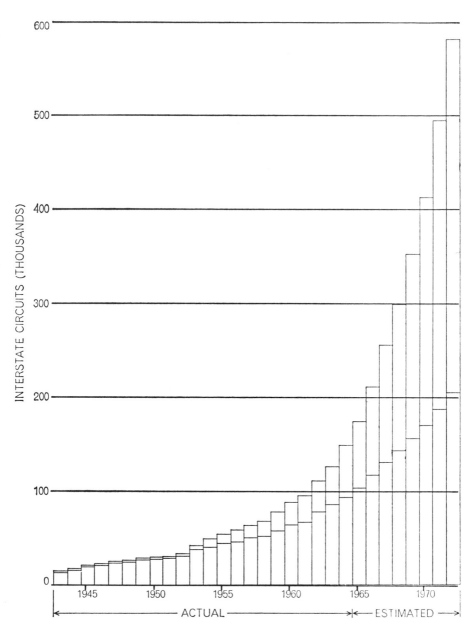

Long-lines circuits of the Bell System are increasing steeply. The lower segment of each bar represents circuits used for conventional telephone messages. The upper segment represents equivalent voice circuits used for special services, such as facsimile, television and data of various kinds. Such circuits are expected to exceed message circuits in 1967.

used by the Bankers Trust Company the computer responds over the line by a recorded voice.

We should also realize that in an up-to-date computer center much of the output may be graphs, diagrams and drawings rather than tabular print-out. The most efficient means for transmitting graphical material is to transmit the coded directions that would ordinarily be fed to the output device that makes the drawing. This means that a graphical output device with a considerable logical capability—a small computer in itself—must be used at the receiving end. In some cases this may prove impractical, and less efficient television or facsimile transmission may then be employed.

Similarly, computers can make use of graphical inputs. Again the efficient mode of transmission is to have a small computer to encode the input at the transmitting end, but again facsimile or even television might find a place putting graphical material into computers.

In the more distant future it may be possible to control computers, including telephone switching systems, by the human voice. Progress is being made in the automatic identification of speakers by voice, as a substitute for a handwritten signature, and this could play an important part in banking and other credit transactions.

The prospect before us, then, is a large growth in the use of all kinds of special signals in communicating with computers as well as with human beings. The flexible and universal nature of electrical communication will continue to make it possible for communication to grow freely and flexibly in meeting needs that have been and will continue to be less than completely predictable.

If we were to start afresh in building a universally adaptable communication network, there are persuasive arguments that it should transmit digital signals exclusively. Voice and other signals can now be converted economically to and from digital form at telephone offices. Digital signals could then be used in terminal equipment and throughout the switching apparatus. Such primitive signals are unspecialized, and can be used easily for any form of communication. About 64,000 binary pulses a second will provide a telephone circuit and about 64 million suffice for commercial television.

In the days of the vacuum tube such a digital network would have been uneconomical, but the transistor has made digital transmission practical, and the impending microelectronic revolution will steadily lower the cost of both digital transmission and digital processing, including digital switching.

Using today's technology, we could construct apparatus that would economically:

Transmit pulses over a single pair of wires at rates up to six million bits per second.

Transmit pulses through a coaxial channel at rates up to 300 million bits per second (a total capacity of three billion bits per second each way through a 20-unit coaxial cable).

Transmit six billion bits per second each way through a two-inch wave guide by means of radio waves whose wavelength is measured in millimeters.

Transmit a total of six billion bits per second between various pairs of telephone offices by means of a single hovering artificial satellite.

For better or worse, it would be idle to assume that there will be all-digital transmission in any near future. For an all-digital system to be useful it would have to extend to anyone who wanted communication service. For the cost of such a system to be bearable the traffic would have to be great. One cannot start entirely afresh and build a universal digital-transmission system, first because the undertaking would be impractically large and second because the initial traffic such a system would handle is already accommodated by existing facilities.

What, then, do we have, and where are we going? There are in the country a number of private transmission systems (predominantly microwave-radio systems) owned by large users. The bulk of traffic, however, goes over common-carrier telephone and telegraph company lines. Of the traffic borne by common carriers the bulk of the facilities are those of the telephone companies, both Bell System and independent. These facilities have a capital value of some $30 billion. They consist of a great many kinds of equipment, old and new, which through a process of orderly development and evolutionary accommodation can work together in handling a variety of traffic.

A small part of the Bell System transmission equipment is already digital. The "T1" transmission system sends 1.5 million binary pulses per second for distances between five and 50 miles. A twisted pair of wires in a cable is used for each direction, and regenerative repeaters every mile amplify and reshape the train of pulses. The T1 system is widely installed. In Massachusetts, for example, a nework of T1 systems will soon cover the entire state. The system is used predominantly for telephony, but it is also used for data transmission, including facsimile. It is well suited to the visual telephone ("Picturephone"). Other digital-transmission systems are under development, including a T2 system with four times the bit capacity of the T1 and a T4 coaxial-cable system with nearly 200 times the capacity of the T1.

The rest of the common-carrier plant—transmission and switching—was designed primarily for sending analogue signals such as voice. The amplitude of an analogue signal varies over a period of time in a smooth way, and in certain respects this variation must be reproduced with high precision.

To achieve the universality necessary for effective communication, common-carrier facilities are interconnected in a hierarchical manner. Let me illustrate by describing the switched-message telephone plant.

Although most of the world's 182 million telephones are interconnected, we shall consider only the 95 million telephones in North America. Among the 95 million telephones there are more than 4×10^{15} possible interconnections. It is ridiculous to imagine this number of individual circuits interconnecting the telephones of the country. Clearly some more sensible means of interconnection must be employed. That is, of course, the telephone switchboard in the local "central office" [see illustration on the facing page].

The "subscriber's loop" from your house goes to a local central office, along with between a few hundred and as many as 50,000 other subscriber's loops. When you talk with another subscriber who is connected to the same central office your loop is connected to his right at that office. In a large metropolitan area there will be many central offices. When there is heavy

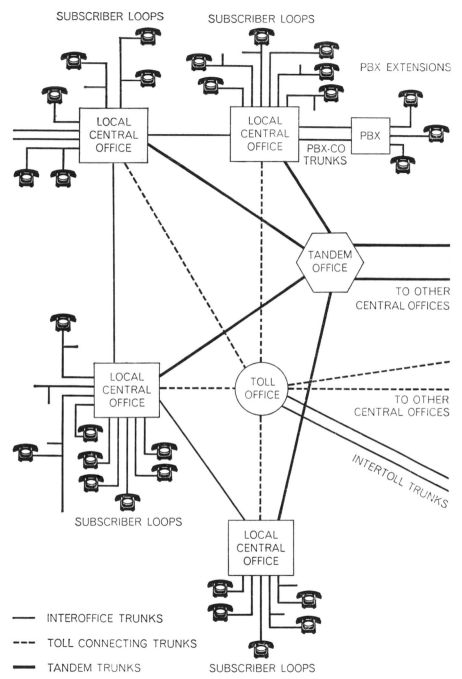

SUBSCRIBER LOOPS

SUBSCRIBER LOOPS

PBX EXTENSIONS

LOCAL CENTRAL OFFICE

LOCAL CENTRAL OFFICE

PBX

PBX-CO TRUNKS

TANDEM OFFICE

TO OTHER CENTRAL OFFICES

LOCAL CENTRAL OFFICE

TOLL OFFICE

TO OTHER CENTRAL OFFICES

INTERTOLL TRUNKS

SUBSCRIBER LOOPS

LOCAL CENTRAL OFFICE

——— INTEROFFICE TRUNKS

--- TOLL CONNECTING TRUNKS

▬▬ TANDEM TRUNKS

SUBSCRIBER LOOPS

Telephone network is designed in hierarchical fashion. When a call is placed to someone in the immediate neighborhood, the connection is usually made in the local central office. Calls to more distant points may involve "toll offices" or "tandem offices."

traffic between nearby offices, those offices will be connected by interoffice trunks.

When there are a large number of central offices in one area, it is uneconomical to provide an adequate number of trunks between all central offices, just as it is uneconomical to interconnect all telephones pair by pair. Instead a tandem office is set up, connected to each of the local central offices it serves by tandem trunks. Finally, one may wish to talk with someone else in a distant city. In that case the call will go from the local central office to a toll office and thence over an intertoll trunk to some other toll office.

There is also a hierarchical organization of the facilities used to transmit signals between various parts of the system. The subscriber's loop is a twisted pair of copper wires in a cable, without means of amplification. (Amplifiers are sometimes needed for a long loop.) The subscriber's loop is a two-wire circuit, that is, voice signals are transmitted simultaneously in both directions over the same pair of wires. Because the means of suppressing interference between the signals going in opposite directions is not quite perfect, some of the signal going toward a subscriber is reflected back toward the sender. Although this defect is unobjectionable in voice communication, it makes it impractical to use simple two-wire circuits for the simultaneous two-way transmission of data.

The next level in the hierarchy employs four-wire systems, which provide independent circuits for the two directions of transmission. In these systems, which interconnect toll offices, the band of frequencies constituting a telephone channel is shifted up in frequency so that many channels can be "stacked" one above another in frequency and transmitted through amplifiers and over cables without interference. This technique is known as frequency-division multiplex.

For long-haul transmission hundreds of channels are transmitted over one coaxial cable, or one microwave link, or one submarine cable, or one communication satellite. At present all long-haul systems use frequency-division multiplex. They all employ a standard pattern in shifting the frequencies of voice channels and combining them. A "channel bank" is used to combine 12 voice channels into a group by shifting their frequencies.

A "group bank" is used to combine five groups into a supergroup (60 channels) by another frequency shift. A "supergroup bank" is used to combine 10 supergroups into a master group (600 channels) by means of still another frequency shift. By a further frequency shift several master groups can be sent over one long-haul system.

Because of this hierarchical procedure various channels with a bandwidth broader than a telephone channel are readily available in the telephone network. These are the group, with a bandwidth of about 48,000 cycles; the supergroup, with a bandwidth of about 240,000 cycles; and the master group, with a bandwidth of about 2.4 million cycles. Such broad-band channels are commonly employed in data transmission and facsimile transmission. If the demand arises, data can be sent over the channels of still wider bandwidth (about 4.1 million cycles) developed to carry television signals.

For some years in the future common-carrier circuits that were designed primarily for voice signals will be used to transmit a wide variety of new kinds of signal, including digital, facsimile and Picturephone signals. Special end links, such as those provided by the T1 digital system, will come into play, and long-haul digital transmission will be introduced gradually in such a way that it can operate interchangeably with present facilities. Nonetheless, new kinds of communication cannot wait for the construction of an entirely new common-carrier plant.

Present circuits derived from frequency-division multiplex systems are rather sophisticated from the point of view of information theory. They are tailored to the statistical analysis of voice signals and conversations. If they are required to carry a large number of data signals that "talk" all the time with the same "loudness," they can be overloaded.

Furthermore, the ear does not mind if some frequency components of a signal arrive a little earlier or a little later than others, but this is intolerable in the transmission of pulses. To transmit pulses efficiently over a circuit designed for voice a device called an equalizer must be used, and this device must be tailored to the particular circuit.

Finally, our sense of hearing is insensitive to moderate, gradual changes in level. In transmitting digital signals efficiently over a circuit, however, it may be necessary to distinguish among 16 or more precise amplitudes. The control of level is therefore another problem.

In the economics of data transmission the cost of the "data set," which adapts a circuit for data transmission, may be paramount. On the other hand, a high rate of transmission in bits per second may be the most important factor. Therefore cheap data terminals that will squeeze more bits per second through a circuit are also needed.

Let us consider sending data over a telephone circuit. A simple data set will transmit up to 300 bits per second over any circuit. A slightly better set will transmit up to 600 bits per second. A set that does not use a binary signal but transmits four different kinds (frequencies) of signals will transmit up to 2,400 bits per second. All these data sets are available commercially.

Beyond this level of performance experiments have been done showing that it is possible to transmit over a telephone channel up to 5,400 bits per second, and perhaps more than 9,000 bits per second. Such transmission calls for error-correcting codes and automatic equalizers, which adjust themselves to the characteristics of the particular circuit.

These rates are not high enough for many applications. Accordingly data sets are available that will transmit up to 19,200 bits per second over six voice channels, up to 50,000 bits per second over 12 voice channels (a group) and up to 230,400 bits per second over 60 voice channels (a supergroup). Finally, it is possible to use a standard television channel for transmission at rates up to several million bits per second. In addition to development work on a long-haul coaxial-cable system for more economical data transmission over long distances, experimental work is under way on the transmission of more bits per second over existing long-haul coaxial and microwave systems.

Providing broad-band transmission of various kinds is complicated by the fact that long-haul transmission systems in general link only toll offices. Therefore, although it is easy to extend voice circuits from any central office to a subscriber over existing wires, special arrangements must be made in order to supply broad-band data or other services to a subscriber. Fortunately the T1 digital-transmission system, which works over a pair of wires in a cable, provides an economical means for doing so. An alternative is simple short-haul microwave systems.

Transmission is, of course, only part of the problem. Various services are now available that supply circuits for a user's exclusive use. Telephone message service provides connections of any duration for the transmission of voice, data or other kinds of information. Some users, however, want channels of greater bandwidth than voice channels on a switched, or nonprivate, basis.

At present Western Union's Telex system provides medium-band switched service, but only between locations near certain key cities. Telephone companies have provided switched data service for group bandwidths on a "private line," or "private network," basis and plan to introduce a general wide-band switched data network.

New uses of communication provide new operational problems. Switched data circuits may be in operation for hours at a time; this is much longer than a telephone call. Some users would occasionally like to have a narrow-band or a broad-band circuit for a minute or less at a time. This means that the switching time required for setting up the connection might be comparable to the time the connection was in use. No doubt electronic switching, employing transistors, will ultimately lead to much shorter switching times than is now possible with electromechanical switching systems employing relays, but the electronic switching capacity now installed is small, and electromechanical switching will predominate for many years.

One obstacle to rapid progress in new uses of communication is the weight of tradition. New uses, even of existing equipment, call for new "packaging." The user wants to buy a service he needs right now, not a service someone else needed years ago. It is not easy to devise standard packages that are acceptable and economical. Moreover, no new service can be offered without the consent of regulatory bodies, and without their first assuring themselves that the new service is "compensatory" according to traditional standards.

The evolution of electronic computers, together with many other advances, is extending communication and the need for communication facilities of a great variety. Even in communication with computers, however, one cannot be sure how much of the communication will be data, how much voice and how much graphical material. The immediate problem is to send all kinds of signals, including data signals, over existing circuits. Only in that way can we have from the start the universality of communication to which telephony has accustomed us.

The fact remains that digital transmission is increasingly attractive for sending all kinds of signals. Indeed, we are probably in a period of evolution that will lead us more and more toward completely digitalized communication service—from the subscriber, through the switching operations and to the farthest reaches of the earth.

ANTHONY G. OETTINGER

The Uses of Computers in Science

The main impact of the computer on science
promises to come not in its role as a powerful
research instrument but rather as an active
participant in the development of scientific theories.

In its scientific applications the computer has been cast in two
quite distinct but complementary roles: as an instrument and as
an actor. Part of the success of the computer in both roles can be
ascribed to purely economic factors. By lowering the effective
cost of calculating compared with experimenting the computer
has induced a shift toward calculation in many fields where once
only experimentation and comparatively direct measurement were
practical.

The computer's role as an instrument is by far the more clear-
cut and firmly established of the two. It is in its other role, however, as an active participant in the development of scientific
theories, that the computer promises to have its most profound
impact on science. A physical theory expressed in the language of
mathematics often becomes dynamic when it is rewritten as a
computer program; one can explore its inner structure, confront
it with experimental data and interpret its implications much
more easily than when it is in static form. In disciplines where
mathematics is not the prevailing mode of expression the language
of computer programs serves increasingly as the language of science. I shall return to the subject of the dynamic expression of

theory after considering the more familiar role of the computer as an instrument in experimental investigations.

The advance of science has been marked by a progressive and rapidly accelerating separation of observable phenomena from both common sensory experience and theoretically supported intuition. Anyone can make at least a qualitative comparison of the forces required to break a matchstick and a steel bar. Comparing the force needed to ionize a hydrogen atom with the force that binds the hydrogen nucleus together is much more indirect, because the chain from phenomenon to observation to interpretation is much longer. It is by restoring the immediacy of sensory experience and by sharpening intuition that the computer is reshaping experimental analysis.

The role of the computer as a research instrument can be readily understood by considering the chain from raw observations to intuitively intelligible representations in the field of X-ray crystallography. The determination of the structure of the huge molecules of proteins is one of the most remarkable achievements of contemporary science. The labor, care and expense lavished on the preparation of visual models of protein molecules testify to a strong need for intuitive aids in this field. The computational power required to analyze crystallographic data is so immense that the need for high-speed computers is beyond doubt.

The scope and boldness of recent experiments in X-ray crystallography have increased in direct proportion to increases in computer power. Although computers seem to be necessary for progress in this area, however, they are by no means sufficient. The success stories in the determination of protein structures have involved an interplay of theoretical insight, experimental technique and computational power.

In work of this kind a rotating protein crystal is bombarded by a beam of X rays; the rays diffracted by the crystal are recorded on a photographic plate, where they produce characteristic patterns of bright spots on the dark background. Measurements of the relative positions and intensities of the spots in the diffraction pattern are the raw material for calculations that have as their result a table of coordinates of the three-dimensional distribution of electrons in the molecule. The electron-density data are then used to draw density-contour maps, which are interpreted as a three-dimensional model of the particular protein molecule under study.

Many of the links in this chain are now automated. The laborious manual measurement of photographs, for example, is no longer necessary. In the laboratory of William N. Lipscomb, Jr., at Harvard University a mounted crystal is rotated automatically through the required sequence of orientations while a photomultiplier tube measures the intensity of the diffracted X rays. Machines convert information about position and intensity into digital form and record it on punched cards for input to a computer.

At the other end of the chain Cyrus Levinthal of the Massachusetts Institute of Technology and Robert Langridge of Harvard have used the time-shared computer and display facilities of M.I.T.'s Project MAC to develop a remarkable set of programs that accept electron densities calculated for a three-dimensional region and turn these into an image of molecular structure on an oscilloscope. Gone is the time-consuming task of drawing and building the electron-density map. Once the picture of a molecule has been calculated for a standard orientation the orientation can be changed at will by simple controls that actuate special circuits for transforming the coordinates of the picture before displaying it. Slight motions provide excellent depth perception without the expense of stereoscopic image pairs. The molecule can be turned in order to view it from any angle, or it can be sliced by a plane in order to see it in cross section.

Joining these two links is the next step. A new coaxial-cable network will soon carry Lipscomb's raw data directly to a computer at the Harvard Computing Center. No technical obstacle bars the further transmission of calculated electron densities to the system at M.I.T., where the molecular display could be prepared and then sent back for direct viewing on a screen at the experimental site. Once the time-shared computer utility emerges from its present experimental stage to spread throughout institutions and regions, such doings will very likely be commonplace [see "Time-sharing on Computers," by R. M. Fano and F. J. Corbató, page 76]. It is only tame speculation to visualize a graduate student "looking through" a computer at a protein molecule as directly as he now looks at a cell through a microscope.

The metaphor of the transparent computer describes one of the principal aims of contemporary "software" engineering, the branch of information engineering concerned with developing the complex programs (software) required to turn an inert mound of apparatus (hardware) into a powerful instrument as easy to use as pen and paper. As anyone can testify who has waited a day or more for a conventional computing service to return his work only to find that a misplaced comma had kept the work from being done at all, instant transparency for all is not yet here. Nevertheless, the advances described in the other chapters of this book toward making computer languages congenial and expressive, toward making it easy to communicate with the machine and toward putting the machine at one's fingertips attest to the vigor of the pursuit of the transparent computer.

A few critics object to the principle of transparency because they fear that the primary consequence will be atrophy of the intellect. It is more likely that once interest in the *process* of determining molecular structure becomes subordinate to interest in the molecule itself, the instrument will simply be accepted and intellectual challenge sought elsewhere. It is no more debasing, unromantic or unscientific in the 1960's to view a protein crystal through the display screen of a computer than it is to watch a paramecium through the eyepiece of a microscope. Few would wish to repeat the work of Christian Huygens each time they need to look at a microscope slide. In any case, computers are basically so flexible that nothing but opaque design or poor engineering can prevent one from breaking into the chain at any point, whenever one thinks human intuition and judgment should guide brute calculation.

It is essential, of course, for anyone to understand his instrument well enough to use it properly, but the computer is just like other commonplace instruments in this regard. Like any good tool, it should be used with respect. Applying "data reduction" techniques to voluminous data collected without adequate experimental design is a folly of the master not to be blamed on the servant. Computer folk have an acronym for it: GIGO, for "garbage in, garbage out."

X-ray crystallography is the most advanced of many instances

Plates

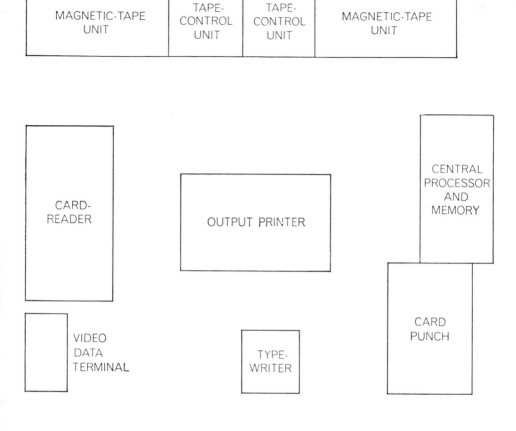

1. *Typical computer installation includes components of the kind shown in front and top views on the facing page; the components are identified in the diagram above. The heart of the system, a computer in the Spectra 70 series of the Radio Corporation of America, is the central processor and memory unit; the other units serve for input, output and storage of data. The input devices are the typewriter, with which the operator communicates with the machine, and the card-reader, for which the card-punch is an adjunct. The main output devices are the printer and the video data terminal, which employs a cathode ray tube. The tape units store data.*

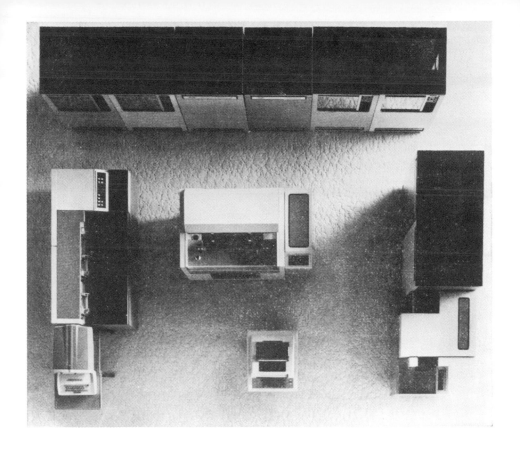

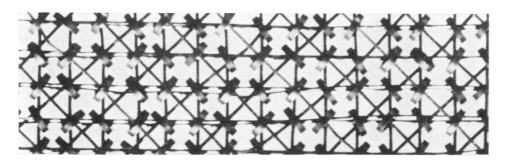

2. Magnetic-core memory has been the standard high-speed memory in computers for many years. A typical core memory plane is shown at about actual size above; a portion of the plane is enlarged about 15 diameters below. This example, made by Fabri-Tek Incorporated, contains 16,384 ferrite cores, each a fiftieth of an inch in diameter.

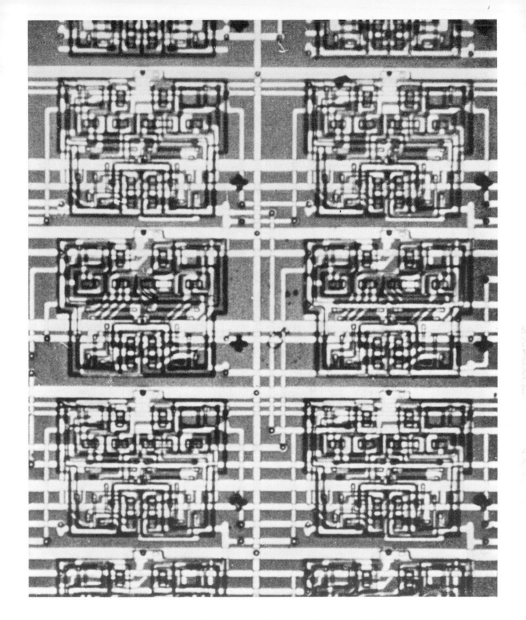

3. Microelectronic circuits of the kind shown here can be regarded as the nerve tissue of the next generation of computers. The circuits, which are enlarged about 125 diameters, are part of a "complex bipolar array chip" made by Fairchild Semiconductor. Each of the complete circuits shown (dark gray) is a functional unit consisting of 18 transistors and 18 resistors. These units are connected by a larger microelectronic network (white); there are 28 units in the entire chip. Some recent computers incorporate microelectronic circuits, but the circuits are not connected microelectronically as they are in this chip. Possibly microelectronic circuits will be used not only as logic elements but also as memory elements in future computers

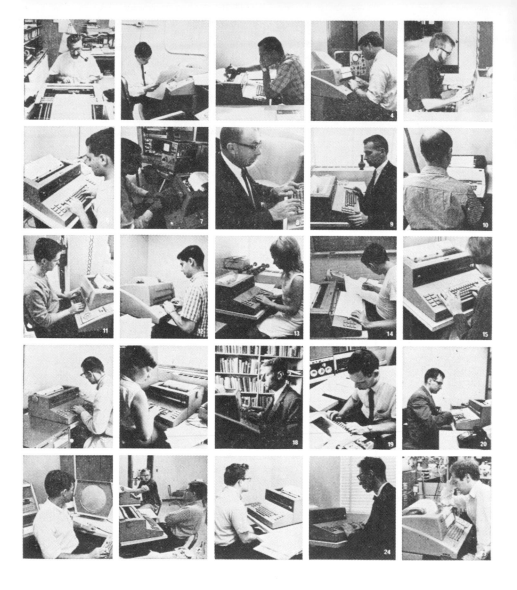

4. Project MAC *time-sharing system at the Massachusetts Institute of Technology has 160 terminals on the M.I.T. campus and nearby and is also available from distant terminals. As many as 30 terminals can be connected at one time, with each user carrying on a direct and in effect uninterrupted dialogue with the computer. The terminals are for the most part simple teletypewriters such as the* IBM *1050 (6) and Teletype models 33 (19), 35 (5) or 37 (10). Some are in offices, some in large "pool" rooms, some in laboratories and a few in private homes (1). In addition to students and staff members doing their own research, the users shown here include secretaries preparing papers for publication (13), authors Fano (8) and Corbató (24) and a psychiatrist at the Massachusetts General Hospital (18).*

5. *Computer-assisted instruction in elementary arithmetic is facilitated by cathode-ray-tube display and light pen. A first-grade pupil, receiving "readiness" work preparatory to instruction in addition, is shown two possible answers to a question implicit in the symbols occupying the top line of the cathode-ray-tube display. As he watches (top photograph), his earphones carry a spoken message asking him to select from the symbolic statements of union shown in the second and third lines of the display the one that is identical with the equation shown in the top line. The pupil signals his choice (bottom photograph) by pointing to the statement he prefers with machine's light pen; the computer then records the answer.*

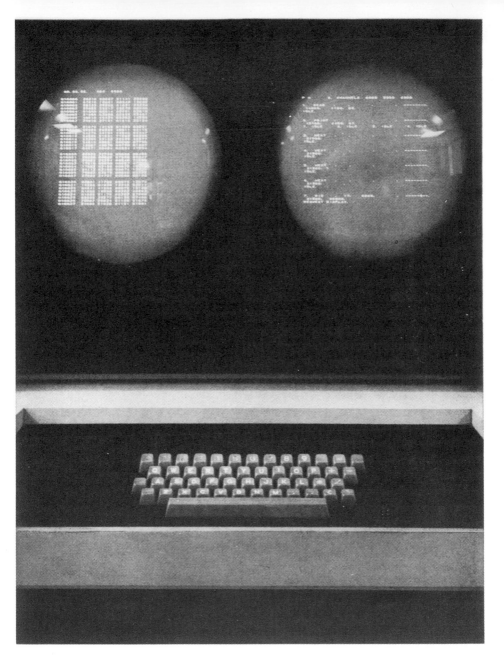

6. *Control console of a computer representative of the most recent generation of computers is much simpler in appearance than the large panels of some earlier machines. This is the console of a Control Data Corporation 6600 computer at the Courant Institute of Mathematical Sciences at New York University. The keyboard is for input of instructions; the cathode ray tubes display (left) data from the computer's core memory and (right) the status of the seven problems the computer can handle at once.*

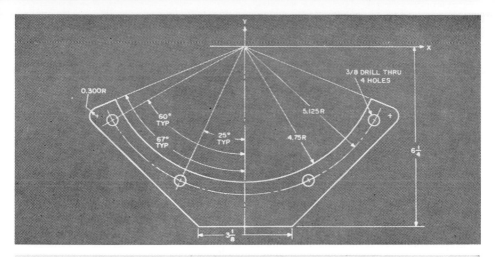

7. *Machine tools can be controlled by computers. At the IIT Research Institute the process begins with a conventional engineering drawing of a part to be machined, in this case a small "radius plate" (top). From the drawing the part programmer, writing in the APT (Automatic Programming for Tools) language, prepares a set of instructions that describe the part (second from top) and also the path to be followed by the tool. A computer calculates the detailed motions required to move the tool along that path, translating the programmer's word-symbols into numerical signals in the form of a punched tape. The tape controls the machine (third from top), in this case an "Omnimil" with 60 tools that are automatically interchangeable. A milling tool (bottom left) shapes the part (bottom right).*

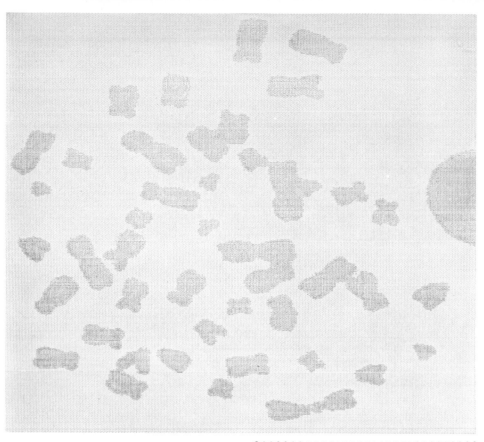

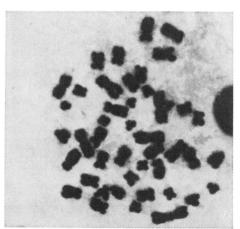

8. *Chromosome analysis by computer makes it possible to examine automatically large numbers of cells for chromosome abnormalities. A photomicrograph of a complement of human chromosomes is shown at bottom left. An image of the photomicrograph is provided by the grid of numerals in computer print-out at top. Enlargement of a single chromosome appears at bottom right. Print-outs were made with a scanning device called* FIDAC *and an* IBM *7094 computer at the National Biomedical Research Foundation.*

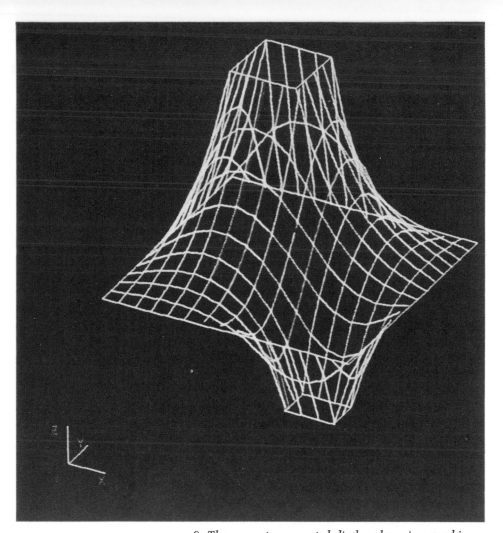

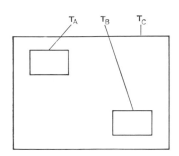

9. *The computer-generated display above is a graphical solution of a typical "equilibrium" problem in engineering: to show the heat distribution in a slab. The rectangular slab (see illustration at left) has two regions whose boundaries are maintained at temperatures (T_A and T_B) that are respectively the same amount higher and lower than the temperature (T_C) at which the boundary of the slab itself is maintained. The curves connecting the three rectangles in the display give the heat distribution, with the temperatures indicated by the z coordinate. The display was generated on a Project MAC terminal at the Massachusetts Institute of Technology; the computer program was Equilibrium Problem-Solver, designed by Coyt Tillman of M.I.T.*

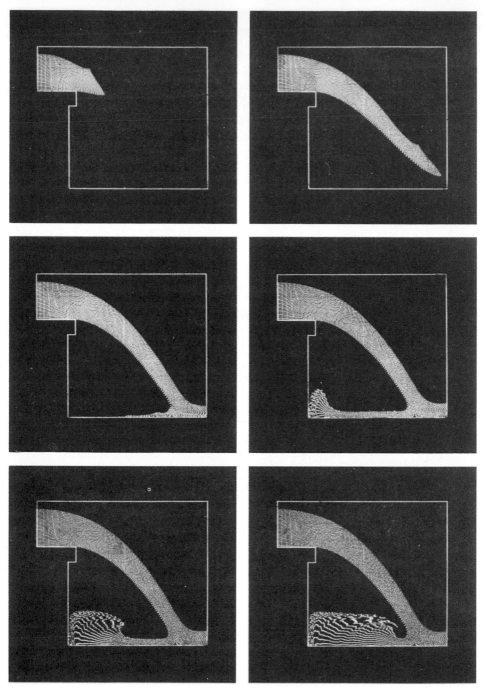

10. *Simulated waterfall spills over the edge of a cliff and splashes into a pool in this computer experiment performed by John P. Shannon at the Los Alamos Scientific Laboratory as part of a study of dynamic behavior of fluids with the aid of numerical models.*

11. *Specialized terminal of Project* MAC *has a small computer, the Digital Equipment Corporation's* PDP-8, *operating a braille printer (foreground) for a blind staff member.*

12. *Chemical publications from all over the world are collected, abstracted and indexed by Chemical Abstracts Service. The magnetic-tape storage vault above contains coded information on 416,000 chemical structures and a complete bibliography on each.*

13. *Evolution of circuits is reflected in these close-ups showing the central processing units in four generations of computers.* UNIVAC I *(top), the first large commercial electronic computer, used vacuum-tube logic circuits. The first model was delivered to the Bureau of the Census in 1951. International Business Machines' Model 704 (second from top) was a widely used large-scale vacuum-tube computer with a magnetic-core memory. The first 704 was installed in late 1955. In 1963* IBM *delivered the first 7040 (third from top), a typical transistorized computer using discrete components. The Spectra 70/45 (bottom), recently delivered by the Radio Corporation of America, represents the latest generation. It uses monolithic integrated circuits.*

14. *Early Bird, built by Hughes Aircraft, was placed in a synchronous orbit some 22,300 miles above the equator in April, 1965. At that altitude its period of rotation is exactly 24 hours, with the result that it appears to stay fixed above a point in the South Atlantic. From that position Early Bird can relay radio and television signals uninterruptedly between the U.S. and Europe. It seems likely that far more capacious synchronous satellites will soon be needed to supply communication channels between cities within the U.S.*

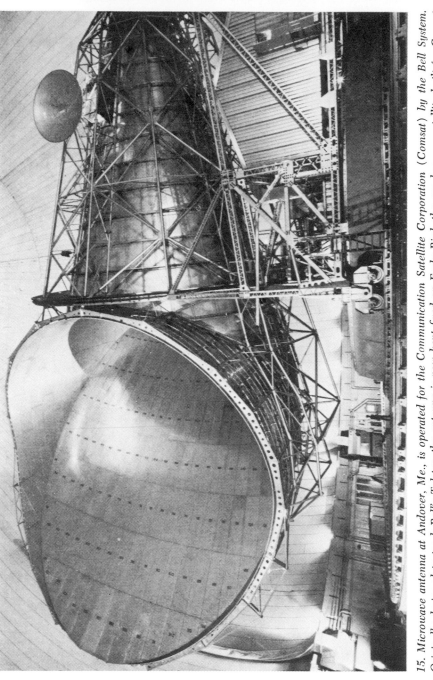

15. *Microwave antenna at Andover, Me., is operated for the Communication Satellite Corporation (Comsat) by the Bell System. Originally designed to track Bell's Telstar, the antenna is now kept fixed on Early Bird, the synchronous satellite built for Comsat by the Hughes Aircraft Company (see Plate 14).*

in which similar instrumentation is being developed. Four experimental stations at the Cambridge Electron Accelerator, operated jointly by Harvard and M.I.T., are currently being connected to a time-shared computer at the Harvard Computing Center to provide a first link. A small computer at each experimental station converts instrument readings from analogue to digital form, arranges them in a suitable format and transmits them to the remote computer. There most data are stored for later detailed calculation; a few are examined to instruct each of the small local machines to display information telling the experimenter whether or not his experiment is going well. Heretofore delays in conventional batch-processing procedures occasionally led to scrapping a long experiment that became worthless because poor adjustments could not be detected until all calculations were completed and returned.

This type of experiment is described as an "open loop" experiment, since the computer does not directly affect the setting of experimental controls. Closed-loop systems, where the experiment is directly controlled by computer, are currently being developed. Their prototypes can be seen in industrial control systems, where more routine, better-understood devices, ranging from elevators to oil refineries, are controlled automatically.

The problem of "reading" particle-track photographs efficiently has been a persistent concern of high-energy physicists. Here the raw data are not nearly as neat as they are in X-ray diffraction patterns, nor can photography as readily be bypassed. Automating the process of following tracks in bubble-chamber photographs to detect significant events presents very difficult and as yet unsolved problems of pattern recognition, but computers are now used at least to reduce some of the tedium of scanning the photographs. Similar forms of man-machine interaction occur also in the study of brain tumors by radioactive-isotope techniques. Where the problem of pattern recognition is simpler, as it is in certain types of chromosome analysis, there is already a greater degree of automation.

Let us now turn from the computer as instrument to the computer as actor, and to the subject of dynamic expression of theory. To understand clearly words such as "model," "simulation" and others that recur in this context, a digression is essential to distinguish the functional from the structural aspects of a model or a theory.

A robot is a functional model of man. It walks, it talks, but no one should be fooled into thinking that it is a man or that it explains man merely because it acts like him. The statements that "the brain is like a computer" or that "a network of nerve cells is like a network of computer gates, each either on or off," crudely express once popular structural theories, obviously at different levels. Both are now discredited, the first because no one has found structures in the brain that look anything like parts of any man-made computer or even function like them, the second because nerve-cell networks were found to be a good deal more complicated than computer networks.

A functional model is like the electrical engineer's proverbial "black box," where something goes in and something comes out, and what is inside is unknown or relevant only to the extent of somehow relating outputs to inputs. A structural model emphasizes the contents of the box. A curve describing the current passing through a semiconductor diode as a function of the voltage applied across its terminals is a functional model of this device that is exceedingly useful to electronic-circuit designers. Most often such curves are obtained by fitting a smooth line to actual currents and voltages measured for a number of devices. A corresponding structural model would account for the characteristic shape of the curve in terms that describe the transport of charge-carriers through semiconductors, the geometry of the contacts and so forth. A good structural model typically has greater predictive power than a functional one. In this case it would predict changes in the voltage-current characteristic when the geometry of the interfaces or the impurities in the semiconductors are varied.

If the black box is opened, inspiration, luck and empirical verification can turn a functional model into a structural one. Physics abounds with instances of this feat. The atom of Lucretius or John Dalton was purely functional. Modern atomic theory is structural, and the atom with its components is observable. The phlogiston theory, although functional enough up to a point, evaporated through lack of correspondence between its components and reality. Although the description of the behavior of matter by thermodynamics is primarily functional and its description by statistical mechanics is primarily structural, the consistency of these two approaches reinforces both.

The modern computer is a very versatile and convenient black box, ready to act out an enormous variety of functional or structural roles. In the physical sciences, where the script usually has been written in mathematics beforehand, the computer merely brings to life, through its program, a role implied by the mathematics. Isaac Newton sketched the script for celestial mechanics in the compact shorthand of differential equations. Urbain Leverrier and John Couch Adams laboriously fleshed out their parts in the script with lengthy and detailed calculations based on a wealth of astronomical observations. Johann Galle and James Challis pointed their telescopes where the calculations said they should and the planet Neptune was discovered. In modern jargon, Leverrier and Adams each ran Neptune simulations based on Newton's model, and belief in the model was strengthened by comparing simulation output with experiment. Computers now routinely play satellite and orbit at Houston, Huntsville and Cape Kennedy. Nevertheless, there is little danger of confusing Leverrier, Adams or a computer with any celestial object or its orbit. As we shall see, such confusion is more common with linguistic and psychological models.

The determination of protein structures provides an excellent example of how computers act out the implications of a theory. Finding a possible structure for a protein molecule covers only part of the road toward understanding. For example, the question arises of why a protein molecule, which is basically just a string of amino acid units, should fold into the tangled three-dimensional pattern observed by Kendrew. The basic physical hypothesis invoked for explanation is that the molecular string will, like water running downhill, fold to reach a lowest energy level. To act out the implications of this hypothesis, given an initial spatial configuration of a protein chain, one might think of calculating the interactions of all pairs of active structures in the chain, minimizing the energy corresponding to these interactions over all possible configurations and then displaying the resultant molecular picture. Unfortunately this cannot be done so easily, since no simple formula describing such interactions is available and, with present techniques, none could be written down and manipulated with any reasonable amount of labor. Sampling more or less cleverly the energies of a finite but very large number of configurations is the only possibility. An unsupervised computer searching through a set of samples for a minimum would, more likely than not, soon find itself blocked at some local minimum—unable, like a man in a hollow at the top of a mountain, to see deeper valleys beyond the ridges that surround him.

The close interaction of man and machine made possible by new "on line" time-sharing systems, graphical display techniques and more convenient programming languages enables Levinthal and his collaborators to use their intuition and theoretical insight to postulate promising trial configurations. It is then easy for the computer to complete the detail work of calculating energy levels for the trial configuration and seeking a minimum in its neighborhood. The human operator, from his intuitive vantage point, thus guides the machine over the hills and into the valley, each partner doing what he is best fitted for.

Even more exciting, once the details of the interactions are known theoretically, the X-ray diffraction pattern of the molecule can be calculated and compared with the original observations to remove whatever doubts about the structure are left by ambiguities encountered when going in the other direction. This closing of the circle verifies not only the calculation of molecular structure but also the theoretical edifice that provided the details of molecular interactions.

In this example the computer clearly mimics the molecule according to a script supplied by underlying physical and chemical theory. The computer represents the molecule with a sufficient degree of structural detail to make plausible a metaphorical identification of the computer with the molecule. The metaphor loses its force as we approach details of atomic structure, and the submodels that account for atomic behavior are in this case merely functional.

The remarkable immediacy and clarity of the confrontation of acted-out theory and experiment shown in the preceding example is by no means an isolated phenomenon. Similar techniques are emerging in chemistry, in hydrodynamics, and in other branches of science. It is noteworthy, as Don L. Bunker has pointed out, that computers used in this way, far from reducing the scientist to a passive bystander, reinforce the need for the creative human element in experimental science, if only because witless calculation is likely to be so voluminous as to be beyond the power of even the fastest computer. Human judgment and intuition must be injected at every stage to guide the computer in its search for a solution. Painstaking routine work will be less and less useful for making a scientific reputation, because such "horse work" can be reduced to a computer program. All that is left for the scientist to contribute is a creative imagination. In this sense scientists are subject to technological unemployment, just like anyone else.

In the "softer" emerging sciences such as psychology and linguistics the excitement and speculation about the future promise of the computer both as instrument and as actor tend to be even stronger than in the physical sciences, although solid accomplishments still are far fewer.

From the time modern computers were born the myth of the "giant brain" was fed by the obvious fact that they could calculate and also by active speculation about their ability to translate from one language into another, play chess, compose music, prove theorems and so on. That such activities were hitherto seen as peculiar to man and to no other species and certainly to no machine lent particular force to the myth. This myth (as expressed, for example, in *New Yorker* cartoons) is now deeply rooted as the popular image of the computer.

The myth rests in part on gross misinterpretation of the nature of a functional model. In the early 1950's, when speculation about whether or not computers can think was at the height of fashion, the British mathematician A. M. Turing proposed the following experiment as a test. Imagine an experimenter communicating by teletype with each of two rooms (or black boxes), one containing a man, the other a computer. If after exchanging an appropriate series of messages with each room the experimenter is unable to tell which holds the man and which the computer, the computer might be said to be thinking. Since the situation is symmetrical, one could equally well conclude that the man is computing. Whatever the decision, such an experiment demonstrates at most a more or less limited functional similarity between the two black boxes, because it is hardly designed to reveal structural details. With the realization that the analogy is only functional, this approach to the computer as a model, or emulator, of man loses both mystery and appeal; in its most naïve form it is pursued today only by a dwindling lunatic fringe, although it remains in the consciousness of the public.

In a more sophisticated vein attempts continue toward devising computer systems less dependent on detailed prior instructions and better able to approach problem-solving with something akin to human independence and intelligence. Whether or not such systems, if they are achieved, should have anything like the structure of a human brain is as relevant a question as whether or not flying machines should flap their wings like birds. This problem of artificial intelligence is the subject of speculative research described in the chapter by Marvin L. Minsky beginning on page 193. Once the cloud of misapplied functional analogy is dispelled the real promise of using the computer as an animated structural model remains.

Mathematics has so far made relatively few inroads in either linguistics or psychology, although there are now some rather beautiful mathematical theories of language. The scope of these theories is generally limited to syntax (the description of the order and formal relations among words in a sentence). Based as they are on logic and algebra, rather than on the now more familiar calculus, these theories do not lend themselves readily to symbolic calculation of the form to which mathematicians and natural scientists have become accustomed. "Calculations" based on such theories must generally be done by computer. Indeed, in their early form some of these theories were expressed only as computer programs; others still are and may remain so. In such cases the language of programs is the language of science; the program is the original and only script, not just a translation from mathematics.

Early claims that computers could translate languages were vastly exaggerated; even today no finished translation can be produced by machine without human intervention, although machine-aided translation is technically possible. Considerable progress has been made, however, in using computers to manipulate languages, both vernaculars and programming languages. Grammars called phrase-structure grammars and transformational grammars supply the theoretical backdrop for this activity. These grammars describe sentences as they are generated from an initial symbol (say S for sentence) by applying rewrite rules followed (if the grammar is transformational) by applying transformation rules. For example, the rewrite rule $S \to SuPr$, where Su can be thought of as standing for subject and Pr as standing for predicate, yields the string $SuPr$ when it is applied to the initial symbol S. By adding the rules $Su \to John$ and $Pr \to sleeps$ one can turn this string into the sentence "John sleeps." Transformations can then be applied in order to turn, for example, the active sentence "John followed the girl" into the passive one "The girl was followed by John."

Under the direction of Susumu Kuno and myself a research group at Harvard has developed, over the past few years, techniques for inverting this generation process in order to go from a sentence as it occurs in a text to a description of its structure or, equivalently, to a description of how it might have been generated by the rules of the grammar. Consider the simple sentence "Time flies like an arrow." To find out which part of this sentence is the subject, which part the predicate and so on, a typical program first looks up each word in a dictionary. The entry for "flies" would show that this word might serve either as a plural noun denoting an annoying domestic insect or as a verb denoting locomotion through the air by an agent represented by a subject in the third person singular.

The specific function of a word in a particular context can be found only by checking how the word relates to other words in the sentence, hence the serious problem of determining which of the many combinations of possible functions do in fact fit together as a legitimate sentence structure. This problem has been solved essentially by trying all possibilities and rejecting those that do not fit, although powerful tests suggested by theory and intuition can be applied to eliminate entire classes of possibilities at one fell swoop, thereby bringing the process within the realm of practicality [see illustration on page 124].

A grammar that pretends to describe English at all accurately must yield a structure for "Time flies like an arrow" in which "time" is the subject of the verb "flies" and "like an arrow" is an

```
*****  ANALYSIS NUMBER   1         SENTENCE NUMBER  000001                  CORPUS  NUMBER
ENGLISH   SENTENCE STRUCTURE   SWC   SWC MNEMONIC    SYNTACTIC ROLE             RL NUM  PREDICTION POOL
                                                                                       SE
TIME      1S                   NOUS  NOUN 1          SUBJECT OF PREDICATE VERB  SENNNO
FLIES     1V                   VIIS  COMPLETE VI     PREDICATE VERB             VXVII0  PD VSA
LIKE      1VPR                 PRE   PREPOSITION     PREPOSITION                PDPREO  PD
AN        1VPOA                ART   PRO-ADJECTIVE   OBJECT OF PREPOSITION      NQAAAO  PD NQG
ARROW     1VPO                 NOUS  NOUN 1          OBJECT OF PREPOSITION      N5MMMO  PD N5G
.         1.                   PRD   PERIOD          END OF SENTENCE            PDPRDO  PQ
-------------------------------------------------------------------------------------------------------

*****  ANALYSIS NUMBER   2         SENTENCE NUMBER  000001                  CORPUS  NUMBER
ENGLISH   SENTENCE STRUCTURE   SWC   SWC MNEMONIC    SYNTACTIC ROLE             RL NUM  PREDICTION POOL
                                                                                       SE
TIME      1SA                  NOUS  NOUN 1          SUBJECT OF PREDICATE VERB  SENOUO
FLIES     1S                   NOUP  NOUN 1          SUBJECT OF PREDICATE VERB  7XMMMO  PD VZA7ZA
LIKE      1V                   VT1P  NOUN-OBJECT VT  PREDICATE VERB             VXVT11  PD VPA
AN        1QA                  ART   PRO-ADJECTIVE   OBJECT OF PREDICATE VERB   N2AAAO  PD N2A
ARROW     1Q                   NOUS  NOUN 1          OBJECT OF PREDICATE VERB   N5MMMO  PD N5A
.         1.                   PRD   PERIOD          END OF SENTENCE            PDPRDO  PQ
-------------------------------------------------------------------------------------------------------

*****  ANALYSIS NUMBER   3         SENTENCE NUMBER  000001                  CORPUS  NUMBER
ENGLISH   SENTENCE STRUCTURE   SWC   SWC MNEMONIC    SYNTACTIC ROLE             RL NUM  PREDICTION POOL
                                                                                       SE
TIME      3V                   IT1   INFINITE VT1    IMPERATIVE VERB            SEIT10
FLIES     3Q                   NOUP  NOUN 1          OBJECT OF IMPERATIVE VERB  N2NNNO  PD N2B
LIKE      3QPR                 PRE   PREPOSITION     PREPOSITION                PDPREO  PD
AN        3QPOA                ART   PRO-ADJECTIVE   OBJECT OF PREPOSITION      NQAAAO  PD NQG
ARROW     3QPQ                 NOUS  NOUN 1          OBJECT OF PREPOSITION      N5MMMO  PD N5G
.         3.                   PRD   PERIOD          END OF SENTENCE            PDPRDO  PD
-------------------------------------------------------------------------------------------------------
```

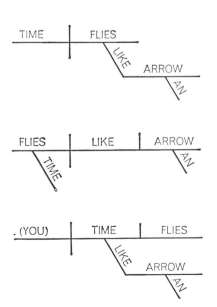

Syntactic analysis by computer of the sentence "Time flies like an arrow" yields three different structural interpretations, which are represented here by computer print-out (above) and by conventional sentence-structure diagrams (left). The first structure is one in which "time" is the subject of the verb "flies" and "like an arrow" is an adverbial phrase modifying the verb (Analysis Number 1). "Time" can also serve attributively, however, as in "time bomb," and "flies" of course can serve as a noun. Together with "like" interpreted as a verb, this yields a structure that becomes obvious only if one thinks of a kind of domestic insect called "time flies," which happen to like an arrow, perhaps as a meal (2). Moreover, "time" as an imperative verb with "flies" as a noun also yields a structure that makes sense as an order to someone to take out his stopwatch and time flies with great dispatch, or like an arrow (3). No computer techniques now known can deal effectively with semantic problems of this kind, but research is continuing.

adverbial phrase modifying the verb. "Time" can also serve attributively, however, as in "time bomb," and "flies" of course can serve as a noun. Together with "like" interpreted as a verb, this yields a structure that becomes obvious only if one thinks of a kind of flies called "time flies," which happen to like an arrow, perhaps as a meal. Moreover, "time" as an imperative verb with "flies" as a noun also yields a structure that makes sense as an order to someone to take out his stopwatch and time flies with great dispatch, or like an arrow.

A little thought suggests many minor modifications of the grammar sufficient to rule out such fantasies. Unfortunately too much is then lost. A point can be made that the structures are legitimate even if the sentences are meaningless. It is, after all, only an accident of nature, or for that matter merely of nomenclature, that there is no species of flies called "time flies." Worse yet, anything ruling out the nonexisting species of time flies will also rule out the identical but legitimate structure of "Fruit flies like a banana."

Still more confusing, the latter sentence itself is given an anomalous structure, namely that which is quite sensible for "Time flies . . ." but which is nonsensical here since we know quite well that fruit in general does not fly and that when it does, it flies like maple seeds, not like bananas.

A theory of syntax alone can help no further. Semantics, the all too nebulous notion of what a sentence means, must be invoked to choose among the three structures syntax accepts for "Time flies like an arrow." No techniques now known can deal effectively with semantic problems of this kind. Research in the field is continuing in the hope that some form of man-machine interaction can yield both practical results and further insight into the deepening mystery of natural language. We do not yet know how people understand language, and our machine procedures barely do child's work in an extraordinarily cumbersome way.

The outlook is brighter for man-made programming languages. Since these can be defined almost at will, it is generally possible to reduce ambiguity and to systematize semantics well enough for practical purposes, although numerous challenging theoretical problems remain. The computer is also growing in power as an instrument of routine language data processing. Concordances, now easily made by machine, supply scholars in the humanities and social sciences with tabular displays of the location and context of key words in both sacred and profane texts.

Psychologists have used programming languages to write scripts for a variety of structural models of human behavior. These are no more mysterious than scripts for the orbit of Neptune or the structure of hemoglobin. The psychological models differ from the physical ones only in their subject and their original language. Convincing empirical corroboration of the validity of these models is still lacking, and the field has suffered from exaggerated early claims and recurrent confusion between the functional and the structural aspects of theory. Psychology and the study of artificial intelligence are both concerned with intelligent behavior, but otherwise they are not necessarily related except to the extent that metaphors borrowed from one discipline may be stimulating to the other.

In actuality it is the languages, not the scripts, that are today the really valuable products of the attempts at computer modeling of human behavior. Several languages, notably John McCarthy's LISP, have proved invaluable as tools for general research on symbol manipulation. Research on natural-language data processing, theorem-proving, algebraic manipulation and graphical display draws heavily on such languages. Nevertheless, the computer as instrument is rapidly making a useful place for itself in the psychology laboratory. Bread-and-butter applications include the administration, monitoring and evaluation of tests of human or animal subjects in studies of perception and learning.

The business of science, both in principle and in practice, is inextricably involved in the business of education, particularly on the university level. The paradigm of the computer as instrument and as actor, although described in terms of research, seems to apply to instruction as well. Because on-line, time-shared systems are still experimental and expensive, especially with graphical display facilities, their use for instruction lags somewhat behind their use for research.

Hopes for computers in education at the elementary or secondary level are described in the chapter by Patrick Suppes beginning on page 157. My own current exploration of the potential value of technological aids to creative thought focuses rather on the undergraduate or graduate student and on the transition from learning in the classroom to learning when practicing a profession.

The desire to keep labor within reasonable bounds generally leads to oversimplified and superficial experiments in student laboratories. Where the observation and intelligent interpretation of a variety of significant phenomena are the primary objectives of a laboratory exercise, using a transparent computer should reduce unnecessary drudgery to the point where judgment and interpretation, even of realistic experiments, can prevail.

The transparent computer also promises to be effective as a kind of animated blackboard. This hardly implies the disappearance of chalk, films or books. The computer merely adds another powerful and versatile tool to the teacher's kit. In fact, where repetition or polish is necessary, the computer itself can serve to make films or equivalent visual recordings. We have found that whereas films cannot be interrupted or altered, a recorded computer sequence can easily be stopped in response to a student's question; the lecturer can then explore alternatives by returning either to the informal direct use of the computer or to the conventional blackboard. The prerecorded sequence can then be resumed.

Best of all, there need be no distinction between the classroom tool and that available to students for homework assignments, laboratory calculations or individual research projects. The transition from classroom to life therefore promises to be made smoother. Since computers are not yet either as transparent or as cheap as one might wish, many problems of technique and finance remain to be faced. In any case, no panacea has been found for education's ills, only a richer range of choices to be made.

An example based on our experimental use in Harvard classrooms of a keyboard-and-display system developed by Glen Culler at the University of California at Santa Barbara will illustrate both the promise and the problems. Since the static printed page cannot adequately portray the effect of dynamic display, the problems may be more evident than the promise. The topic chosen is mathematical in nature, since such problems are best suited for the equipment currently available. The objective is to develop a natural and perspicuous presentation of topics traditionally reserved for more advanced treatment, to develop others in greater depth than conventional methods allow and to stimulate the student's intuition and his resourcefulness in solving problems. The objective is not to eliminate theory and rigor in favor of witless calculation, but rather to restore the close link between theory and calculation that characterized mathematics before the advent of rigor late in the 19th century led to the aberrant but currently fashionable split between pure and applied mathematics.

It is well known that any periodic function can be approximated by the sum of a series of terms that oscillate harmonically, converging on the curve of the function. Culler's apparatus makes possible quick intuitive exploration of the nature of this approximation. Computer-generated curves present an immediate visual plot of the rich content of the mathematical statement [see illustration on the facing page].

The accompanying computer-generated curves show the effect of increasing the number of terms in the partial sum of the series. The spikes near the corners of the square wave are caused by nonuniform convergence near a discontinuity. For the pure mathematician this demonstration can motivate a more formal treatment of nonuniform convergence. For the engineer the phenomenon can be clarified by displaying the components of the approximation in such a way as to make it obvious intuitively why the spikes occur. In principle the instructor, or an interested student on his own, could follow up such a demonstration by modeling the effect of a linear circuit element, say a resistor or a simple amplifier, on a square wave, on its individual components and on their sum.

At present any concurrent formal algebraic manipulations require pencil or chalk. Current progress toward machine-aided algebraic manipulation raises the exciting possibility that machines will eventually help with both symbolic and numerical manipulation and with easy transitions between these two modes of expression. Working in both modes simultaneously or in whatever combination rigor and intuition demand would profoundly affect the thought of pure and applied mathematicians alike.

Other types of teaching experiment can be conducted by building an appropriate structural model into the computer. One might assume the structure and examine its behavior, as is frequently done in management games, or one might treat only the

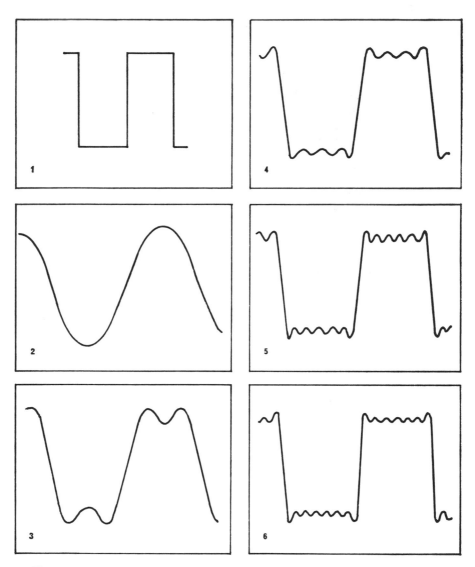

Problem in mathematics illustrates the author's experimental use in Harvard classrooms of a keyboard-and-display system developed by Glen Culler of the University of California at Santa Barbara. It is well known that any periodic function (in this example the square wave at top left) can be approximated by the sum of a series of terms that oscillate harmonically, converging on the curve of the function. Culler's apparatus makes possible quick intuitive exploration of this approximation. The other curves show the effect of increasing the number of terms in the partial sum of the series. The spikes at the corners of the square wave are caused by nonuniform convergence near a discontinuity.

behavior as observable, leaving the model to be determined as an exercise in theory-building. As paradigms are developed by research in some area, these paradigms could then be applied as well to teaching in that area. It will be interesting, for example, to experiment with the teaching of a foreign language for which a transformational grammar of the type I described earlier has been implemented on a computer.

It is also interesting to speculate on the use of on-line computers as tools for the investigation of the psychology of learning and problem-solving. Experiments in this area have been difficult, contrived and unrealistic. When the interactive computer serves as a problem-solving tool, it is also easily adapted to record information about problem-solving behavior. Here again the problem will not be the collection of data but rather devising appropriate experimental designs, since an hour's problem-solving session at a computer console can accumulate an enormous amount of data.

In short, computers are capable of profoundly affecting science by stretching human reason and intuition, much as telescopes or microscopes extend human vision. I suspect that the ultimate effects of this stretching will be as far-reaching as the effects of the invention of writing. Whether the product is truth or nonsense, however, will depend more on the user than on the tool.

STEVEN ANSON COONS

The Uses of Computers in Technology

In most technological applications computers have
been used to execute a specific program of instructions.
Now they are beginning to fulfill their promise of
interacting directly with men in engineering design.

The uses of computers in technology fall into two categories. One
is traditional (if so new a field can be said to have a tradition),
the other quite novel. The first category includes the multifarious
applications in which the computer carries out a program of
instructions with little or no intervention by human beings. This
is a powerful way to use an information-processing machine, and
it has dominated the early years of the computer era. The second
category embraces a new class of applications in which the
computer is an active partner of man. I believe that within the
next few years this new way of using computers will bring about
deep changes in the large segment of technology that might be
called "creative engineering."

As the computer is traditionally applied to a technological
task, it acts as it is told to act. This is not to say that a machine so
instructed cannot accomplish impressive tasks. Its program can
be quite elaborate—so complex that no human being could follow
it in a reasonable length of time (even, in some instances, in an
unreasonable length of time). In obeying instructions a computer
often deals appropriately with changing circumstances and
adjusts to variations in its environment, achieving its purpose by

a process so subtle as to give the impression of adaptive intelligence. The machine is nonetheless acting as an automaton. Its behavior, although complex, is mechanical and predictable. Man's ingenuity is applied to presenting the problem of setting up the task; thereafter the machine grinds away at the solution or execution.

This is not the case when the computer and man are linked in what J. C. R. Licklider of the International Business Machines Corporation calls a symbiotic relationship, a relationship in which each can perform the kind of activity for which it is best suited. Man is quite good at inventing and organizing ideas, making associations among apparently unrelated notions, recognizing patterns and stripping away irrelevant detail; he is creative, unpredictable, sometimes capricious, sensitive to human values. The computer is almost exactly what man is not. It is capable of paying undivided attention to unlimited detail; it is immune to distraction, precise and reliable; it can carry out the most intricate and lengthy calculation with ease, without a flaw and in much less than a millionth of the time that would be required by its human counterpart. It is emotionless, or so we suppose. It suffers from neither boredom nor fatigue. It needs to be told only once; thereafter it remembers perfectly until it is told to forget, whereupon it forgets instantly and absolutely.

When man and machine work together, the shortcomings of each are compensated by the other, which leaves both partners free to exercise their individual powers in a common enterprise. The potential of such a combination is greater than the sum of its parts.

It was clear when the first electronic computers were being developed that the machines could by their nature deal easily with repetitive calculations. During World War II computers worked out firing tables for artillery. Another early application was the calculation of logarithmic and trigonometric tables to a large number of significant figures. It was startling to find that some of the classic tables that had been calculated "by hand" contained errors that were discovered only after computer calculation. Computers have continued to specialize in bulky calculations, particularly those in which the procedure is either involved and complicated or repetitive.

It soon became apparent, however, that the computer could also maintain quite sophisticated control over its own procedures and could successfully attack problems of a more difficult kind. Specifically, the ability of the computer to compare two numbers and to elect any one of two or three courses of action based on the outcome of the comparison, although simple in principle, has led to some sophisticated applications. A computer can in fact be relied on to carry out the most intricate processes in the manipulation and transformation of information, provided that these processes are understood well enough by humans to be described in complete detail to the computer.

A computer can, for example, control industrial processes. Not all "automated" industrial plants have computer systems and not all computerized plants are equally automatic. It is possible to construct complex control systems based on continuous monitoring and feedback loops without including computers. Sometimes computers are introduced to make calculations and inform a human operator what needs to be done. Moreover, a computer can on its own control an individual subprocess or regulate an important variable in a production line. In some cases (still largely confined to the petroleum and chemical industries) a computer system actually controls the routine operations of the plant.

The control of chemical plants is a good example of an application in which the computer can deal with a large amount of information, monitoring the many variables involved in such a way as to maintain optimum production and quality of product. The variables in a chemical process—temperature, pressure, flow, valve settings, viscosity, color and many others—are interrelated in complicated ways, and usually the relations are highly non-linear. If two ingredients must flow into a reaction vessel in a certain ratio, and the flow rate of one ingredient is deficient for some reason, it does no good for the computer system to attempt to rectify the deficiency by opening the supply valve wider if the valve is already fully open; instead the computer should take account of the state of affairs and close the valve on the other supply line until the desired ratio of flows is achieved.

A computer is able to receive information from many measuring stations located at strategic places in the process plant, to perform the necessary calculations and comparisons of these detailed data, to make decisions on how to monitor the control mechanisms and to send commands back to them in such a way as to maintain optimum operation. This capability is highly reliable, and since there is essentially no limit to the complexity of the information with which the computer can deal, industrial engineers can now devise processes so intricate that it would be difficult, if not impossible, to control them with human workers.

Another industrial application of computers lies in the numerical control of machine tools. A great many parts of machines are produced by either milling or routing, processes in which a cutting tool moves so as to cut some contoured shape out of sheet metal or heavier stock. In conventional methods this demands the constant attention of a skilled machine operator, particularly if the contour to be formed is irregularly curved. Under the control of a computer the cutter can be made to move in any desired path, and it is in principle no more difficult to produce "sculptured" shapes bounded by complex curved surfaces than it is to produce objects with flat faces. The numerical control of machine tools has enjoyed an extraordinary success because it guarantees the reliability and reproducibility of even the most elaborate shapes. The spoilage due to human error is reduced to the vanishing point, and many parts are now practicable that would be prohibitively expensive to produce if a human operator had to monitor the settings of the machine [see Plate 7].

A striking example is the milling of airplane-wing "skins" from slabs of aluminum alloy. For structural reasons these sheet metal skins need to be thicker near the wing roots, where the bending stress is high, than they do near the wing tips, where it is less. For a long time this has been accomplished by assembling an elaborate laminated structure, with sheets of varying thickness fastened together by hundreds of rivets and stiffened by bulkheads and frames. The assembly of such structures is complicated and time-consuming. Now it has been found that much of the wing structure can literally be cut out of solid slabs—tapered thickness, stiffening members and all—at a cost and in a time substantially less than is needed for conventional assembly methods. Wing skins cut from slabs two inches thick, 10 feet wide and 40 feet long are not at all uncommon.

The increasing capabilities of modern computers suggested that a more direct partnership between the machines and their human operators would be effective, and several developments described in other chapters of this book combined to make this possible. First, the languages by which men communicate with computers have evolved rapidly. Language forms have now begun to appear that are much more "problem-oriented" or "user-oriented" than the original languages; they are easy to learn because they resemble ordinary English and involve more or less conventional mathematical notation.

Another important development that makes the man-machine combination feasible is time-sharing [see "Time-sharing on Computers," by R. M. Fano and F. J. Corbató, page 76]. Computers can be operated economically only if they are kept constantly busy at productive work. A man working at a computer console cannot keep the machine busy, because the machine can receive a command, interpret and act on it and return a reply or a result in a few microseconds; then it must wait while the human operator digests the reply, thinks about it and decides on his next action. Enough people at individual consoles can provide the time-shared computer with a work load that will keep it gainfully employed.

A third development is the display console, on which the computer can create symbols, graphs and drawings of objects and can maintain the display statically or cause it to move, simulating dynamic behavior. Together with input devices such as the "light pen," the display console becomes a window through which information can be transferred between the man and the machine.

The comfortable and congenial combination of man and machine made possible by these three developments has found some of its first applications in computer-aided design. By "design" I mean the creative engineering process, including the analytical techniques of testing, evaluation and decision-making and then the experimental verification and eventual realization of the result in tangible form. In science and engineering (and perhaps in art as well) the creative process is a process of experimentation with ideas. Concepts form, dissolve and reappear in different contexts; associations occur, are examined and tested for validity on a conscious but qualitative level, and are either accepted tentatively or rejected. Eventually, however, the concepts and conjectures must be put to the precise test of mathematical analysis. When these analytical procedures are established ones (as they are in such disciplines as stress analysis, fluid mechanics and electrical-network analysis), the work to be done is entirely mechanical. It can be formulated and set down in algorithms: rituals of procedure that can be described in minute detail and can be performed by a computer. Indeed, this part of the creative process *should* be done by the computer in order to leave man free to exercise his human powers and apply his human values.

There is much talk of "automated design" nowadays, but usually automated design is only part of the design process, an optimization of a concept already qualitatively formed. There are, for example, computer programs that produce complete descriptions of electrical transformers, wiring diagrams or printed-circuit boards. There are programs that design bridges in the sense that they work out the stresses on each structural member and in effect write its specifications. Such programs are powerful new engineering tools, but they do not depend on an internal capability of creativity; the creativity has already been exercised in generating them.

I can best give some idea of the potentialities of computer-aided design by describing one of the tools that makes it possible. One of the early and epochal instances of man-machine symbiosis was the program called Sketchpad, which was completed late in 1962 by Ivan E. Sutherland of the Massachusetts Institute of Technology [see "Computer Inputs and Outputs," by Ivan E. Sutherland, page 40]. Sutherland used the TX-2 computer, an experimental machine that was built at the Lincoln Laboratory of M.I.T. with the idea of providing direct man-machine interaction at the console long before such a notion had much currency in computer technology and long before the notion of multiple users of a machine was much more than a dream.

When Sutherland began work on Sketchpad, the TX-2 had a cathode-ray-tube screen and a light pen as existing rudimentary pieces of equipment, but little had been done to exploit their possibilities. Sutherland set out to develop a system that would make possible direct conversation between man and machine in geometric, graphical terms. In the course of the development of

Sketchpad he would invite people in to try out his system so that he could observe their reactions. On one occasion Claude E. Shannon, Sutherland's adviser on his doctoral thesis, wanted to perform a geometric construction. Rather than work out the construction on the console screen, Shannon automatically turned to paper and pencil to make a preliminary sketch. This came as a disappointment to Sutherland, who intended the system to be so congenial to the user that it would not intrude on his thought processes. He thereupon disassembled his program and rewrote it. It went through several such revisions, and it stands today as a classic of well-considered human engineering.

Learning to use Sketchpad is so easy that it can scarcely be thought of as learning; one simply begins and then becomes more skillful with experience. The program is remarkably versatile. Using Sketchpad, I was able one evening to set up and experiment with the following problems and constructions:

1. Evaluate a cubic polynomial equation. There is a simple geometric construction for polynomials of any degree and for real and complex values of the various terms. By manipulating the x variable with the light pen I could cause y to vanish, thus "solving" the cubic equation.

2. Construct a general conic section, or second-degree curve, using the basic principles of projective geometry.

3. Draw and set in simulated motion a "four-bar" mechanical linkage. Although such linkages are simple in outward form, their analysis is troublesome and is still the subject of investigation.

4. Draw a pin-jointed structure (such as a bridge), displace one of the joints (as if loading the structure) and observe the "relaxation" that is thereupon carried out by the computer to minimize the energy of the system, thereby simulating the actual deflection.

5. Plot the potential field typical of the flow of an ideal fluid within a region of specified shape.

Now, it is clear that these five problems are not much related to one another and that a conventional computer program written to deal with one of them would not be of the slightest use for any of the others. The computer did not contain a set of programs —one for each of the problems. Instead it had a flexible and quite general capability for performing a set of primitive geometric constructions and for applying a set of primitive geometric constraints. The computer played the role of an intelligent but innocent assistant, and together the machine and I set up and solved the problems. The time it took to do so was not more than 10 or 15 minutes in each case, so that something less than two hours was spent in not only achieving solutions but also experimenting with these solutions by changing the input variables. During this time the computer was mostly idle, waiting for me to decide what to do next. It probably spent not much more than five minutes in actual cooperative work.

This experiment in man-machine interaction is described not because the problems are significant or because the solutions were obtained efficiently. On the contrary, the computer was compelled to obtain solutions in an inefficient way compared with what might have happened if special conventional programs had been written for each problem. Five such special programs, however, could well have taken weeks to write and "debug."

Whereas Ivan Sutherland's Sketchpad is purely geometric, William R. Sutherland, also of M.I.T., has extended his brother's work to include abstractions. With his program one can draw diagrams, attach meanings to them and then cause the computer to take appropriate action based on the diagrams and their associated meanings. One can draw a circuit diagram, for example, stipulate the characteristics and functional behavior of the elements of the diagram and then simulate the actual circuit performance. One can also draw a logical flow diagram of a computational procedure and then "activate" the diagram, so to speak, to obtain numerical results from numerical inputs to the procedural diagram.

The two Sutherlands' systems illustrate the striking possibilities of direct and natural communication with the machine. It is perhaps no mere coincidence that these highly congenial systems are graphical, and that the two-dimensional nature of their communicative form greatly enhances the ease of their use and the "transparency" of the interface they create between man and computer. The line of type from conventional typewriter keyboards has until recently been the only economically available means of "on line" communication with the computer. This one-dimensional string of symbols has had a somewhat stultifying influence on computer technology, partly because it bears little resemblance to standard and familiar mathematical notation and perhaps partly because its awkward syntactic constructions force some unnatural formulations in programming.

In many fields of engineering the geometric description of objects is a fundamentally important task. Airplane fuselages, ship hulls and automobile bodies are all complex free forms (as opposed to simpler specified forms such as spheres, cones, toruses or ellipsoids) and take many months to design and define by conventional methods. All kinds of smaller objects are also free forms: the hand set of a telephone, the bowl of a tobacco pipe, a differential housing of an automobile. In the design and ultimate detailed description of all such shapes the computer can make an extremely important contribution.

Objects are bounded by surfaces, and once the surfaces are designed and described we know a great deal about the object. The computer has made it possible, at least in principle, to perform all kinds of geometric operations on surfaces, provided that they can be described in mathematical terms. Unfortunately the traditional mathematical treatment of surfaces says a great deal about the analytical relations of surfaces that already exist and are expressible mathematically but very little about the problem of bringing them into existence. The emphasis has been on analysis, and until recently the study of the synthesis of surfaces has been neglected.

The design of a free-form shape begins with the design of a few salient outlines; once these important design curves are established, the complete and detailed description of the object's surface is to some extent a matter of mechanical extension of the implicit information. For example, an engineer can define a few contour curves for a casting. His drawing goes to a patternmaker in the shop, who creates a pattern in wood. The surface of the pattern is suggested by the design curves but is necessarily more completely specified; the patternmaker extends the original meager information by interpreting the intent of the designer. In the process he has done nothing inherently creative, but he has behaved like a benevolent, experienced and skillful machine.

Within the past few years a way has been found to make the

computer play the part of the experienced patternmaker. The designer need only draw a few descriptive design curves; the computer immediately generates a surface that incorporates these curves, and the designer can either accept the surface or modify it by drawing additional curves. The surface so designed is contained in the computer in definite mathematical form and is constructed automatically in a fraction of a second. If the designer wishes, he can command the computer to operate a plotter and draw out a full-size contour map or other graphical representation of the object, or he can require that the computer control a multiaxis milling machine to carve out a model. If the designer sees in the drawing or model features that do not please him or do not satisfy the purpose of the shape, he can either make changes graphically with the light pen or indicate dimensional changes on the keyboard. The computer will immediately and obediently incorporate these modifications in its internal mathematical description of the surface of the object and will display the modified shape on the screen. The full-scale drawing can then be redrawn or the model recarved. When the shape is satisfactory, it can be machined from metal or any other desired material.

The saving in time and effort can be great. Five grossly modified versions of a ship hull were designed in the space of a few minutes on a Project MAC computer console at M.I.T.; each version was completely described by the computer in about a tenth of a second. A point anywhere on the hull could have been determined with a precision of one part in 10 million—certainly more than adequate precision for most engineering purposes. The mathematical algorithm that makes this possible is extremely simple in concept, and it is designed to be quick and easy for computer implementation. It is also quite general. It will accept virtually any kind of design curve: polynomials, transcendental functions and even freehand sketched curves possessing no descriptive mathematical formula whatever.

Given this power to do what might be called mathematical sculpture, the engineer can use the computer representation of an object as the base for a variety of analytical treatments. He can perform stress analyses, predict pressures and other fluid forces on airplane and ship shapes, simulate dynamic effects such as vibration, study heat flow or do any of a number of calculations that depend partly on precise knowledge of the shape in question. The surface algorithm is easily extended to hyper-surfaces of any dimensionality, making possible the graphical presentation of multidimensional functions. It has been learned that such surfaces, even though they do not exist in our three-dimensional universe, can be exhibited on a cathode-ray-display tube and, when they are observed in dynamic motion, can convey meaning and elicit understanding.

In the near future—perhaps within five and surely within 10 years—a handful of engineer-designers will be able to sit at individual consoles connected to a large computer complex. They will have the full power of the computer at their fingertips and will be able to perform with ease the innovative functions of design and the mathematical processes of analysis, and they will even be able to effect through the computer the manufacture of the product of their efforts. Through their consoles they will be in communication with one another to ensure that the separate elements of the design are compatible. Engineering standards, parts catalogues and other data will be accessible through the display screens of their consoles. Some mechanical parts will be produced directly from the design information generated within the computer, without the necessity of drawings. (When drawings are required to provide information for final assembly or for maintenance manuals, these drawings will be prepared by the computer from the primary design information, and the drawings will even be tailored to match the use. For example, electrical wiring drawings will subordinate actual structure, showing only enough to clarify the task of the electrician.)

It would be difficult to compile even a representative list of the agencies and individuals who are making contributions toward the realization of this new age of the computer. At M.I.T., Douglas Ross and I have been directing efforts toward this goal under Air Force sponsorship for about seven years. In the Electronic Systems Laboratory, Ross is engaged in a formidable effort in the areas of data structures, computer languages and general compilers for engineering design. My group in the department of mechanical engineering has been working on graphical displays and on design tasks such as three-dimensional stress analysis, the solution of equilibrium field problems, kinematics and data storage and retrieval. Almost all universities with computer facilities are engaged in some phase of the problem. Work closely parallel to the work at M.I.T. is being done by Bertram Herzog and his colleagues at the University of Michigan. In industry the Lockheed Aircraft Corporation, the General Motors Corporation and the Ford Motor Company have experimental computer-aided design systems in operation, and these systems are beginning to be used to a limited extent in production engineering. The Boeing Company and the Douglas Aircraft Company are involved in similar activities.

Much energy and talent is being devoted to making computer-aided design and man-machine interaction a convenient everyday reality, and as time goes on more fresh effort is being channeled into this exciting enterprise. One may hope that engineers, economists, psychologists, sociologists and other men can help to provide the appropriate human adjustments to it.

MARTIN GREENBERGER

The Uses of Computers in Organizations

As computer systems take up more tasks in human organizations they come to resemble the organizations themselves. Ultimately they will serve the organization's key functions of communication and control.

The computer systems under development today are beginning to mirror man and his industrial society, both in structure and in the pattern of their evolution. Our industrial civilization is characterized by the division of labor, the specialization and routinization of functions, mechanization, stratification of control and a hierarchical form of organization that integrates the activities of planning, management and operations. Coordination is accomplished by an elaborate system of information-handling and communication. The computer is being brought into the organization primarily to help with information-handling, but in the process it is incorporating in its programs almost all the characteristics of the organization as a whole.

This may come as no surprise, since computer systems and programs are designed by human beings and might therefore be expected to assume aspects of man and his organizations. Indeed, all the machines man has devised possess the characteristics of organizations to some extent. But the computer is not just another machine. It has a versatility, a logical flexibility and an open-endedness—an ability to grow—that is not matched by anything short of the living organism. The computer, a comparatively recent addition to the organization, has within it the potential for completely remolding the organization. Accordingly it has new and important implications for the future of human society. In this chapter we shall first consider the past and present uses of the computer in the organizational setting and then explore the computer's possible future in that setting.

The use of the digital computer as a generally available (that is, commercially produced) tool is only 15 years old. Its first applications were in science and engineering. Its early users took a rather restricted view of its capabilities. It was put to work composing lengthy numerical tables and performing other prosaic calculations. Soon, however, its wider potentialities gained the interest of the military authorities, among others, and substantial amounts of money were made available to promote its evolution. The digital computer became a yeast in research and development. Without the computer there might be no nuclear power plants today, no communication satellites, no space program, perhaps no commercial fleets of jet airplanes. In the laboratories of science the computer likewise grew rapidly in power, versatility and esteem [see "The Uses of Computers in Science," by Anthony G. Oettinger, page 113]. By expanding the ability to deal with complex problems, the computer has stepped up the rate of scientific and technological advance.

The story is much the same for the use of the computer in business and government. Its first employment outside the fields of science and engineering was by the Bureau of the Census in 1951. There and in the business firms that began to use the machine it was assigned exclusively to standard clerical and statistical tasks. Most engineers and business executives foresaw little use for the computer in business except for record-keeping and other mechanical operations. The General Electric appliance division installed a UNIVAC I in 1954 and gave it the job of preparing the payroll, which was successfully achieved only after a certain amount of agony and mishap. A few banks, insurance companies, mass-circulation magazines and public utilities arranged to use digital computers for customer accounting and billing; some manufacturers and distributors applied the computer to inventory control.

It is startling to recall that this was the situation barely a decade ago. Today tens of thousands of digital computers are employed in business and government in the U.S. By virtue of their flexibility and great improvements in their speed, capacity and reliability, they have been able to take on a wide variety of new jobs. The computer has been graduated from a specialist in drudgery to an information processor adept in a broad range of functions. Interestingly enough, this broadening of the computer's capability has been achieved in part by creating a high degree of specialization within the machine. As the art of programming advances, the devices used for the organization of computer programs are coming to resemble those that have proved useful in the organization of human society. The large programs today contain a considerable array of differentiated services and multiple levels of control.

The programmed unit of specialization in a computer system is called a routine. It is a set of instructions for performing a distinguishable task; it can be likened to a human worker doing a specific job or using a particular skill. There are routines that exercise control (managers) and others that execute operations (workers). Subserving the specialized operations are standardized routines, called subroutines, that perform functions of general utility.

Computer routines are the programmer's device for coping with complexity. They not only enable him to break down a complex program into manageable parts but also confer other important advantages. A program can be organized in modules, or building blocks, consisting of self-contained routines, and this makes it easy to reach in and replace a defective module or to add a new one. Most large computer systems have been built by the modular approach. Those that have not have demonstrated how important it is to allow for change and growth. Modularity facilitates growth. Just as new workers, skills, machines and instruments can be added to an industrial or research establishment to enlarge its scope of operations or deepen its capabilities, so in a modular computer system new routines can be added to improve its operation.

The modular structure is also a great convenience when a team of programmers undertakes to collaborate on a large project, as a group of us at Harvard University did in 1957 in the course of building a demographic model of the U.S. economy. Each member was assigned to an independent section. We were able to work in relative isolation; responsibilities were clearly established; program checking was simplified, and the project proceeded along several lines simultaneously.

A good illustration of modular design is our system called OPS (for "On-Line Process Synthesis") at the Massachusetts Institute of Technology. It was developed within the time-sharing system of Project MAC, which is itself constructed on the modular plan [see "Time-sharing on Computers," by R. M. Fano and F. J. Corbató, page 76]. OPS is one of numerous user programs filed in the memory of the time-sharing system. This particular program, however, like a division of a large corporation, is a complete operating system in its own right. It has its own retinue of control routines and a wide assortment of subroutines and operational programs known as "operators." There is an operator corresponding to each of the customary statements in an algebraic programming language, such as FORTRAN or ALGOL, and there are also operators for individually tailored and complex compounds of these statements. One operator solves general linear programming problems. Another does a multiple regression analysis. A third locates the critical path in a network. A fourth performs a general computation involving vectors and matrices. A fifth smooths a time series, providing an economic forecast. A sixth schedules an event during a simulation run. A seventh presents information in tabular format. And so on. The user can add operators that are particularly relevant to his own interests. By its modular structure the OPS system makes room within the physical limitations of the machine for a high degree of growth and variety.

A user of the OPS system addresses each operator by its name, which may be an English word such as SET, PRINT or READ. He can combine operators into a compound operator and give it a name of its own. Since the OPS system runs in a time-sharing environment, the user can program himself into the computer operation and from his on-line terminal perform those aspects of the operation that call for human judgment or are amorphous and undefined. In the same way he can control the operation of the program externally.

Thus time-sharing makes possible the flexible inclusion of people in a computer operation. The potential for human participation is particularly significant in operations conducted in "real time." This term simply means that the computer interacts with the external environment and carries out appropriate operations as the situation develops. In other words, the computer is linked directly to the work to be done in the real world. A straightforward example is the guidance of a missile or space vehicle to its destination by continual computer adjustments to the changing conditions en route. A more elaborate example is the SAGE computer, which receives information on possible enemy activity from radar stations, aircraft and picket ships spread over a vast area. The computer must rapidly summarize on display screens the information coming in from all these sources, and it must act as adviser and controller for any defensive action that is indicated.

It is with the advent of real-time systems that the organization of programming has begun to resemble human organizations most closely. A real-time system requires considerably more complicated programming than the more conventional batch-processing operation does. Whereas in batch processing jobs typically are fed to the computer continuously and serially from a single tape on which they have previously been accumulated, in a real-time operation they can enter instantly, sporadically and simultaneously from any of many remote terminals connected to the computer. Jobs are processed transaction by transaction rather than batch by batch. Since the execution of the program is interrupted whenever external conditions dictate, a variety of special routines must be provided to handle each of the contingencies. To make the system workable, information within the computer must be arranged in randomly accessible form, and programs are needed to make storage and retrieval of this information convenient. The result may be a complex organization of specialized routines whose coordination and control are a central function of the real-time operation.

The technology for real-time systems is already fairly well advanced, thanks largely to military developments such as SAGE. The available terminal equipment, however, particularly that providing for the input and output of information in graphical form, is still too expensive. Moreover, such "conversational" teleprocessing is costly, because present communication systems are designed for voice signals and continuous transmission of data, not for scattered bursts of data. Nevertheless, in spite of the temporary obstacles of high cost and the relative difficulty of real-time programming, real-time systems are already entrenched in the military sphere and have been making decided progress in business and industry.

The first commercial application of a real-time system on a large scale was the SABRE reservation system of American Airlines. Its computer center is in Briarcliff Manor, N.Y. To this center more than 1,000 reservation clerks at airports and offices throughout the U.S. address their queries and instructions. The clerks type their messages into the computer from their typewriter terminals, using a code SABRE can comprehend. The transactions occur at unpredictable times, placing an uneven load and a wide variety of demands on the system. Yet SABRE is tuned to respond to a request within three seconds.

Several airlines and railroads have followed this lead and installed reservation systems of the same type. Real-time computers soon will also be landing airliners in fog and scheduling railroad freight-yard activities and the movement of boxcars. A computer will control the running and spacing of the high-speed passenger trains of the new rapid-transit line in the San Francisco-Oakland bay area. Real-time systems are being set up to control automobile traffic in large cities, including New York. It is not farfetched to anticipate that someday an integrated information-and-control system will link together not only transportation facilities but also hotels, motels, car rentals and all other agencies of travel.

In the field of finance real-time systems are being put to work by banks, insurance companies and stock markets. Many savings banks have installed on-line systems in which deposits and withdrawals are recorded directly in a computer. Commercial banks are beginning to use random-access computers for handling demand-deposit accounting and recording stock transfers. Insurance companies are planning to make the files of their policyholders available to their agents in field offices through on-line queries to the central office. Several stock-quotation services enable brokers and their clients to obtain the price of a security simply by dialing the computer. The New York and American stock exchanges are embarked on programs that will facilitate the eventual automation of all their floor activities, with the possible exception of the setting of prices. It is perhaps not overly fanciful to foresee a day when most trading and financial transactions will be carried out not on the floors of exchanges and in the conference rooms of banks but over computer communication networks linking together widely separated offices of the transactors. Such a development might have important implications for the future of our cities, one of whose chief functions at present is to serve as financial centers.

Real-time computers have also entered the fields of retail and wholesale commerce. There are now service companies that make real-time computation available in the manner of public utilities to enterprises of modest size. One such company is the Keydata Corporation in Cambridge, Mass. Some of its subscribers are wholesale distributors. When a sale is made, a clerk types an invoice for the customer on a teletypewriter that is connected to the Keydata computer by a leased telephone line. The clerk identifies the customer simply by a number; the items he has bought are also identified by number, and the only other information supplied is the amount of each item bought. The computer fills in, from information stored in its files, all the rest of the necessary data for the invoice: the date, the invoice number, the name and address of the customer, descriptions of the items sold and their prices. It calculates and prints the total amount of the sale and checks for clerical errors. All in all it types about 80 percent of the information on a typical invoice. The computer retains information concerning the transaction and therefore is equipped to provide the services of inventory control and sales analysis.

In industry one of the pioneers in the development of real-time systems has been the Lockheed Missiles and Space Company. Its computer center at Sunnyvale, Calif., operates an "automatic data-acquisition system" that collects information on work flow from more than 200 factory stations spread over a 300-mile radius from the center. The system records and controls the movement of more than 200,000 separate items manufactured or stored at these locations. Also connected to the computer are 25 stations from which, on inquiry, prompt information can be obtained about the location of shop and purchase orders, inventory levels and labor charges. The system, which has been operating since 1962, has saved the company millions of dollars in its Polaris and Agena programs. It has relieved supervisory personnel of much pressure and confusion and has freed them to devote more time to planning. It has also eliminated hundreds of jobs in the areas of purchasing, expediting and production scheduling.

The reduction of jobs by the computer and its acquisition of detailed data about the activities of workers produced an eruption of resentment among the workers. This subsided after Lockheed put restrictions on the use of the data by management, instituted training programs and assigned to other jobs employees who had been displaced by the machine.

Probably the most extensive and advanced use of a real-time system in industry today is that at the Westinghouse Electric Corporation. Its telecomputer center in Pittsburgh is becoming the nerve center of the corporation. The center started operating in 1962 as an automatic switchboard for messages in the teletype network that serves all the Westinghouse divisions. Today this system, in continual communication with about 300 plants, field offices, warehouses, distributors and appliance-repair centers, is taking over the functions of inventory control and order processing on a vast scale. It has also begun to take a hand in production control and is steadily moving into new fields [see illustration on pages 152–153].

The improvements in the company's operations have been dramatic. By directing shipments to customers from the nearest warehouse that has the ordered item in stock the system has speeded up deliveries and reduced transportation costs. It provides salesmen with information about the availability of products and about prices within minutes. It updates sales statistics continuously. It automatically requisitions replenishments when inventories fall below a given level. The data captured by the computer from the messages it is continually receiving and transmitting give the management a growing fund of timely information.

One interesting application of the Westinghouse computer system is a "cash-management information program" that keeps a running account of the cash flow. All receipts and disbursements of the various Westinghouse divisions are immediately transmitted by teletype to the telecomputer center and recorded in the appropriate accounts. When the balance in any of the corporation's 250 regional bank accounts falls below a preset level, the computer automatically orders a transfer of cash from the central bank account. When the balance in the central account is higher than necessary, the treasury office invests the excess in marketable securities, notifying the computer as it does so. The net result is that the company's management knows the company's cash position at all times and is able to put formerly idle funds to work earning interest.

A device for the graphical display of financial information has been installed at Westinghouse headquarters and is now being tested and "debugged." It will picture for the Westinghouse executives trends in the company's financial operations and will compare financial forecasts with actual accomplishments. The system has important implications for planning by top management. Other applications of the computer to planning are being made at the General Electric Company, the International Business Machines Corporation, the Standard Oil Company (New Jersey) and many other large corporations.

What has occurred in real-time programming up to now is obviously only a prelude to much more far-reaching developments that are likely to follow in the coming years. Let us speculate a bit on the nature of these developments and their possible broad-scale effects on our business and industrial organizations.

One aspect of the organization that is likely to be affected is the degree to which its control is centralized. Over the past 30 years, as enterprises have grown enormously in size, the trend has been toward decentralization of company operations through the setting up of divisions and profit centers. The giant corporations have found, however, that decentralization can be a mixed blessing. It tends to multiply jobs, duplicate functions and establish local goals that may run orthogonally to the objectives of the organization as a whole. It also places a burden on the company's information system by multiplying the need for information at the same time that it disperses information in a multitude of separate files spread through the organization. It may be

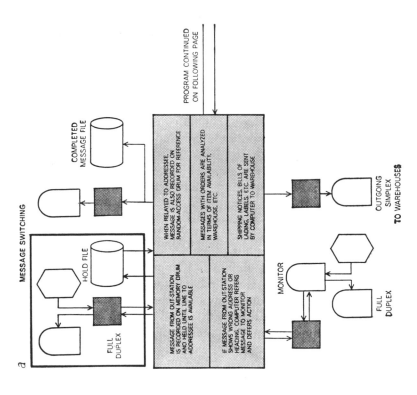

MESSAGE SWITCHING

a

COMPLETED MESSAGE FILE

HOLD FILE

FULL DUPLEX

MONITOR

FULL DUPLEX

OUTGOING SIMPLEX
TO WAREHOUSES

MESSAGE FROM OUT STATION IS RECORDED ON MEMORY DRUM AND HELD UNTIL LINE TO ADDRESSEE IS AVAILABLE

IF MESSAGE FROM OUT STATION SHOWS WRONG ADDRESS OR HEADING, COMPUTER DEFERS MESSAGE TO MONITOR AND DEFERS ACTION

WHEN RELAYED TO ADDRESSEE, MESSAGE IS ALSO RECORDED ON RANDOM-ACCESS DRUM FOR REFERENCE

MESSAGES WITH ORDERS ARE ANALYZED IN TERMS OF ITEM AVAILABILITY, WAREHOUSE, ETC

SHIPPING NOTICES, BILLS OF LADING, LABELS, ETC. ARE SENT BY COMPUTER TO WAREHOUSE

PROGRAM CONTINUED ON FOLLOWING PAGE

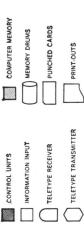

CONTROL UNITS

INFORMATION INPUT

TELETYPE RECEIVER

TELETYPE TRANSMITTER

COMPUTER MEMORY

MEMORY DRUMS

PUNCHED CARDS

PRINT-OUTS

Corporation nerve center has evolved from a computer-assisted message-relay system developed by the Westinghouse Electric Corporation in the early 1960's. The diagram on this and the facing page shows the scope of the system's activities. The center, located in Pittsburgh, was planned as a control point for teletype communications between Westinghouse's more than 300 sales offices, distributors, warehouses, factories and repair centers throughout the U.S. At first the center's computers served such simple purposes as overnight memory storage of a West Coast message to an East Coast addressee received after close of business and automatic forwarding of the message the following day (a). The computers were also programmed to analyze incoming orders and to check them automatically against continuously revised inventory compilations. This program directed the computers to forward orders selectively to the stocked warehouses closest to the originators of the orders (b). Computer analysis of sales and purchases soon produced an additional bonus (c). A running record of nationwide cash receipts and disbursements has permitted banking practices that substantially reduce cash surpluses and allow investment of these once idle funds,

ORDER PROCESSING AND CASH MANAGEMENT

days or weeks before new information is processed, summarized, transmitted and made available to the people who need it for operations and decisions.

Clearly the computer can help to correct this situation. Data from the many divisions and hierarchical levels of the organization will flow directly into a central computer memory, in the same way that information about hundreds of thousands of inventory items now feeds into Lockheed's automatic data-acquisition system from hundreds of remote terminals. The computer programs will promptly sort the information, place each item in an appropriate list or report, link it to related information already stored and make the processed information quickly accessible to those who need it for authorized purposes.

Some investigators in this field believe that systems for integrating the company files will eventually reverse the trend toward decentralization. That is a moot question; the centralization of information need not imply the centralization of control. It will surely streamline operations, however, and save the company money. Most important, it will give the company a new coherence and sense of unity, and it will pave the way to further mechanization of the company's activities.

Much of this mechanization may take place within the computer. The further evolution of computer programs may repeat the history of industrialization: in the first phase, the division of labor into easy-to-execute tasks; in the second phase, the delegation of these tasks to machines. The first phase was demonstrated by Adam Smith two centuries ago in *The Wealth of Nations*. Smith observed how the division of labor speeded the manufacture of pins: "One man draws out the wire, another straightens it, a third cuts it, a fourth points it, a fifth grinds it at the top for receiving the head; to make the head requires two or three distinct operations; to put it on, is a peculiar business, to whiten the pins is another . . . and the important business of making a pin is, in this manner, divided into about 18 distinct operations. . . . I have seen a small manufactory of this kind where . . . ten persons could make among them upwards of 48,000 pins in a day." Today a single machine, going through much the same process Smith described, turns out several hundred thousand pins per hour.

In the future enactment of this process programs will play the part of machines. Suppose a company has a real-time, time-shared computer that participates as a central instrument of operations. Suppose its body of programming is open-ended, like the OPS system, and is able to grow and assume new functions easily. The routine the computer employs to store away incoming transaction data does the work of a team of file clerks. The routines it has to make this data available on demand to customer representatives and to summarize the data in periodic reports to management are like staff assistants.

The company will be able to expand its work force by hiring employees with the requisite skills, or by extending its real-time computer program, or by a combination of both. Additions and modifications to the program can be kept tentative and flexible until they are judged to perform satisfactorily by human monitors at the consoles. Programs may be refined and made more efficient by a continual policy of replacement and improvement. Over a period of time the computer system will become larger in scope, better in detail and a vital part of the company organization. There will be an intriguing interplay of centripetal and centrifugal forces, tasks for which the computer shows an aptitude being drawn into the body of programming and tasks that are better performed by the human touch or mind drifting outward to the operators at the consoles (and beyond). Ultimately the parallel organizations of people and programs in an enterprise may blend together and appear as one, just as organizations of people and machines have done in the past.

What this means for the future of our economy and society remains to be seen. It appears likely that our organizations and institutions will function more efficiently and smoothly and thus become significantly more productive. As others have remarked, there is no reason to suppose this will result in a glut of goods and services or in massive unemployment, even though job descriptions may change drastically.

Much has been written about the dangers that may lie in wait for a computerized society: the cult of the machine, overdelegation of our activities to the computer, too much faith in its simplifications and quantifications, the invasion of privacy and individual rights by overzealous programs of industry or government, criminal misuses of the computer. These possibilities are real and should not be waved aside. Computer scientists take them seriously and are today in an uncomfortable position somewhat like that of the nuclear physicists after the discovery of uranium fission.

It should be perfectly clear, however, that the dangers arise from the way man may use the computer, not from the machine itself. The computer remains under human control. The programs of the future will have the character man designs into them, and prevention of abuses is an important part of the design problem.

PATRICK SUPPES

The Uses of Computers in Education

The huge information-processing capacities of
computers make it possible to use them to adapt
mechanical teaching routines to the needs and the
past performance of the individual student.

As other chapters in this book make abundantly clear, both the processing and the uses of information are undergoing an unprecedented technological revolution. Not only are machines now able to deal with many kinds of information at high speed and in large quantities but also it is possible to manipulate these quantities of information so as to benefit from them in entirely novel ways. This is perhaps nowhere truer than in the field of education. One can predict that in a few more years millions of schoolchildren will have access to what Philip of Macedon's son Alexander enjoyed as a royal prerogative: the personal services of a tutor as well-informed and responsive as Aristotle.

The basis for this seemingly extravagant prediction is not apparent in many examinations of the computer's role in education today. In themselves, however, such examinations provide impressive evidence of the importance of computers on the educational scene. As an example, a recent report of the National Academy of Sciences states that by mid-1965 more than 800 computers were in service on the campuses of various American universities and that these institutions spent $175 million for computers that year. The report goes on to forecast that by 1968 the universities' annual budget for computer operations will reach $300 million and that their total investment in computing facilities will pass $500 million.

A similar example is represented by the fact that most colleges of engineering and even many high schools now use computers to train students in computer programming. Perhaps just as important as the imposition of formal course requirements at the college level is the increasingly widespread attitude among college students that a knowledge of computers is a "must" if their engineering or scientific training is to be up to date. Undergraduates of my generation who majored in engineering, for instance, considered a slide rule the symbol of their developing technical prowess. Today being able to program a computer in a standard language such as FORTRAN or ALGOL is much more likely to be the appropriate symbol.

At the graduate level students in the social sciences and in business administration are already making use of computers in a variety of ways, ranging from the large-scale analysis of data to the simulation of an industry. The time is rapidly approaching when a high percentage of all university graduates will have had some systematic training in the use of computers; a significant percentage of them will have had quite sophisticated training. An indication of the growth of student interest in computers is the increase in student units of computer-science instruction we have had at Stanford University over the past four years. Although total enrollment at Stanford increased only slightly during that period, the number of student units rose from 2,572 in 1962–1963 to 5,642 in 1965–1966.

The fact that time-sharing programs are rapidly becoming operational in many university computation centers justifies the forecast of another increase in the impact of computers on the universities [see "Time-sharing on Computers," by R. M. Fano and F. J. Corbató, page 76]. Under time-sharing regimes a much larger number of students can be given direct "on line" experience, which in itself is psychologically attractive and, from the practical viewpoint, facilitates deeper study of the use of computers. There is still another far from trivial way in which the computer serves the interests of education: The large school system that does not depend on computers for many administrative and service functions is today the exception rather than the rule.

The truly revolutionary function of computers in education, however, lies in the novel area of computer-assisted instruction. This role of the computer is scarcely implemented as yet but, assuming the continuation of the present pace of technological development, it cannot fail to have profound effects in the near future. In this article I shall describe some experiments in computer-assisted instruction that are currently being conducted at levels ranging from the comparatively simple to the quite complex and then examine some unsuspected problems that these experiments have revealed. First, however, the reader deserves an explanation of why computer-assisted instruction is considered desirable at all.

The single most powerful argument for computer-assisted instruction is an old one in education. It concerns the advantages, partly demonstrated and partly conjectured, of individualized instruction. The concept of individualized instruction became the core of an explicit body of doctrine at the end of the 19th century, although in practice it was known some 2,000 years earlier in ancient Greece. For many centuries the education of the aristocracy was primarily tutorial. At the university level individualized tutorial instruction has been one of the glories of Oxford and Cambridge. Modern criticisms of the method are not directed at its intrinsic merit but rather at its economic inefficiency. It is widely agreed that the more an educational curriculum can adapt in a unique fashion to individual learners—each of whom has his own characteristic initial ability, rate and even "style" of learning—the better the chance is of providing the student with a successful learning experience.

The computer makes the individualization of instruction easier because it can be programmed to follow each student's history of learning successes and failures and to use his past performance as a basis for selecting the new problems and new concepts to which he should be exposed next. With modern information-storage devices it is possible to store both a large body of curriculum material and the past histories of many students working in the curriculum. Such storage is well within the capacity of current technology, whether the subject is primary school mathematics, secondary school French or elementary statistics at the college level. In fact, the principal obstacles to computer-assisted instruction are not technological but pedagogical: how to devise ways of individualizing instruction and of designing a curriculum that are suited to individuals instead of groups. Certain obvious steps that take account of different rates of learning can be made with little difficulty; these are the main things that have been done so far. We have still, however, cut only a narrow path into a rich jungle of possibilities. We do not have any really clear scientific idea of the extent to which instruction can be individualized. It will probably be some time before a discipline of such matters begins to operate at anything like an appropriately deep conceptual level.

A second important aspect of computers in education is closer in character to such familiar administrative functions as routine record-keeping. Before the advent of computers it was extremely difficult to collect systematic data on how children succeed in the process of learning a given subject. Evaluative tests of achievement at the end of learning have (and will undoubtedly continue to have) a place both in the process of classifying students and in the process of comparing different curriculum approaches to the same subject. Nonetheless, such tests remain blunt and insensitive instruments, particularly with respect to detailed problems of instruction and curriculum revision. It is not possible on the basis of poor results in a test of children's mastery of subtraction or of irregular verbs in French to draw clear inferences about ways to improve the curriculum. A computer, on the other hand, can provide daily information about how students are performing on each part of the curriculum as it is presented, making it possible to evaluate not only individual pages but also individual exercises. This use of computers will have important consequences for all students in the immediate future. Even if students are not themselves receiving computer-assisted instruction, the results of such instruction will certainly be used to revise and improve ordinary texts and workbooks.

Let me now take up some of the work in computer-assisted instruction we have been doing at Stanford. It should be emphasized that similar work is in progress at other centers, including the University of Illinois, Pennsylvania State University, the University of Pittsburgh, the University of Michigan, the University of Texas, Florida State University and the University of California at Santa Barbara, and within such companies as the International Business Machines Corporation, the Systems Development Corporation and Bolt, Beranek and Newman. This list is by no means exhaustive. The work at these various places runs from a primary emphasis on the development of computer hardware to the construction of short courses in subjects ranging from physics to typing. Although all these efforts, including ours at Stanford, are still in the developmental stage, the instruction of large numbers of students at computer terminals will soon (if academic and industrial soothsayers are right) be one of the most important and socially beneficial fields of application for computers [see Plate 5].

At Stanford our students are mainly at the elementary school level; the terminals they use, however, are also suitable for secondary school and university students. At each terminal there is a visual device on which the student may view displays brought up from the computer memory as part of the instruction program. A device that is coming into wide use for this purpose is the cathode ray tube; messages can be generated directly by the computer on the face of the tube, which resembles a television screen. Mounted with the cathode ray tube is a typewriter keyboard the student can use to respond to problems shown on the screen. At some additional cost the student can also have a light pen that enables him to respond directly by touching the pen to the screen instead of typing on the keyboard. Such a device is particularly useful for students in the lowest elementary grades, although when only single-digit numerical responses or single-character alphabetical ones are required, the use of a keyboard is quite easy even for kindergarten children to learn.

After the display screen and the keyboard the next most important element at a terminal is the appropriate sound device. Presenting spoken messages to students is desirable at all educational levels, but it is particularly needed for younger children. It would be hard to overemphasize the importance of such spoken messages, programmed to be properly sensitive to points at which the student may encounter difficulty in learning. Such messages are the main help a good tutor gives his pupil; they are the crucial missing element in noncomputerized teaching machines. All of us have observed that children, especially the younger ones, learn at least as much by ear as they do by eye. The effectiveness of the spoken word is probably stronger than any visual stimulus, not only for children but also most of the time for adults. It is particularly significant that elementary school children, whose reading skills are comparatively undeveloped, comprehend rather complicated spoken messages.

A cathode ray tube, a keyboard and a loudspeaker or earphones therefore constitute the essential devices for computer-assisted instruction. Additional visual displays such as motion pictures or line drawings can also be useful at almost all levels of instruction. Ordinary film projectors under computer control can provide such displays.

So far three levels of interaction between the student and the computer program have received experimental attention. At the most superficial level (and accordingly the most economical one) are "drill and practice" systems. Instruction programs that fall under this heading are merely supplements to a regular curriculum taught by a teacher. At Stanford we have experimented a great deal with elementary school mathematics at the drill-and-practice level, and I shall draw on our experience for examples of what can be accomplished with this kind of supplementation of a regular curriculum by computer methods.

Over the past 40 years both pedagogical and psychological studies have provided abundant evidence that students need a great deal of practice in order to master the algorithms, or basic procedures, of arithmetic. Tests have shown that the same situation obtains for students learning the "new math." There seems to be no way to avoid a good deal of practice in learning to execute the basic algorithms with speed and accuracy. At the elementary level the most important way in which computer-assisted instruction differs from traditional methods of providing practice is that we are in no sense committed to giving each child the same set of problems, as would be the case if textbooks or other written materials were used. Once a number of study "tracks," representing various levels of difficulty, have been prepared as a curriculum, it is only a matter of computer programming to offer students exercises of varying degrees of difficulty and to select the appropriate level of difficulty for each student according to his past performance.

In the program we ran in elementary grades at schools near Stanford during the academic year 1965–1966 five levels of difficulty were programmed for each grade level. A typical three-day block of problems on the addition of fractions, for example, would vary in the following way. Students at the lowest level (Level 1) received problems involving only fractions that had the same denominator in common. On the first two days levels 2 and 3 also received only problems in which the denominators were the same. On the third day the fraction problems for levels 2 and 3 had denominators that differed by a factor of 2. At Level 4 the problems had denominators that differed by a factor 2 on the first day. At Level 5 the denominators differed by a factor of 3, 4, 5 or 6 on the first day. Under the program the student moved up and down within the five levels of difficulty on the basis of his performance on the previous day. If more than 80 percent of his exercises were done correctly, he moved up a level. If fewer than 60 percent of the exercises were done correctly, he moved down a level. The selection of five levels and of 80 and 60 percent has no specific theoretical basis; they are founded on practical and pedagogical intuition. As data are accumulated we expect to modify the structure of the curriculum.

Our key effort in drill-and-practice systems is being conducted in an elementary school (grades three through six) a few miles from Stanford. The terminals used there are ordinary teletype machines, each connected to our computer at Stanford by means of individual telephone lines. There are eight teletypes in all, one for each school classroom. The students take turns using the teletype in a fixed order; each student uses the machine once a day for five to 10 minutes. During this period he receives a number of exercises (usually 20), most of which are devoted to a single concept in the elementary school mathematics curriculum. The concept reviewed on any given day can range from ordinary two-digit addition to intuitive logical inference. In every case the teacher has already presented the concept and the pupil has had some classroom practice; the computer-assisted drill-and-practice work therefore supplements the teacher's instruction.

The machine's first instruction—PLEASE TYPE YOUR NAME—is already on the teletype paper when the student begins his drill.

The number of characters required to respond to this instruction is by far the longest message the elementary student ever has to type on the keyboard, and it is our experience that every child greatly enjoys learning how to type his own name. When the name has been typed, the pupil's record is looked up in the master file at the computer and the set of exercises he is to receive is determined on the basis of his performance the previous day. The teletype now writes, for example, DRILL 604032. The first digit (6) refers to the grade level, the next two digits (04) to the number of the concept in the sequence of concepts being reviewed during the year, the next two digits (03) to the day in terms of days devoted to that concept (in this case the third day devoted to the fourth concept) and the final digit (2) to the level of difficulty on a scale ranging from one to five.

The real work now begins. The computer types out the first exercise. The carriage returns to a position at which the pupil should type in his answer. At this point one of three things can happen. If the pupil types the correct answer, the computer immediately types the second exercise. If the pupil types a wrong answer, the computer types WRONG and repeats the exercise without telling the pupil the correct answer. If the pupil does not answer within a fixed time (in most cases 10 seconds), the computer types TIME IS UP and repeats the exercise. This second presentation of the exercise follows the same procedure regardless of whether the pupil was wrong or ran out of time on the first presentation. If his answer is not correct at the second presentation, however, the correct answer is given and the exercise is typed a third time. The pupil is now expected to type the correct answer, but whether he does or not the program goes on to the next exercise. As soon as the exercises are finished the computer prints a summary for the student showing the number of problems correct, the number wrong, the number in which time ran out and the corresponding percentages. The pupil is also shown his cumulative record up to that point, including the amount of time spent at the terminal [see illustration on facing page].

A much more extensive summary of student results is available to the teacher. By typing in a simple code the teacher can receive a summary of the work by the class on a given day, of the class's work on a given concept, of the work of any pupil and of a num-

```
PLEASE TYPE YOUR NAME

ROBERT VALENTINE

DRILL NUMBER 604032

L.C.M.  MEANS  LEAST COMMON MULTIPLE

___  IS THE L.C.M. OF  4 AND  9

TIME IS UP

_36 IS THE L.C.M. OF  4 AND  9

_23 IS THE L.C.M. OF 12 AND  8

WRONG

_24 IS THE L.C.M. OF 12 AND  8

_1_ IS THE L.C.M. OF 15 AND 10

WRONG

___  IS THE L.C.M. OF 15 AND 10

TIME IS UP, ANSWER IS 30

_30 IS THE L.C.M. OF 15 AND 10

_60 IS THE L.C.M. OF 12 AND 30

_12 IS THE L.C.M. OF  2,  4, AND  6

_40 IS THE L.C.M. OF  8, 10, AND  5

S. FOR SUMMARY S.

                NUMBER    PERCENT
CORRECT           14        70
WRONG              5        25
TIMEOUT            1         5
70% CORRECT IN BLOCK, 70% OVERALL TO DATE
GOOD BYE, O FEARLESS DRILL TESTER.
TEAR OFF ON DOTTED LINE
```

•••

Drill-and-practice exercise, shown in abbreviated form, is typical of a simple computer-assisted instruction program that is designed to be responsive to the needs of individual students. The illustrated exercise is one of five that differ in their degree of difficulty; when the student types his name, the exercise best suited to him on the basis of computer-memory records of his previous performance is selected automatically. The first three questions and answers exemplify the ways in which the computer is programmed to deal with various shortcomings. The student fails to answer the first question within the allotted 10-second time limit; the computer therefore prints TIME IS UP *and repeats the question, which the student then answers correctly. A wrong answer to the next question causes the computer to announce the error and repeat the question automatically; a second chance again elicits a correct answer. A wrong answer to the third question is compounded by failure to respond to the reiterated question within the time limit. Because this question has now drawn two unsatisfactory responses the automatic* TIME IS UP *statement is followed by a printing of the correct answer. The question is now repeated for a third and last time. Whether or not the student elects to copy the correct answer (he does so in this instance), the computer automatically produces the next question. Only six of the 20 questions that compose the drill are shown in the example. After the student's last answer the computer proceeds to print a summary of the student's score for the drill as well as his combined average for this and earlier drills in the same series. The drill-and-practice exercise then concludes with a cheery farewell to the student and an instruction to tear off the teletype tape.*

ber of other descriptive statistics I shall not specify here. Indeed, there are so many questions about performance that can be asked and that the computer can answer that teachers, administrators and supervisors are in danger of being swamped by more summary information than they can possibly digest. We are only in the process of learning what summaries are most useful from the pedagogical standpoint.

A question that is often asked about drill-and-practice systems is whether we have evidence that learning is improved by this kind of teaching. We do not have all the answers to this complex question, but preliminary analysis of improvement in skills and concepts looks impressive when compared with the records of control classes that have not received computer-assisted instruction. Even though the analysis is still under way, I should like to cite one example that suggests the kind of improvement that can result from continued practice, even when no explicit instructions are given either by the teacher or by the computer program.

During the academic year 1964–1965 we noticed that some fourth-grade pupils seemed to have difficulty changing rapidly from one type of problem format to another within a given set of exercises. We decided to test whether or not this aspect of performance would improve with comparatively prolonged practice. Because we were also dissatisfied with the level of performance on problems involving the fundamental commutative, associative and distributive laws of arithmetic, we selected 48 cases from this domain.

For a six-day period the pupils were cycled through each of these 48 types of exercise every two days, 24 exercises being given each day. No specific problem was repeated; instead the same problem types were encountered every two days on a random basis. The initial performance was poor, with an average probability of success of .53, but over the six-day period the advance in performance was marked. The proportion of correct answers increased and the total time taken to complete the exercises showed much improvement (diminishing from an average of 630 seconds to 279 seconds). Analysis of the individual data showed that every pupil in the class had advanced both in the proportion of correct responses and in the reduction of the time required to respond.

The next level of interaction of the pupil and the computer program is made up of "tutorial" systems, which are more complex than drill-and-practice systems. In tutorial systems the aim is to take over from the classroom teacher the main responsibility for instruction. As an example, many children who enter the first grade cannot properly use the words "top" and "bottom," "first" and "last" and so forth, yet it is highly desirable that the first-grader have a clear understanding of these words so that he can respond in unequivocal fashion to instructions containing them. Here is a typical tutorial sequence we designed to establish these concepts: 1. The child uses his light pen to point to the picture of a familiar object displayed on the cathode-ray-tube screen. 2. The child puts the tip of his light pen in a small square box displayed next to the picture. (This is the first step in preparing the student to make a standard response to a multiple-choice exercise.) 3. The words FIRST and LAST are introduced. (The instruction here is spoken rather than written; FIRST and LAST refer mainly to the order in which elements are introduced on the screen from left to right.) 4. The words TOP and BOTTOM are introduced. (An instruction to familiarize the child with the use of these words might be: PUT YOUR LIGHT PEN ON THE TOY TRUCK SHOWN AT THE TOP.) 5. The two concepts are combined in order to select one of several things. (The instruction might be: PUT YOUR LIGHT PEN ON THE FIRST ANIMAL SHOWN AT THE TOP.)

With such a tutorial system we can individualize instruction for a child entering the first grade. The bright child of middle-class background who has gone to kindergarten and nursery school for three years before entering the first grade and has a large speaking vocabulary could easily finish work on the concepts I have listed in a single 30-minute session. A culturally deprived child who has not attended kindergarten may need as many as four or five sessions to acquire these concepts. It is important to keep the deprived child from developing a sense of failure or defeat at the start of his schooling. Tutorial "branches" must be provided that move downward to very simple presentations, just as a good tutor will use an increasingly simplified approach when he realizes that his pupil is failing to understand what is being said. It is equally important that a tutorial program have enough flexibility to avoid boring a bright child with repeti-

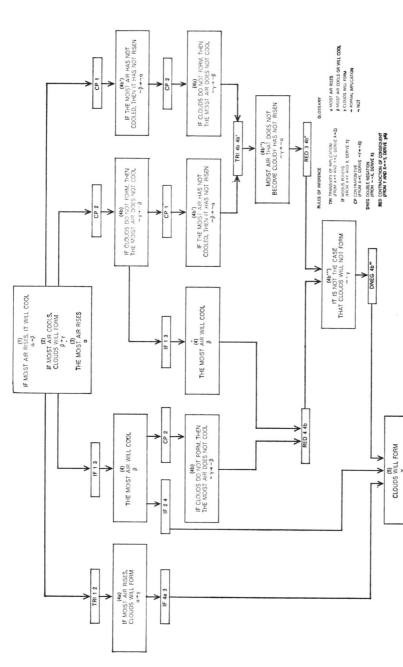

Tutorial exercise in mathematical logic is an example of a more complex variety of computer-assisted instruction. The student may proceed from a set of given hypotheses (top) to a given conclusion (bottom) by any one of several routes. Each of the il-lustrated downward paths represents a legitimate logical attack on the problem and each constitutes a unique sequence of in-ferences (see legend and statements in logical notation below each of the numbered verbal statements). Ideally a tutorial com-puter program will show no preference for one path over another but will check the soundness of each step along any path.

tive exercises he already understands. We have found it best that each pupil progress from one concept in the curriculum to another only after he meets a reasonably stiff criterion of performance. The rate at which the brightest children advance may be five to 10 times faster than that of the slowest children.

In discussing curriculum materials one commonly distinguishes between "multiple-choice responses" and "constructed responses." Multiple-choice exercises usually limit the student to three, four or five choices. A constructed response is one that can be selected by the student from a fairly large set of possibilities. There are two kinds of constructed response: the one that is uniquely determined by the exercise and the one that is not. Although a good part of our first-grade arithmetic program allows constructed responses, almost all the responses are unique. For example, when we ask for the sum of 2 plus 3, we expect 5 as the unique response. We have, however, developed a program in mathematical logic that allows constructed responses that are not unique. The student can make any one of several inferences; the main function of the computer is to evaluate the validity of the inference he makes. Whether or not the approach taken by the student is a wise one is not indicated until he has taken at least one step in an attempt to find a correct derivation of the required conclusion. No two students need find the same proof; the tutorial program is designed to accept any proof that is valid. When the student makes a mistake, the program tells him what is wrong with his response; when he is unable to take another step, the program gives him a hint.

It will be evident from these examples that well-structured subjects such as reading and mathematics can easily be handled by tutorial systems. At present they are the subjects we best understand how to teach, and we should be able to use computer-controlled tutorial systems to carry the main load of teaching such subjects. It should be emphasized, however, that no tutorial program designed in the near future will be able to handle every kind of problem that arises in student learning. It will remain the teacher's responsibility to attempt the challenging task of helping students who are not proceeding successfully with the tutorial program and who need special attention.

Thus a dual objective may be achieved. Not only will the

tutorial program itself be aimed at individualized instruction but also it will free the teacher from many classroom responsibilities so that he will have time to individualize his own instructional efforts. At Stanford we program into our tutorial sessions an instruction to the computer that we have named TEACHER CALL. When a student has run through all branches of a concept and has not yet met the required criterion of performance, the computer sends a teacher call to the proctor station. The teacher at the proctor station then goes to the student and gives him as much individualized instruction as he needs.

At the third and deepest level of student-computer interaction are systems that allow a genuine dialogue between the student and the program. "Dialogue systems" exist only as elementary prototypes; the successful implementation of such systems will require the solving of two central problems. The first may be described as follows: Suppose in a program on economic theory at the college level the student types the question: WHY ARE DEMAND CURVES ALWAYS CONVEX WITH RESPECT TO THE ORIGIN? It is difficult to write programs that will recognize and provide answers to questions that are so broad and complex, yet the situation is not hopeless. In curriculum areas that have been stable for a long time and that deal with a clearly bounded area of subject matter, it is possible to analyze the kinds of questions students ask; on the basis of such an analysis one can make considerable progress toward the recognition of the questions by the computer. Nonetheless, the central intellectual problem cannot be dodged. It is not enough to provide information that will give an answer; what is needed is an ability on the part of the computer program to recognize precisely what question has been asked. This is no less than asking the computer program to understand the meaning of a sentence.

The second problem of the dialogue system is one that is particularly critical with respect to the teaching of elementary school children. Here it is essential that the computer program be able to recognize the child's spoken words. A child in the first grade will probably not be able to type even a simple question, but he can voice quite complex ones. The problem of recognizing speech adds another dimension to the problem of recognizing the meaning of sentences.

In giving an example of the kind of dialogue system we are currently developing at Stanford I must emphasize that the program I am describing (which represents an extension of our work in mathematical logic) is not yet wholly operational. Our objective is to introduce students to simple proofs using the associative and commutative laws and also the definitions of natural numbers as successors of the next smallest number (for example, $2 = 1 + 1$, $3 = 2 + 1$ and $4 = 3 + 1$). Our aim is to enable the student to construct proofs of simple identities; the following would be typical instances: $5 = 2 + 3$ and $8 = (4 + 2) + 2$. We want the student to be able to tell the computer by oral command what steps to take in constructing the proof, using such expressions as REPLACE 2 BY $1 + 1$ or USE THE ASSOCIATIVE LAW ON LINE 3. This program is perfectly practical with our present computer system as long as the commands are transmitted by typing a few characters on the keyboard. A major effort to substitute voice for the keyboard is planned for the coming year; our preliminary work in this direction seems promising.

But these are essentially technological problems. In summarizing some other problems that face us in the task of realizing the rich potential of computer-assisted individual instruction, I should prefer to emphasize the behavioral rather than the technological ones. The central technological problem must be mentioned, however; it has to do with reliability. Computer systems in education must work with a much higher degree of reliability than is expected in computer centers where the users are sophisticated scientists, or even in factory-control systems where the users are experienced engineers. If in the school setting young people are put at computer terminals for sustained periods and the program and machines do not perform as they should, the result is chaos. Reliability is as important in schools as it is in airplanes and space vehicles; when failure occurs, the disasters are of different kinds, but they are equally conclusive.

The primary behavioral problem involves the organization of a curriculum. For example, in what order should the ideas in elementary mathematics be presented to students? In the elementary teaching of a foreign language, to what extent should pattern drill precede expansion of vocabulary? What mixture of phonics and look-and-say is appropriate for the beginning stages of reading? These are perplexing questions. They inevitably arise in the practical context of preparing curriculum materials; unfortunately we are far from having detailed answers to any of them. Individualized instruction, whether under the supervision of a computer or a human tutor, must for some time proceed on the basis of practical judgment and rough-and-ready pedagogical intuition. The magnitude of the problem of evolving curriculum sequences is difficult to overestimate: the number of possible sequences of concepts and subject matter in elementary school mathematics alone is in excess of 10^{100}, a number larger than even generous estimates of the total number of elementary particles in the universe.

One of the few hopes for emerging from this combinatorial jungle lies in the development of an adequate body of fundamental theory about the learning and retention capacity of students. It is to be hoped that, as systematic bodies of data become available from computer systems of instruction, we shall be able to think about these problems in a more scientific fashion and thereby learn to develop a more adequate fundamental theory than we now possess.

Another problem arises from the fact that it is not yet clear how critical various kinds of responses may be. I have mentioned the problem of interpreting sentences freely presented by the student, either by the written or by the spoken word. How essential complex constructed responses to such questions may be in the process of learning most elementary subjects is not fully known. A problem at least as difficult as this one is how computer programs can be organized to take advantage of unanticipated student responses in an insightful and informative way. For the immediate future perhaps the best we can do with unanticipated responses is to record them and have them available for subsequent analysis by those responsible for improving the curriculum.

The possible types of psychological "reinforcement" also present problems. The evidence is conflicting, for instance, whether students should be immediately informed each time they make a mistake. It is not clear to what extent students should be forced to seek the right answer, and indeed whether this search should take place primarily in what is called either the discovery mode or the inductive mode, as opposed to more traditional methods wherein a rule is given and followed by examples and then by exercises or problems that exemplify the rule. Another central weakness of traditional psychological theories of reinforcement is that too much of the theory has been tested by experiments in which the information transmitted in the reinforcement procedure is essentially very simple; as a result the information content of reinforcement has not been sufficiently emphasized in theoretical discussions. A further question is whether or not different kinds of reinforcement and different reinforcement schedules should be given to children of different basic personality types. As far as I know, variables of this kind have not been built into any large-scale curriculum effort now under way in this country.

Another pressing problem involves the effective use of information about the student's past performance. In standard classroom teaching it is impossible to use such records in a sensitive way; we actually have little experience in the theory or practice of the use of such information. A gifted tutor will store in his own memory many facts about the past performance of his pupil and take advantage of these facts in his tutorial course of study, but scientific studies of how this should be done are in their infancy. Practical decisions about the amount of review work needed by the individual, the time needed for the introduction of new concepts and so forth will be mandatory in order to develop the educational computer systems of the future. Those of us who are faced with making these decisions are aware of the inadequacy of our knowledge. The power of the computer to assemble and provide data as a basis for such decisions will be perhaps the most powerful impetus to the development of education theory yet to appear. It is likely that a different breed of education research worker will be needed to feel at home with these vast masses of data. The millions of observational records that computers now process in the field of nuclear physics will be rivaled in quantity and complexity by the information generated by computers in the field of instruction.

When students are put to work on an individualized basis, the problem of keeping records of their successes and failures is enormous, particularly when those records are intended for use in making decisions about the next stage of instruction. In planning ways to process the records of several thousand students at

Stanford each day, we found that one of the most difficult decisions is that of selecting the small amount of total information it is possible to record permanently. It is not at all difficult to have the data output run to 1,000 pages a day when 5,000 students use the terminals. An output of this magnitude is simply more than any human being can digest on a regular basis. The problem is to reduce the data from 1,000 pages to something like 25 or 30. As with the other problems I have mentioned, one difficulty is that we do not yet have the well-defined theoretical ideas that could provide the guidelines for making such a reduction. At present our decisions are based primarily on pedagogical intuition and the traditions of data analysis in the field of experimental psychology. Neither of these guidelines is very effective.

A body of evidence exists that attempts to show that children have different cognitive styles. For example, they may be either impulsive or reflective in their basic approach to learning. The central difficulty in research on cognitive styles, as it bears on the construction of the curriculum, is that the research is primarily at an empirical level. It is not at all clear how evidence for the existence of different cognitive styles can be used to guide the design and organization of individualized curriculum materials adapted to these different styles. Indeed, what we face is a fundamental question of educational philosophy: To what extent does society want to commit itself to accentuating differences in cognitive style by individualized techniques of teaching that cater to these differences? The introduction of computers in education raises this question in a new and pressing way. The present economics of education is such that, whatever we may think about the desirability of having a diverse curriculum for children of different cognitive styles, such diversity is not possible because of the expense. But as computers become widely used to offer instruction in the ways I have described here, it will indeed be possible to offer a highly diversified body of curriculum material. When this occurs, we shall for the first time be faced with the practical problem of deciding how much diversity we want to have. That is the challenge for which we should be prepared.

BEN-AMI LIPETZ

Information Storage and Retrieval

Computers and various means of storing information
in highly reduced form are making libraries more
efficient, but the goal of providing instant access
to almost everything ever published remains distant.

One of man's unique characteristics is his ability to communicate
his thoughts and experience to his fellows. He communicates not
only by means of transient sounds and gestures, as various other
animals do to some extent, but also by means of durable packets
of intelligible information in such forms as handwriting, printing, drawings, photographs, sound recordings and instrument
traces. These durable packets of information—which accumulate
by the millions, if not the billions, each year—can be collectively
described as records. Records can be, and frequently are, gathered into organized collections from which they can be re-
covered as the need arises. The field of information storage and
retrieval is thus concerned with methods of creating and managing collections of records to facilitate the recovery of pertinent
records as they are needed.

Ideally the individual would like to have both access to large
numbers of potentially useful records and the ability to retrieve
rapidly and accurately the particular records that pertain to each
of his specific needs as it arises. Some 20 years ago the emergence
of electronic technology for computation and data processing,
and the rapid improvement of photographic technology, in-

spired in people working in these fields the dream of putting huge collections of records, such as the entire Library of Congress, at the fingertips of any user anywhere, and of giving each user the means to search such a collection almost instantaneously. The transmission of records, the translation of foreign languages, the integration of newly acquired information into the collection—all would be accomplished automatically.

In spite of the extraordinary advances in computer technology, described by the authors of other chapters in this book, we are still a long way from the implementation of this dream. Why has it proved so elusive?

Exceptional progress has been made in providing high-speed access to carefully defined and limited stores of records. With progress, however, has come the realization that the ultimate goal is far more difficult to achieve than had been thought earlier. It involves not only the development of techniques for storing and manipulating records but also the improvement of our understanding and simulation of the ways in which people make associations and value judgments, together with the development of more reliable methods of predicting human information needs. The problem is largely an intellectual one, not simply one of developing faster and less expensive machinery.

The use of information storage and retrieval systems is a matter of everyday experience for literate people. The public lending library is perhaps the most widely known example. Most readers will be familiar also with specialized research libraries and technical information centers of various kinds. But information storage and retrieval is not confined to libraries; it is commonplace in everyday life. Correspondence files, accounting systems, inventory-control systems, directories—all are information storage and retrieval systems. So are collections of cooking recipes or of amateur color slides. Even the ubiquitous dictionary, as well as the index to a book or a journal, is an example of information storage and retrieval systems. All these examples are comprised of records to which one may address a variety of allowable questions (that is, questions within the intended scope of the collection) with a reasonable expectation of retrieving a selection of records in response to each question.

Many seemingly different activities can be observed in information storage and retrieval systems. Operationally, however, all such systems employ only three basic processes: the analysis of records, the derivation of new records from old ones and the physical displacement of records over a distance. Analysis is the central ingredient that determines whether and how new records should be created and whether existing records should be transferred or transmitted. In analyzing a record one compares it with something—another record, a list of significant features to be examined or information already assimilated in one's mind. Subsequent action is determined by the finding of a match or a mismatch between the record and the thing with which it is being compared. Finding or not finding a specified feature in a record implies comparison. Satisfactory comparison, however, requires the ability to recognize the important features in a record. This is not an easy task to turn over to a machine.

Provided that effective methods of analysis can be devised, an information storage and retrieval system operates as follows. Records are gathered or inserted into the collection in some orderly manner, possibly with indexing. A would-be user addresses a question to the collection. On the basis of the question a search of the collection is conducted and pertinent records are identified or retrieved. Note that the collection of records in a system has been created and organized *before* the specific questions it is to answer have been stated. In other words, the system is created in *anticipation* of needs that are not fully known. Yet the measure of adequacy of a system is its ability to satisfy its users' needs as they arise.

It is possible to devise an information storage and retrieval system that will conveniently retrieve pertinent records in response to all possible questions? Unfortunately it is not. Any record we might choose to examine has an infinite number of real or potential attributes, any one of which could serve by its existence or absence to answer a possible question.

This can be illustrated by considering an ordinary color slide that is to be inserted in a collection of other slides. We can think at once of a number of attributes by which it could be retrieved: the date of the photograph, the location at which it was made, the names of individuals in the picture. To this we might add the name of the photographer, the type of camera, the lens, the film, the exposure, the light or weather conditions under which the photograph was taken, the date of developing, the developing solutions used, the specific developing procedures. Each of these items could be detailed and embroidered indefinitely. If we took another tack, we could go into almost infinite detail on the content of the photograph: we could describe the relationship of the people photographed to one another or to the photographer; we could specify the presence or absence of all known or conjectured geological formations, plant or animal species, cloud formations, man-made structures and so on ad infinitum. Not only is it impossible to create an information storage and retrieval system that will respond fully to all possible questions but also it would be prohibitively expensive to try to approach such a condition. In practice all information storage and retrieval systems must adopt more modest objectives.

Designing systems to satisfy unstated needs may sound like an impossible task, yet it is being done all the time. It is accomplished by specialization. All systems, even the largest libraries, are designed with intentional or implicit limitations in scope and purpose. They do not attempt to be all things to all people. They are founded with some degree of knowledge of what kind of records are available and what general type of questions interest (or should interest) the intended users. A system can be designed for the future by extrapolating from past interests and trends; indeed, this is the only rational approach to design. As experience with a system accumulates, the requirements can often be predicted more accurately, although never with complete accuracy.

A system that is fully responsive to its users will react not only by conducting immediate searches but also by adapting its collecting and organizing activities over the long run to accommodate indicated interests and probable needs. Conversely, the users will also adapt in time to an existing system. If the system has failed to provide its users with adequate responses, and seems to them unlikely to do so in the future, unusual demands on the system may diminish as the users take their problems elsewhere. Accordingly the stability of a pattern of usage does not in itself indicate that a system is being successful in anticipating needs. Success must be related to the satisfaction and the creativeness of the *intended* users of a system, not merely of the current users. The performance of a system that is intended for highly specialized and highly restricted application is obviously far easier to gauge than the performance of a system with only vaguely defined objectives and clientele.

Two different strategies can be followed in operating an information storage and retrieval system. One is to analyze and organize the collection with great precision in the anticipation of questions. This is usually done by means of indexing. When a question arises, one would presumably have the pertinent records or their index entries already segregated from the rest of the collection, making retrieval rapid and routine. The second strategy is to avoid any unnecessary prior processing of records. When a specific question is received, a record-by-record search of the collection is made. The first strategy makes sense where needs can be anticipated precisely, where rapid retrieval is essential or where processing costs (which are proportional to the number of records processed and the detail of processing) are low compared with the alternative searching costs (which are proportional to the number of records examined in a search and the frequency of searching). The second strategy makes sense where the opposite conditions exist.

In practice virtually all systems employ a blend of the two strategies. Since the users' needs cannot be fully anticipated, some degree of record-by-record searching in response to questions is unavoidable. But some degree of prior organization of the collection according to anticipated general areas of interest will almost certainly eliminate large portions of the collection from consideration and thus make the search more efficient. The proper balance of the two strategies will vary greatly between one system and another. An example of a system at one extreme would be a military defense system, such as the SAGE air defense system or the newer missile defense system, which can be regarded as "real time" information storage and retrieval systems. In such systems rapid response or completeness of response may be all-important; therefore they tend to be elaborately organized to facilitate automatic searching of available records or data. At the other extreme a small collection of family snapshots may do

a COLLECTION OF RECORDS

b ANALYSIS OF RECORDS

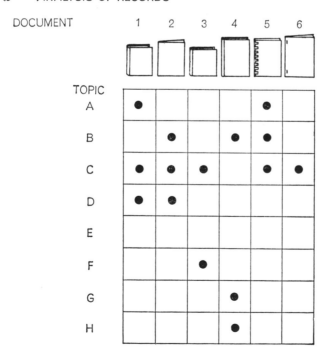

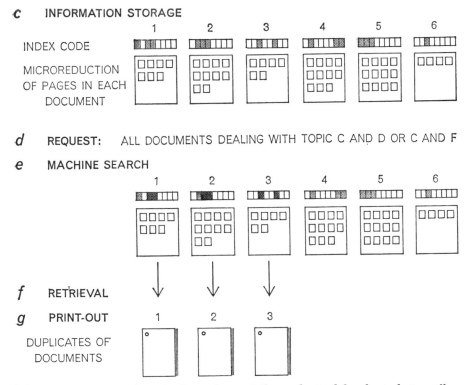

c INFORMATION STORAGE

INDEX CODE

MICROREDUCTION OF PAGES IN EACH DOCUMENT

d REQUEST: ALL DOCUMENTS DEALING WITH TOPIC C AND D OR C AND F

e MACHINE SEARCH

f RETRIEVAL

g PRINT-OUT

DUPLICATES OF DOCUMENTS

Information storage and retrieval can be partially mechanized by the technique illustrated here. Human judgment is still required in the first two stages. The first stage (a) is the collection of records and the identification of those (gray tint) that deal with a common area of interest, for example electrical communication. In the second stage (b) someone must analyze each record, or document, and decide whether or not it covers particular topics, arbitrarily limited here to eight (A through H). The individual pages of each document are recorded on microfilm (c) or other microstorage medium that provides a space for indexing in code the topics covered by each document. Here the eight spaces in the index code correspond to the letters A through H. When a request is received for information on any of the listed topics (d), a machine can rapidly search the index code (e) and retrieve the pertinent documents (f). The individual pages of these documents can be displayed in enlarged form for quick inspection or printed out as "hard copy" (g). In the request illustrated here ("All documents dealing with topics C and D or C and F") C might stand for "microwave relays," D for "coaxial cables" and F for "wave guides." One can imagine that the request has been placed by someone who wants to read about microwave relays only if they are discussed in conjunction with coaxial cables and wave guides. One may assume that two other documents (No. 5 and No. 6) that mention microwave relays are not comprehensive enough to go into these alternative ways of transmitting information.

very well with virtually no organization at all; on the rare and leisurely occasions when such a collection is reviewed the labor involved is neither great nor distasteful.

Most information systems will be organized to achieve the best compromise somewhere between these extremes. The compromise is shaped by economic forces that are by no means well understood. There are as yet no reliable quantitative guidelines for selecting the best mixture of service activities for a system, or for determining the precise emphasis to be given each aspect of record-processing. The intent of system planners and operators is to find a blend of processing and service activities that will give the best results for the particular operating environment, in terms of the benefits afforded to the users of the system and the costs of operating the system.

Advances in technology have had a major impact on the constituent costs of operating an information storage and retrieval system and have also widened to some extent the scope of activities that can be undertaken by a system. There is widespread and rapidly increasing use of automatic data-processing equipment, often in association with computers, to accomplish routine clerical tasks. Techniques and machines that were evolved to handle accounting and inventory control in commerce and industry are being adopted generally in the larger libraries and in many types of specialized information storage and retrieval systems.

The parallels are clear. If machines have been developed to help process purchase orders in a business, they can be applied to help process purchase orders in a library. If machines can handle customer billing in a business, they can be used to keep track of borrowing transactions in a library. If machines can be used to manage asset accounts in a business, they can be used to help keep track of the inventory of records in a collection. If machines can produce statistical summaries of business activity, they can do the same for information-handling activity.

These functions all involve the manipulation of digital information. Therefore they can be handled by machines, with great savings in time and labor over manual techniques, provided that the basic records are available in a machine-readable medium such as punched cards. It takes human effort, of course, to commit these records to a machine-readable form. Since some kind of record would have to be typed or written by hand in any case, there is usually little or no added labor involved in making machine-readable records instead. Thus without even introducing any marked change in the nature of the services offered by an information storage and retrieval system, automatic data-processing techniques can often reduce the cost of routine activities and simultaneously increase the accuracy and responsiveness of the system.

A fairly typical example of how business methods have been applied to information systems is the system used for keeping track of borrowed books at the library of the Oak Ridge National Laboratory. Each authorized borrower is supplied with a permanent machine-readable identification card, much like the credit card a department store or an oil company might supply to a customer. A similar card, bearing a different number, is kept with the book. When a book is to be borrowed, both cards are placed in a reading device that transmits the numbers to a computer together with the date. When the book is returned, the book card is used again to transmit a message to the computer indicating that the transaction has been completed. If the book is not returned on time, a notice addressed to the borrower is prepared automatically. Reports to the management on borrowing traffic, and on the precise holdings of each borrower, are also prepared routinely.

The ability of data-processing equipment and computers to generate new records by rearranging and copying from old records is extremely useful in other areas of information storage and retrieval. In the preparation of an alphabetical index to some body of literature the sorting of index entries into alphabetical order can be done by machine if the individual entries are first recorded in machine-readable form. If the final product is to be an attractive publication, the poor aesthetics of typography from early computer-driven printers (unit-spaced capital letters) is no longer a limitation. High-quality typesetting machines are now available that can be activated by the same machine-readable records computers require, or that can be coupled directly to a computer; such machines can generally set type much faster than a human operator. An advanced computer-driven typesetter is used at the National Library of Medicine in publishing *Index Medicus,* the world's largest index journal.

When numerous index entries are to be derived from a single packet of information, the use of data-processing techniques can make it unnecessary to create each index entry manually. At a library, for example, a set of catalogue cards that is to be produced for a newly acquired book may consist of seven different cards; all these cards are identical except that each has a different heading inserted to indicate where it is to be filed. This heading information is obtained from statements within the text on the card. If a computer can be made to recognize each of the items in the text that is to serve as a heading, then the computer should be able to accept a single typing of the text and from it generate the full set of seven cards, each augmented with a different heading. Indeed, this is now being done at the Yale Medical Library and elsewhere.

The same techniques that can be applied in sorting and in augmenting records by computer can be used in searching a collection of machine-readable records. If the machine can recognize in a record the specific code, word or phrase, or the coincidence of two or more such key terms called for by the search question, it can seek out the pertinent records and list them, copy them, compile them or cause them to be physically retrieved or transmitted [see illustrations on pages 180 and 181].

This has been the basis for much mechanization of specialized information systems. Usually only a brief description of the primary record plus a number of index terms describing the record are committed to machine-readable form. The result of a machine search may be a series of document numbers, bibliographic descriptions of documents, abstracts or even full copies of pertinent documents, depending on the money and human effort that can be invested in creating the system. This mechanized searching ability can be found in an increasing number of systems in Federal agencies and also in industrial information systems. In the pharmaceutical and chemical industries considerable success has been achieved in developing methods to describe chemical compounds in machine-usable languages that make possible mechanized searching for particular chemical groups within complex molecules.

Although computers can scan coded records at speeds that are thousands of times faster than humans can achieve, it does not always follow that a machine search will be faster or more convenient than a manual search of a corresponding collection. For example, a file of records in alphabetical order may be stored on a magnetic tape, and a corresponding file may exist either as a card file or as a printed index. To conduct a search for a specific item on the tape by computer might take, on the average, some five minutes, since the tape must be scanned until the item is found. The same item might be found in the manual card file or book index in a few seconds because rapid access to the appropriate area is possible and irrelevant material can be skipped. Rapid-access capabilities can be given to computers too (by means of disk memories and magnetic-card memories, for example), but at present the cost of storing genuinely large collections of records in this way would usually be prohibitive. Accordingly if the questions that will be asked are known to be fairly standard and can be handled by indexing methods that are not too elaborate, the traditional manual file and printed index may still be competitive with computers. The scanning speeds of computers can make them far superior, however, in responding to questions that have not been anticipated and that require record-by-record examination of a large collection.

If we turn now from the clerical activities of information storage and retrieval systems to the activities usually regarded as intellectual, such as selecting index terms, translating records and evaluating records, we find that computer techniques have made far less impact. Computers are still notoriously deficient in the ability to recognize concepts. A computer will search for a given word with great success, but it will not select a synonymous word unless it has also been given that word to search for or has been given a definition of "synonym" in machine language. This can necessitate large and expensive computer memories, excessive programming work and slowed operation where it can be done at all. Similarly, when concepts buried in multiple-word phrases must be recognized or. when a foreign language must be translated, the human specialist is still quite able to compete with the computer. This is not to say that useful applications for computers are entirely lacking in these areas or that improvements cannot be expected.

One technique that achieves indexing of a sort has found considerable acceptance. This is the KWIC (Key Word in Context) index, a form of concordance generally used to index documents by the words in their titles. A computer reads all the words in all the titles and alphabetizes these words. Then it prints out these words for all the titles in alphabetical order on successive lines but keeps with these words the context of the titles and a code for locating full information. No attempt is made to associate synonyms. The user of such a list faces the chore of searching for synonyms himself. To eliminate useless printing and searching effort the computer can be instructed not to print entries for commonplace words such as "and," "the" and so on, which have no value as index terms. The journal *Chemical Titles* is such an index; it has been published for several years and serves as an express alerting service to apprise chemists of recent articles that have appeared in selected journals.

Other approaches to indexing by computer have been tried and are under development. A statistical approach takes advantage of the computer's ability to count. Occurrences of different words in a text are counted. The terms that occur most often (other than commonplace words) are designated as index terms, on the assumption that they correlate closely with the intended topic of the record being scanned. Tests of this approach have not demonstrated the validity of the assumption. Similar statistical methods have been tried in the hope of isolating meaningful concepts by counting instances of co-occurrence of groups of words within sentences or paragraphs. A quite different approach attempts to build into computers, through programming, the capability to analyze the structure of language as humans would analyze it. This is in effect a denial that there is any inexpensive and reliable shortcut. The method is promising but requires immense human effort to develop and immense machine capability to execute.

There have been, of course, other technical developments, not involving computers, that have been of great value for information storage and retrieval systems. For example, there have been important advances in techniques for copying records and making microphotographic images. Copying devices have grown tremendously in importance and have increased in annual sales from relative insignificance 15 years ago to more than $500 million last year. Such devices can make high-quality photocopies reliably without requiring much labor. The impact on information storage and retrieval systems has been profound. Many systems now provide copies of records in preference to lending the originals; in other systems, self-service copying privileges have been accepted eagerly by patrons who would rather have a personal copy of a record than a borrowed original. Offset printing presses and other duplicating machines have also become comparatively inexpensive, reliable and convenient. It is common for information systems of any size to do far more printing now than ever of accession lists, indexes and other compilations, and to do most of it themselves.

The microfilming of records, although not a new technique (microfilming dates back more than a century), has been growing rapidly in acceptance and importance. An almost bewildering number of new techniques and devices for recording, duplicating, reading and manipulating microimages have been developed within the past decade. Although the traditional microfilm on reels is by no means obsolete, there has been increasing use of microfilm in the form of transparent film cards, called microfiche, which contain several rows of images (corresponding to the length of a typical research report) and which can be handled and interfiled easily. Also important has been the use of "aperture cards," which are standard punched cards for data-processing machines in which have been embedded one or more microfilm frames. Aperture cards are key-punched with index codes describing the record they carry in microfilm; when the aperture card is selected in a search, the desired record is immediately available. Aperture cards are particularly attractive as a means of storing, retrieving and duplicating engineering drawings. They have been used on a large scale in the nation's missile and space programs.

The saving of storage space is an obvious objective of the use of microfilm, but it is one that should be approached with caution. Extremely high reductions are possible, but they are rarely economical because of the penalties in higher filming expense, higher projecting expense and the difficulty of handling tiny images. A recently adopted Federal standard for microfiche reflects the view that a reduction ratio of about 1 : 20 is the most economical with present technology. A record reduced by this factor takes up one four-hundredth of its original area.

Probably even more important than space saving to many users at present is the fact that records on microfilm can be duplicated more cheaply than the full-sized originals. Microfiche, which are distributed in quantity by Federal research organizations such as the Atomic Energy Commission and the National Aeronautics and Space Administration, cost only a few cents each to duplicate. To print and distribute full-size copies of the original reports could easily raise the unit cost to a dollar or more. The saving in weight that results from microfilming is also important wherever much transportation of records is required.

Just as computers can be developed to select and retrieve records that exist in the form of punched cards or as records stored in their magnetic memories, a variety of computer-like devices have been developed to select and retrieve records that exist in mediums other than punched paper or magnetic memory. Fully automatic systems have been developed for detecting index codes of various types (optical film reels, film cards, magnetic cards and paper cards) and for retrieving or displaying records on demand. The magnetic-tape-recording technique developed for recording television programs, called videotape, has also been adapted for storage and high-speed searching of suitably indexed graphical records.

The information-storage and -retrieval capacities available in various technologies are compared in the illustration on the facing page.

Progress in communication has had far-reaching effects on information storage and retrieval. The telephone, which we now take for granted, made it possible for people to get much quicker service from libraries where telephone requests were accepted because the need to visit the collection was eliminated. Until now the telephone request has had to go through a human intermediary at the library before a search could be initiated, and

CHARACTERISTICS	MICROFICHE	APERTURE CARDS	RECORDAK MIRACODE	IBM 1350 SYSTEM	AMPEX VIDEOFILE
NORMAL STORAGE CONFIGURATION	4" × 6" SHEET FILM IN PAPER JACKET	35-MM. FILM FRAME IN 3¼" × 7⅞" CARD	100-FOOT REEL 16-MM. FILM	1⅞" × 2¾" SHEET FILM IN PLASTIC CELL	7,200-FOOT REEL 2" WIDE
SIZE OF STORAGE CONTAINER	30 JACKETED SHEETS PER INCH OF FILE	125 CARDS PER INCH OF FILE	4" × 4" × 1"	32 SHEETS IN 1½" × 3" × 1" CELL	16" × 15" × 3"
STORAGE CAPACITY, 8½" × 11" DOCUMENTS (REDUCTION RATIO)	60 PER SHEET (20:1)	UP TO 8 PER CARD (24:1)	2,000 PER REEL (24:1)	256 PER CELL (24:1) MODULES OF 2,250 CELLS	250,000 PER REEL (1,280 LINES PER FRAME)
MAXIMUM DOCUMENTS PER CUBIC INCH	75	42	125	57	350
SEQUENTIAL SEARCH RATE	(MANUAL)	UP TO 33 CARDS PER SECOND	200 DOCUMENTS PER SECOND	(1,000 RANDOM ACCESSIONS PER HOUR)	1,050 DOCUMENTS PER SECOND

Storage mediums are here compared by storage density and other characteristics. Microfiche contain no provision for machine searching. Aperture cards are usually stored in large open bins called tub files. A tub file 26 inches wide and 16 feet long will hold about 50,000 cards. If the file is well organized, a hand search can retrieve a given card at random in less than 10 seconds. To extract the same card by machine search of a small batch of cards will often take much longer. The IBM system is the only one listed that provides automatic random access to a complete store of records. A module of 2,250 plastic cells, each containing 32 film chips, can store nearly 600,000 documents. The system can be expanded to seven modules, providing storage space for more than four million documents. No IBM systems are yet in use; a one-module system sells for $188,000.

the oral report of the search has had to be brief. The human intermediary can for many purposes now be eliminated in two different ways.

First, records can be transmitted rapidly and with increasing economy by automatic devices. Records that are already in machine-readable form can be transmitted easily over wires and microwave channels to printing devices, recording devices or computers. Records not in machine-readable form can be scanned by optical-electric devices and then transmitted, to be reconstituted at the receiving end by facsimile printers or television displays. Second, the capability of controlling the transmitting process, or even interacting with it, can be given to the human or the machine at the receiving end. Thus the individual can make use of a computer or operate scanning equipment from a remote location. With such developments the geographic boundaries of traditional information storage and retrieval systems are beginning to evaporate. In their place are beginning to emerge vast networks of compatible communication devices linking users with many specialized and overlapping collections.

Data-transmission costs are still sufficiently high, however, to keep the dissolution of traditional systems from becoming a runaway revolutionary process. And the competition of alternative means of satisfying the users' needs for information should not be ignored. As in the case of manual systems the compromise persists in automatic systems between the processes of reacting to immediate needs and of acting in anticipation of probable needs. Direct-access, on-line communication between the user and a computer memory is in the former category. In the latter are such things as specialized directories, indexes and alerting services (usually in the form of printed matter), which can be made available to potential users through more traditional channels of communication such as the mails and can often forestall the need for direct and expensive searching of machine memories. For example, many libraries that have been converting their catalogue records to machine-readable form in order to make it possible to search them to answer user requests are finding it desirable to publish these records in books (using the computer to control typesetting) and to distribute the book catalogues to their patrons. Numerous questions regarding holdings in the collection can then be answered by the user at his desk in seconds, without even the need for a telephone call, much less a computer search. Of course the cost of publishing book catalogues can be an argument against this policy where collections are growing so rapidly that catalogues must be revised frequently. There is no "best" solution except in a specific situation.

Another indexing procedure of growing significance is the publishing of records in machine-readable form. For example, the National Library of Medicine is now publishing monthly editions of magnetic tapes that contain the records of new acquisitions listed in *Index Medicus*. These tapes are mailed to a number of distant medical libraries that have access to compatible computer facilities. Special searches can then be made locally without any need for direct communication between the local user and the computer at the National Library of Medicine.

A major limitation in the use of machines for information storage and retrieval is their limited capacity for reading conventional printed text. Automatic print readers are not yet developed to the stage where they can read enough symbols with sufficient reliability at a sufficiently low cost to make them competitive with human transcription, except in special situations. Print readers can be used successfully in some applications where the nature and quality of the typography of the records to be read is under strict control, or where only a few symbols are to be recognized (such as the digits 0 through 9 in postal "ZIP" codes). To improve accuracy or increase symbol capacity or relax controls on input typography introduces decision-making problems that cannot be resolved without greatly complicating the equipment design.

Even when machine-readable records are somehow made available, however, the types of analysis that can be performed automatically are so far quite limited. Individual symbols can be made recognizable by storing a dictionary of symbol codes within the machine to compare with codes in the record being analyzed. Words can be recognized with fair success by giving the machine the capacity for determining boundaries such as spaces and hyphens. Small numbers of words supplied in search questions can be stored and used as templates in scanning text.

To give a machine the capacity for recognizing syllables so that it can hyphenate words when preparing columns of printed text is a major design problem. Instructing a machine to distinguish, say, a person's name from a geographic place name with good reliability is similarly difficult because of the need to bring large amounts of external knowledge to bear on the determination. And the problem of programming a machine to recognize synonymous words and phrases has scarcely been tackled. Different words and phrases are frequently synonymous only to a degree, depending on the context of the records in which they appear. Often words will have alternative—even opposite—meanings, depending on context. We are far from endowing machines with the capacity of the human intellect to associate ideas and to recognize underlying similarities in things expressed in different ways.

The difficulty of handling analytical problems has so far limited the use of mechanical techniques in information storage and retrieval work to applications that never required much analytical judgment on the part of the humans who formerly did the work. Savings in clerical activities have been great, and performance has been accelerated in such applications. But the human indexer, translator, evaluator and abstractor are still very much needed—more than ever in view of the increasing rate of production of new records. There is great need for machines to take over significant portions of the intellectual work. Faster, larger, cheaper computers are not the complete answer, although they will certainly be necessary. The major contribution will probably come from enlarged understanding of how human evaluations are made and from increased effort to design improved programs of instruction that will endow machines with analytical abilities simulating human abilities. In a real sense the problem is one of learning how to educate machines efficiently. In humans the education process takes decades and requires the accumulation of vast amounts of experience, all of which is imperfectly but quite effectively stored. There is no reason to expect that advances in computers and programs will soon yield systems with the equivalent of a college education, but the trend will be increasingly in that direction.

MARVIN L. MINSKY

Artificial Intelligence

Can a machine be made to exhibit intelligence?
An affirmative answer is indicated by programs that enable
a computer to do such things as set up goals, make plans,
consider hypotheses and recognize analogies.

At first the idea of an intelligent machine seems implausible. Can a computer really be intelligent? In this chapter I shall describe some programs that enable a computer to behave in ways that probably everyone would agree seem to show intelligence.

The machine achievements discussed here are remarkable in themselves, but even more interesting and significant than what the programs do accomplish are the methods they involve. They set up goals, make plans, consider hypotheses, recognize analogies and carry out various other intellectual activities. As I shall show by example, a profound change has taken place with the discovery that descriptions of thought processes can be turned into prescriptions for the design of machines or, what is the same thing, the design of programs.

The turning point came sharply in 1943 with the publication of three theoretical papers on what is now called cybernetics. Norbert Wiener, Arturo Rosenblueth and Julian H. Bigelow of the Massachusetts Institute of Technology suggested ways to build goals and purposes into machines; Warren S. McCulloch of the University of Illinois College of Medicine and Walter H. Pitts of M.I.T. showed how machines might use concepts of logic and abstraction, and K. J. W. Craik of the University of Cambridge proposed that machines could use models and analogies to solve problems. With these new foundations the use of psychological language for describing machines became a constructive and powerful tool. Such ideas remained in the realm of theoretical speculation, however, until the mid-1950's. By that time computers had reached a level of capacity and flexibility to permit the programming of processes with the required complexity.

In the summer of 1956 a group of investigators met at Dartmouth College to discuss the possibility of constructing genuinely intelligent machines. Among others, the group included Arthur L. Samuel of the International Business Machines Corporation, who had already written a program that played a good game of checkers and incorporated several techniques to improve its own play. Allen Newell, Clifford Shaw and Herbert A. Simon of the Rand Corporation had constructed a theorem-proving program and were well along in work on a "General Problem Solver," a program that administers a hierarchy of goal-seeking subprograms.

John McCarthy was working on a system to do "commonsense reasoning" and I was working on plans for a program to prove theorems in plane geometry. (I was hoping eventually to have the computer use analogical reasoning on diagrams.) After the conference the workers continued in a number of independent investigations. Newell and Simon built up a research group at the Carnegie Institute of Technology with the goal of developing models of human behavior. McCarthy and I built up a group at M.I.T. to make machines intelligent without particular concern with human behavior. (McCarthy is now at Stanford University.) Although the approaches of the various groups were different, it is significant that their studies have resulted in closely parallel results.

Work in this field of intelligent machines and the number of investigators increased rapidly; by 1963 the bibliography of relevant publications had grown to some 900 papers and books. I shall try to give the reader an impression of the state of the field by presenting some examples of what has been happening recently.

The general approach to creating a program that can solve difficult problems will first be illustrated by considering the game of checkers. This game exemplifies the fact that many problems can in principle be solved by trying all possibilities—in this case exploring all possible moves, all the opponent's possible replies, all the player's possible replies to the opponent's replies and so on. If this could be done, the player could see which move has the best chance of winning. In practice, however, this approach is out of the question, even for a computer; the tracking down of every possible line of play would involve some 10^{40} different board positions. (A similar analysis for the game of chess would call for some 10^{120} positions.) Most interesting problems present far too many possibilities for complete trial-and-error analysis. Hence one must discover rules that will try the most likely routes to a solution as early as possible.

Samuel's checker-playing program explores thousands of board positions but not millions. Instead of tracking down every possible line of play the program uses a partial analysis (a "static evaluation") of a relatively small number of carefully selected features of a board position—how many men there are on each side, how advanced they are and certain other simple relations. This incomplete analysis is not in itself adequate for choosing the best move for a player in a current position. By combining the partial analysis with a limited search for some of the consequences of the possible moves from the current position, however, the program selects its move as if on the basis of a much deeper analysis. The program contains a collection of rules for deciding when to continue the search and when to stop. When it stops, it assesses the merits of the "terminal" position in terms of the static evaluation. If the computer finds by this search that a given move leads to an advantage for the player in all the likely positions that may occur a few moves later, whatever the opponent does, it can select this move with confidence.

What is interesting and significant about such a program is not simply that it can use trial and error to solve problems. What makes for intelligent behavior is the collection of methods and techniques that select what is to be tried next, that size up the situation and choose a plausible (if not always good) move and use information gained in previous attempts to steer subsequent analysis in better directions. To be sure, the programs described below do use search, but in the examples we present the solutions were found among the first few attempts rather than after millions of attempts.

A program that makes such judgments about what is best to try next is termed heuristic. Our examples of heuristic programs demonstrate some capabilities similar in principle to those of the checkers program, and others that may be even more clearly recognized as ways of "thinking."

In developing a heuristic program one usually begins by programming some methods and techniques that can solve comparatively uncomplicated problems. To solve harder problems one might work directly to improve these basic methods, but it is much more profitable to try to extend the problem solver's general ability to bring a harder problem within reach by breaking it down into subproblems. The machine is provided with a program for a three-step process: (1) break down the problems into subproblems, keeping a record of the relations between these parts as part of the total problem, (2) solve the subproblems and (3) combine the results to form a solution to the problem as a whole. If a subproblem is still too hard, apply the procedure again. It has been found that the key to success in such a procedure often lies in finding a form of description for the problem situation (a descriptive "language") that makes it easy to break the problem down in a useful way.

Our next example of a heuristic program illustrates how descriptive languages can be used to enable a computer to employ analogical reasoning. The program was developed by Thomas Evans, a graduate student at M.I.T., as the basis for his doctoral thesis, and is the best example so far both of the use of descriptions and of how to handle analogies in a computer program.

The problem selected was the recognition of analogies between geometric figures. It was taken from a well-known test widely used for college-admission examinations because its level of difficulty is considered to require considerable intelligence. The general format is familiar: Given two figures bearing a certain relation to each other, find a similar relation between a third figure and one of five choices offered. The problem is usually written: "A is to B as C is to (D_1, D_2, D_3, D_4 or D_5?)" [see illustration on the facing page].

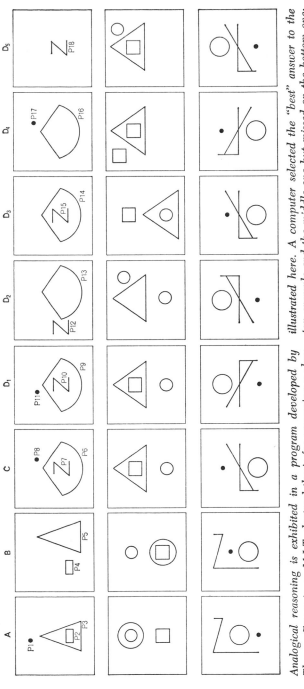

Analogical reasoning is exhibited in a program developed by Thomas Evans in an M.I.T. doctoral thesis for answering a class of problems frequently included in intelligence tests: "A is to B as C is to (D₁, D₂, D₃, D₄, or D₅?)." Three such problems are illustrated here. A computer selected the "best" answer to the top example and the middle one but missed on the bottom one; the program is weak in assessing relations among more than two objects. A typical solution is illustrated on pages 200 and 201.

The particularly attractive feature of this kind of problem as a test of machine intelligence is that it has no uniquely "correct" answer. Indeed, performance on such tests is not graded by any known rule but is judged on the basis of the selections of highly intelligent people on whom the test is tried.

Now, there is a common superstition that "a computer can solve a problem only when every step in the solution is clearly specified by the programmer." In a superficial sense the statement is true, but it is dangerously misleading if it is taken literally. Here we understood the basic concepts Evans wrote into the program, but until the program was completed and tested we had no idea of how the machine's level of performance would compare to the test scores of human subjects.

Evans began his work on the problem of comparing geometric figures by proposing a theory of the steps or processes the human brain might use in dealing with such a situation. His theory suggested a program of four steps that can be described in psychological terms. First, in comparing the features of the figures *A* and *B* one must select from various possibilities some way in which a description of *A* can be transformed into a description of *B*. This transformation defines certain relations between *A* and *B*. (For example, in the top problem in the illustration on page 197 a small rectangle is inside the triangle in the figure *A* and outside the triangle in the figure *B*.) There may be several such explanations "plausible" enough to be considered. Second, one looks for items or parts in *C* that correspond to parts in *A*. There may be several such "matches" worthy of consideration. Third, in each of the five figures offering answer choices one searches for features that may relate the figure to *C* in a way similar to the way in which the corresponding features in *B* are related to those in *A*. Wherever the correspondence, if any, is not perfect, one can make it more so by "weakening" the relation, which means accepting a modified, less detailed version of the relation. Fourth and last, one can select as the best answer the figure that required the least modification of relations in order to relate it to *C* as *B* is related to *A*.

This set of hypotheses became the framework of Evans' program. (I feel sure that rules or procedures of the same general character are involved in any kind of analogical reasoning.) His next problem was to translate this rather complex sketch of mental processes into a detailed program for the computer. To do so he had to develop what is certainly one of the most complex programs ever written. The technical device that made the translation possible was the LISP ("list-processor") programming language McCarthy had developed on the basis of earlier work by Newell, Simon and Shaw. This system provides many automatic services for manipulating expressions and complicated data structures. In particular it is a most convenient method of handling descriptions consisting of lists of items. And it makes it easy to write interlocked programs that can, for example, use one another as subprograms.

The input for a specific problem in Evans' program is in the form of lists of vertices, lines and curves describing the geometric figures. A subprogram analyzes this information, identifies the separate parts of the figure and reconstructs them in terms of points on a graph and the connecting lines. The steps and processes in the solution of a problem are given in some detail in the illustrations on pages 200 and 201.

Briefly, the program takes the following course: After receiving the descriptions of the figures (A, B, C and the five answer choices) it searches out topological and geometric relations between the parts in each picture (such as that one object is inside or to the left of or above another). It then identifies and lists similarities between pairs of pictures (A and B, A and C, C and D_1 and so on). The program proceeds to discover all the ways in which the parts of A and B can be matched up, and on the basis of this examination it develops a hypothesis about the relation of A to B (what was removed, added, moved or otherwise changed to transform one picture into the other). Next it considers correspondences between the parts of A and the parts of C. It goes on to look for matchings of the A-to-B kind between the parts in C and each of the D figures (the answer choices). When it finds something approaching a match that is consistent with its hypothesis of the relation between A and B, it proceeds to measure the degree of divergence of the C-to-D relation from A-to-B relation by stripping away the details of the A-to-B transformation one by one until both relations (A-to-B and C-to-D) are essentially alike. In this way it eventually identifies the D

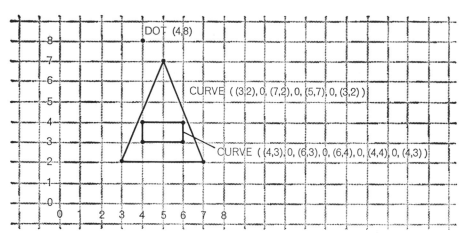

First step of the program describes the parts of each figure in terms of a coordinate system, as shown for A in the top problem on page 197. The triangle and rectangle are "curves" whose apexes are connected by lines of zero curvature, as indicated by the 0.

	RELATIONS WITHIN
(INSIDE (P_2,P_3), ABOVE (P_1,P_3), ABOVE (P_1,P_2)))	A
(LEFT (P_4,P_5)))	B
(INSIDE (P_7,P_6), ABOVE (P_8,P_6), ABOVE (P_8,P_7)))	C
(INSIDE (P_{10},P_9), ABOVE (P_{11},P_9), ABOVE (P_{11},P_{10})))	D_1
(LEFT (P_{12},P_{13})))	D_2
(INSIDE (P_{15},P_{14})))	D_3
(ABOVE (P_{17},P_{16})))	D_4
(NONE)	D_5

	SIMILARITIES BETWEEN
SIM $(P_2,P_4,0°)$ $(P_2,P_4,180°)$ $(P_3,P_5,0°)$	A AND B
SIM $(P_1,P_8,0°)$	A AND C
NIL	B AND C
SIM $(P_6,P_9,0°)$ $(P_7,P_{10},0°)$ $(P_7,P_{10},180°)$ $(P_8,P_{11},0°)$	C AND D_1
SIM $(P_6,P_{13},0°)$ $(P_7,P_{12},0°)$ $(P_7,P_{12},180°)$	C AND D_2
SIM $(P_6,P_{14},0°)$ $(P_7,P_{15},0°)$ $(P_7,P_{15},180°)$	C AND D_3
SIM $(P_6,P_{16},0°)$ $(P_8,P_{17},0°)$	C AND D_4
SIM $(P_7,P_{18},0°)$ $(P_7,P_{18},180°)$	C AND D_5
SIM $(P_1,P_{11},0°)$ $(P_1,P_{17},0°)$	A AND D_1 A AND D_4

Relations and similarities are discovered by the program. It notes, for example, that the rectangle (P_2) is inside the triangle (P_3), the dot (P_1) above both the triangle and the rectangle, and so on. Then it lists similarities between elements in different figures and notes whether or not the similarity persists if an element is rotated 180 degrees.

```
O      (REMOVE A1 ((ABOVE A1 A3) (ABOVE
O         A1 A2) (SIM OB3 A1 (((1.0 . 0.0) .
          (N.N))))))

       (MATCH A2 (((INSIDE A2 A3) (ABOVE
O         A1 A2) (SIM OB2 A2 (((1.0 . 0.0) .
          (N.N)))) . ((LEFT A2 A3) (SIM
          OB2 A2 (((1.0 . 0.0) . (N.N)) ((1.0 .
O         3.14) . (N.N)))) (SIMTRAN (((1.0 .
          0.0) . (N.N)) ((1.0 . 3.14) . (N.N)
          ))))))

O      (MATCH A3 (((INSIDE A2 A3) (ABOVE
          A1 A3) (SIM OB1 A3 (((1.0 . 0.0) .
O         (N.N)))) . ((LEFT A2 A3) (SIM
          OB1 . A3 (((1.0 . 0.0) . (N.N))))
          (SIMTRAN· (((1.0 . 0.0) . (N.N)·
O         ))))))
```

Hypothesis about how A is related to B is constructed by the program, which finds ways in which parts of the two figures can be matched. It lists elements removed, added or matched and the properties, relations and similarities associated with the element.

```
O      (REMOVE A1 ((ABOVE A1 A3) (ABOVE
          A1 A2) (SIM OB3 A1 (((1.0 . 0.0) ·
O         (N.N))))))

       (MATCH A2 (((INSIDE A2 A3) (ABOVE
O         A1 A2)) . ((LEFT A2 A3) (SIMTRAN
          (((1.0 . 0.0) . (N.N)) ((1.0 . 3.14) ·
          (N.N))))))

O      (MATCH A3 (((INSIDE A2 A3) (ABOVE
          A1 A3)) . ((LEFT A2 A3) (SIMTRAN
O         (((1.0 . 0.0) . (N.N)))))))
```

Program concludes, after trying matchings between C and each of the five D figures, that D₂ is the best answer. It does so by considering C-D matchings that are consistent with the A-B hypothesis. By removing details from the hypothesis until it fits the C-D matching, the program selects the C-D match least different from the A-B hypothesis.

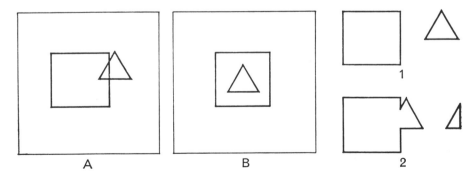

A   B   1   2

Reasoning power of the program is illustrated in a different example by its ability to resolve the overlapping objects in A into a rectangle and triangle (1) rather than the other pieces (2). It makes the distinction by observing that the objects at 1 occur in figure B whereas the others do not. That is, the program is capable of recognizing a "global" aspect of the situation.

figure that seems to come closest to a relation to *C* analogous to the *A* and *B* relation.

Evans' program is capable of solving problems considerably more complex or subtle than the one we have considered step by step. Among other things, in making decisions about the details of a picture it can take into account deductions from the situation as a whole [see bottom illustration on page 201].

No one has taken the trouble to make a detailed comparison of the machine's performance with that of human subjects on the same problems, but Evans' evidence suggests that the present program can score at about the 10th-grade level, and with certain improvements of the program that have already been proposed it should do even better. Evans' work on his program had to stop when he reached the limitations of the computer machinery available to him. His program could no longer fit in one piece into the core memory of the computer, and mainly for this reason it took several minutes to run each problem in the machine. With the very large memory just installed at M.I.T.'s Project MAC the program could be run in a few seconds. The new capacity will make possible further research on more sophisticated versions of such programs.

The Evans program is of course a single-minded affair: it can deal only with problems in geometrical analogy. Although its ability in this respect compares favorably with the ability of humans, in no other respect can it pretend to approach the scope or versatility of human intelligence. Yet in its limited way it does display qualities we usually think of as requiring "intuition," "taste" or other subjective operations of the mind. With his analysis of such operations and his clarification of their components in terms precise enough to express them symbolically and make them available for use by a machine, Evans laid a foundation for the further development (with less effort) of programs employing analogical reasoning.

Moreover, it is becoming clear that analogical reasoning itself can be an important tool for expanding artificial intelligence. I believe it will eventually be possible for programs, by resorting to analogical reasoning, to apply the experience they have gained from solving one kind of problem to the solution of quite different problems. Consider a situation in which a machine is presented with a problem that is too complicated for solution by any method it knows. Ordinarily to cope with such contingencies the computer would be programmed to split the problem into subproblems or subgoals, so that by solving these it can arrive at a solution to the main problem. In a difficult case, however, the machine may be unable to break the problem down or may become lost in a growing maze of irrelevant subgoals. If a machine is to be able to deal, then, with very hard problems, it must have some kind of planning ability—an ability to find a suitable strategy.

What does the rather imprecise word "planning" mean in this context? We can think of a definition in terms of machine operations that might be useful: (1) Replace the given problem by a similar but simpler one; (2) solve this analogous problem and remember the steps in its solution; (3) try to adapt the steps of the solution to solve the original problem. Newell and Simon have actually completed an experiment embodying a simple version of such a program. It seems to me that this area is one of the most important for research on making machine intelligence more versatile.

I should now like to give a third example of a program exhibiting intelligence. This program has to do with the handling of information written in the English language.

Since the beginnings of the evolution of modern computers it has been obvious that a computer could be a superb file clerk that would provide instant access to any of its information—provided that the files were totally and neatly organized and that the kinds of questions the computer was called on to answer could be completely programmed. But what if, as in real life, the information is scattered through the files and is expressed in various forms of human discourse? It is widely supposed that the handling of information of this informal character is beyond the capability of any machine.

Daniel Bobrow, for his doctoral research at M.I.T., attacked this problem directly: How could a computer be programmed to understand a limited range of ordinary English? For subject matter he chose statements of problems in high school algebra. The purely mathematical solution of these problems would be child's play for the computer, but Bobrow's main concern was to provide the computer with the ability to read the informal verbal statement of a problem and derive from that language the equations required to solve the problem. (This, and not solution of the equations, is what is hard for students too.)

The basic strategy of the program (which is named "Student") is this: The machine "reads in" the statement of the problem and tries to rewrite it as a number of simple sentences. Then it tries to convert each simple sentence into an equation. Finally it tries to solve the set of equations and present the required answer (converted back to a simple English sentence). Each of these steps in interpreting the meaning is done with the help of a library (stored in the core memory) that includes a dictionary, a variety of factual statements and several special-purpose programs for solving particular kinds of problems. To write the program for the machine Bobrow used the LISP programming language with some new extensions of his own and incorporated techniques that had been developed by Victor H. Yngve in earlier work on language at M.I.T.

The problems the machine has to face in interpreting the English statements are sometimes quite difficult. It may have to figure out the antecedent of a pronoun, recognize that two different phrases have the same meaning or discover that a necessary piece of information is missing. Bobrow's program is a model of informality. Its filing system is so loosely organized (although it is readily accessible) that new information can be added to the dictionary by dumping it in anywhere. Perhaps the program's most interesting technical aspect is the way it cuts across the linguist's formal distinction between syntax and semantics, thus avoiding problems that, it seems to me, have more hindered than helped most studies of language [see illustrations on pages 205 and 206].

The remarkable thing about Student is not so much that it understands English as that it shows a basic capacity for understanding anything at all. When it runs into difficulty, it asks usually pertinent questions. Sometimes it has to ask the person operating the computer, but often it resolves the difficulty by referring to the knowledge in its files. When, for instance, it meets a statement such as "Mary is twice as old as Ann was when Mary was as old as Ann is now," the program knows how to make the

```
(THE PROBLEM TO BE SOLVED IS)
(MARY IS TWICE AS OLD AS ANN WAS WHEN MARY WAS AS OLD AS ANN
IS NOW . IF MARY IS 24 YEARS OLD , HOW OLD IS ANN Q.)


(WITH MANDATORY SUBSTITUTIONS THE PROBLEM IS)
(MARY IS 2 TIMES AS OLD AS ANN WAS WHEN MARY WAS AS OLD AS
ANN IS NOW . IF MARY IS 24 YEARS OLD , WHAT IS ANN Q.)

(WITH WORDS TAGGED BY FUNCTION THE PROBLEM IS)
((MARY / PERSON) IS 2 (TIMES / OP 1) AS OLD AS (ANN / PERSON)
WAS WHEN (MARY / PERSON) WAS AS OLD AS (ANN / PERSON) IS NOW
(PERIOD / DLM) IF (MARY / PERSON) IS 24 YEARS OLD , (WHAT /
QWORD) IS (ANN / PERSON) (QMARK / DLM))


(THE SIMPLE SENTENCES ARE)

((MARY / PERSON) S AGE IS 2 (TIMES / OP 1) (ANN / PERSON) S
AGE G02521 YEARS AGO (PERIOD / DLM))

(G02521 YEARS AGO (MARY / PERSON) S AGE IS (ANN / PERSON) S
AGE NOW (PERIOD / DLM))

((MARY / PERSON) S AGE IS 24 (PERIOD / DLM))

((WHAT / QWORD) IS (ANN / PERSON) S AGE (QMARK / DLM))


(THE EQUATIONS TO BE SOLVED ARE)

(EQUAL G02522 ((ANN / PERSON) S AGE))

(EQUAL ((MARY / PERSON) S AGE) 24)

(EQUAL (PLUS ((MARY / PERSON) S AGE) (MINUS (G02521))) ((ANN
/ PERSON) S AGE))

(EQUAL ((MARY / PERSON) S AGE) (TIMES 2 (PLUS ((ANN / PERSON)
S AGE) (MINUS (G0252T)))))


(ANN S AGE IS  18)
```

"Student," an English-reading program created by Daniel Bobrow, solves algebra problems. As shown here, Student restates a problem, then analyzes the words in terms of its library of definitions and relations, sets up the proper equations and gives the solution. The machine invented the symbol G02521 for the X used in the text of this chapter.

○ (THE PROBLEM TO BE SOLVED IS)
(THE GAS CONSUMPTION OF MY CAR IS 15 MILES PER GALLON . THE
DISTANCE BETWEEN BOSTON AND NEW YORK IS 250 MILES . WHAT IS
○ THE NUMBER OF GALLONS OF GAS USED ON A TRIP BETWEEN NEW YORK
AND BOSTON Q.)

○ (THE EQUATIONS TO BE SOLVED ARE)

○ (EQUAL G02556 (NUMBER OF GALLONS OF GAS USED ON TRIP BETWEEN
NEW YORK AND BOSTON))

○ (EQUAL (DISTANCE BETWEEN BOSTON AND NEW YORK) (TIMES 250 (MILES)))

○ (EQUAL (GAS CONSUMPTION OF MY CAR) (QUOTIENT (TIMES 15 (MILES))
(TIMES 1 (GALLONS))))

○ THE EQUATIONS WERE INSUFFICIENT TO FIND A SOLUTION

○ (USING THE FOLLOWING KNOWN RELATIONSHIPS)
((EQUAL (DISTANCE) (TIMES (SPEED) (TIME))) (EQUAL (DISTANCE)
(TIMES (GAS CONSUMPTION) (NUMBER OF GALLONS OF GAS USED))))

○ (ASSUMING THAT)
((DISTANCE) IS EQUAL TO (DISTANCE BETWEEN BOSTON AND NEW YORK))

○ (ASSUMING THAT)
((GAS CONSUMPTION) IS EQUAL TO (GAS CONSUMPTION OF MY CAR))

○ (ASSUMING THAT)
((NUMBER OF GALLONS OF GAS USED) IS EQUAL TO (NUMBER OF GALLONS
OF GAS USED ON TRIP BETWEEN NEW YORK AND BOSTON))

○

○ (THE NUMBER OF GALLONS OF GAS USED ON A TRIP BETWEEN NEW YORK
AND BOSTON IS 16.66 GALLONS)

Momentarily stumped at finding unknowns for which it has no equations, Student makes a guess that two phrases describe the same thing and goes on to solve the problem.

○ (THE PROBLEM TO BE SOLVED IS)
(THE GROSS WEIGHT OF A SHIP IS 20000 TONS . IF ITS NET WEIGHT
○ IS 15000 TONS , WHAT IS THE WEIGHT OF THE SHIPS CARGO Q.)

○ THE EQUATIONS WERE INSUFFICIENT TO FIND A SOLUTION

○ TRYING POSSIBLE IDIOMS

○ (DO YOU KNOW ANY MORE RELATIONSHIPS AMONG THESE VARIABLES)

○ (GROSS WEIGHT OF SHIP)

○ (TONS)

○ (ITS NET WEIGHT)

○ (WEIGHT OF SHIPS CARGO)

○ yes
TELL ME

○ (the weight of a ships cargo is the difference between
the gross weight and the net weight)

○ THE EQUATIONS WERE INSUFFICIENT TO FIND A SOLUTION

○ (ASSUMING THAT)
((NET WEIGHT) IS EQUAL TO (ITS NET WEIGHT))

○ (ASSUMING THAT)
((GROSS WEIGHT) IS EQUAL TO (GROSS WEIGHT OF SHIP))

○ (THE WEIGHT OF THE SHIPS CARGO IS 5000 TONS)

Lacking information with which to solve a problem, Student asks for help. The operator (typing in lowercase letters) provides the needed relations but does not use the same words as the problem used, forcing literal-minded Student to make assumptions.

meaning of "was when" more precise by rewriting the statement as two simple sentences: "Mary is twice as old as Ann was X years ago. X years ago Mary was as old as Ann is now."

Bobrow's program can handle only a small part of the grammar of the English language, and its semantic dictionaries are quite limited. Yet even though it can make many kinds of mistakes within its linguistic limitations, it probably surpasses the average person in its ability to handle algebra problems stated verbally. Bobrow believes that, given a larger computer memory, he could make Student understand most of the problems that are presented in high school first-algebra textbooks.

As an example of another kind of intelligence programmed into a machine, a program developed by Lawrence G. Roberts as a doctoral thesis at M.I.T. endows a computer with some ability to analyze three-dimensional objects. In a single two-dimensional photograph of a solid object the program detects a number of the object's geometrical features. It uses these to form a description in terms of lines and then tries to analyze the figure as a composite of simpler building blocks (rectangular forms and prisms). Once the program has performed this analysis it can reconstruct the figure from any requested point of view, drawing in lines that were originally hidden and suppressing lines that should not appear in the new picture. The program employs some rather abstract symbolic reasoning [see illustration on page 208].

The exploration of machine intelligence has hardly begun. There have been about 30 experiments at the general level of those described here. Each investigator has had time to try out a few ideas; each program works only in a narrow problem area. How can we make the programs more versatile? It cannot be done simply by putting together a collection of old programs; they differ so much in their representation of objects and concepts that there could be no effective communication among them.

If we ask, "Why are the programs not more intelligent than they are?" a simple answer is that until recently resources—in people, time and computer capacity—have been quite limited. A number of the more careful and serious attempts have come close to their goal (usually after two or three years of work); others have been limited by core-memory capacity; still others

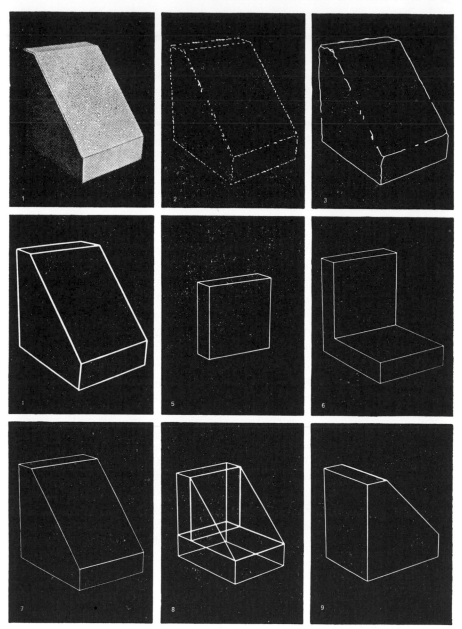

Abstract reasoning is required to complete a figure on the basis of partial information. A program developed by Lawrence G. Roberts at the Massachusetts Institute of Technology allows a computer to interpret a two-dimensional image and reconstruct the three-dimensional object. As shown in this sequence of illustrations, the computer scans a photograph of the object (1), displays its local features (2) and combines line segments (3) to prepare a complete line drawing (4). It accounts for the drawing as a compound of three-dimensional shapes (5–7) and draws in all the interior lines (8). Then it can display the structure from any point of view on request, in the process suppressing any lines that would be hidden (9).

encountered programming difficulties. A few projects have not progressed nearly as much as was hoped, notably projects in language translation and mathematical theorem-proving. Both cases, I think, represent premature attempts to handle complex formalisms without also somehow representing their meaning.

The problem of combining programs is more serious. Partly because of the very brief history of the field there is a shortage of well-developed ideas about systems for the communication of partial results between different programs, and for modifying programs already written to meet new conditions. Until this situation is improved it will remain hard to combine the results of separate research projects. Warren Teitelman of our laboratory has recently developed a programming system that may help in this regard; he has demonstrated it by re-creating in a matter of hours the results of some earlier programs that took weeks to write.

The questions people most often ask are: Can the programs learn through experience and thus improve themselves? Is this not the obvious path to making them intelligent? The answer to each is both yes and no. Even at this early stage the programs use many kinds of processes that might be called learning; they remember and use the methods that solved other problems; they adjust some of their internal characteristics for the best performance; they "associate" symbols that have been correlated in the past. No program today, however, can work any genuinely important change in its own basic structure. (A number of early experiments on "self-organizing" programs failed because of excessive reliance on random trial and error. A somewhat later attempt by the Carnegie Institute group to get their General Problem Solver to improve its descriptive ability was based on much sounder ideas; this project was left unfinished when it encountered difficulties in communication between programs, but it probably could be completed with the programming tools now available.)

In order for a program to improve itself substantially it would have to have at least a rudimentary understanding of its own problem-solving process and some ability to recognize an improvement when it found one. There is no inherent reason why this should be impossible for a machine. Given a model of its own workings, it could use its problem-solving power to work on the problem of self-improvement. The present programs are not quite smart enough for this purpose; they can only deal with the improvement of programs much simpler than themselves.

Once we have devised programs with a genuine capacity for self-improvement a rapid evolutionary process will begin. As the machine improves both itself and its model of itself, we shall begin to see all the phenomena associated with the terms "consciousness," "intuition" and "intelligence" itself. It is hard to say how close we are to this threshold, but once it is crossed the world will not be the same.

It is reasonable, I suppose, to be unconvinced by our examples and to be skeptical about whether machines will ever be intelligent. It is unreasonable, however, to think machines could become *nearly* as intelligent as we are and then stop, or to suppose we will always be able to compete with them in wit or wisdom. Whether or not we could retain some sort of control of the machines, assuming that we would want to, the nature of our activities and aspirations would be changed utterly by the presence on earth of intellectually superior beings.

The Authors

Steven Anson Coons
("The Uses of Computers in Technology") is associate professor of mechanical engineering at the Massachusetts Institute of Technology. He has been at M.I.T. since 1948; for eight years before that he was a design engineer with the Chance-Vought Aircraft Division of the United Aircraft Corporation, where he devised mathematical methods for describing the shape of airplane fuselages by computer. During the past six years Coons has been in charge of the computer-aided design group of the design division of the mechanical engineering department at M.I.T. He has written a number of papers on design and the geometry and description of shapes. He is also coauthor of a textbook on graphics.

F. J. Corbató. See R. M. Fano and F. J. Corbató

David C. Evans
("Computer Logic and Memory") is professor of electrical engineering and director of computer science at the University of Utah. He was graduated from that university in 1949 and obtained a Ph.D. in physics there four years later. From 1953 to 1962 he was director of engineering of the Bendix Corporation's computer division. He then spent three years as professor and associate director of the computing system at the University of California at Berkeley before going to the University of Utah. Evans describes his principal interest as "man-machine systems: the development of interactive computing systems for computer-aided problem-solving."

R. M. Fano and F. J. Corbató
("Time-sharing on Computers") are both at the Massachusetts Institute of Technology. Fano is professor of engineering and of electrical communications; he is also director of Project MAC, an M.I.T. undertaking concerned with research on advanced computer systems. Corbató is professor of electrical engineering and deputy director of the M.I.T. Computation Center. Fano, who was born in Italy and came to the U.S. in 1939, has been at M.I.T. since 1941; he obtained a

doctorate in electrical engineering there in 1947. He is the author of a book, *Transmission of Information,* and coauthor of two textbooks. Corbató received a bachelor's degree from the California Institute of Technology in 1950 and a doctorate in physics at M.I.T. in 1956. He has had much to do with the design and development of multiple-access computer systems. In his spare time he enjoys skiing and hiking. The work reported in the chapter by Fano and Corbató was supported by Project MAC, which is sponsored by the Advanced Research Projects Agency of the Department of Defense under a contract from the Office of Naval Research. The work reported in the chapters by Martin Greenberger and Marvin L. Minsky had the same sponsorship.

Martin Greenberger

("The Uses of Computers in Organizations") is associate professor at the Sloan School of Management at the Massachusetts Institute of Technology. He describes himself as "an applied mathematician by training with growing interests in economics and psychology" and says that his work with computers "sometimes enables me to bring these different affinities together." Greenberger received his bachelor's, master's and doctor's degrees in applied mathematics at Harvard University. Before joining the M.I.T. faculty in 1958 he formed and managed Applied Science Cambridge, a part of the International Business Machines Corporation that cooperated with M.I.T. in the establishment and operation of the M.I.T. Computation Center.

Ben-Ami Lipetz

("Information Storage and Retrieval") is head of the research department of the Yale University Library. He received a degree in mechanical engineering from Cornell University in 1948 and worked for two years as a technical editor at the Brookhaven National Laboratory. Becoming interested in the problems of managing research, he returned to Cornell for a Ph.D. in administration. Before going to Yale he worked on the development and management of specialized technical-information centers at the Battelle Memorial Institute and did research on machine-aided information systems at the Itek Corporation.

John McCarthy

("Information") is professor of computer science at Stanford University. A graduate of the California Institute of Technology in 1948, he received a Ph.D. in mathematics at Princeton University in 1951. Thereafter he taught at Princeton, Stanford, Dartmouth College and the Massachusetts Institute of Technology before taking up his present work. McCarthy's particular interests are computer programming languages, the theory of computation and artificial intelligence.

Marvin L. Minsky

("Artificial Intelligence") is professor of electrical engineering at the Massachusetts Institute of Technology. He is also director of the artificial-intelligence group there. Minsky was graduated from Harvard College in 1950 and received a doctorate in mathematics at Princeton University in 1954. For the next three years he was a member of the Society of Fellows at Harvard, working on neural theories of learning and on optical microscopy. He joined the mathematics department at M.I.T. in 1958 and transferred to the electrical engineering department in 1962.

Anthony G. Oettinger

("The Uses of Computers in Science") is professor of linguistics and of applied mathematics at Harvard University. Except for the academic year 1951–1952, when he was a Henry fellow at the University of Cambridge, he has been at Harvard since 1947; he obtained a bachelor's degree there in 1951 and a doctorate in 1954. He writes: "I have been at work in the linguistics area for a decade, but for the past two years I have shifted to the problems of the educational use of computers."

John R. Pierce

("The Transmission of Computer Data") is executive director of research in the communications sciences division of the Bell Telephone Laboratories. He joined Bell Laboratories in 1936, the year he received a Ph.D. in electrical engineering at the California Institute of Technology, where he had previously obtained bachelor's and master's degrees. Pierce's chief work has concerned microwave tubes and communication, including communication by means of satellites. He has published books on electron beams, traveling-wave tubes, speech and hearing, information theory and quantum electronics.

Christopher Strachey

("System Analysis and Programming") is leader of the Programming Research Group at the Computing Laboratory of the University of Oxford. He was graduated from the University of Cambridge in 1939 and spent the war years as a physicist working on the design of radar tubes. From 1944 to 1951 he taught in preparatory schools; since then he has been working with computers. "My chief interest," he writes, "is to develop the mathematical foundations of programming and, if possible, to simplify programming (particularly that of large "software" systems) and to make the design of machines more rational."

Patrick Suppes

("The Uses of Computers in Education") is professor of philosophy and of statistics at Stanford University and also chairman of the department of philosophy and director of the Institute for Mathematical Studies in the Social Sciences at the university. Suppes went to Stanford as an instructor in 1950, the year he obtained a Ph.D. at Columbia University. He did his undergraduate work at the University of Chicago, from which he was graduated in 1943. His extensive writings include two books, *Introduction to Logic* and *Axiomatic Set Theory*, three other books of which he is a coauthor, and several mathematics books for use in elementary schools. His particular interests are mathematical methods in the social sciences and the philosophy of science.

Ivan E. Sutherland

("Computer Inputs and Outputs") has just left the Department of Defense, where for two years he was director of information-processing techniques at the Advanced Research Projects Agency, to become associate professor of electrical engineering at Harvard University. He received a bachelor's degree in electrical engineering from the Carnegie Institute of Technology in 1959, a master's degree from the California Institute of Technology in 1960 and a Ph.D. at the Massachusetts Institute of Technology in 1963. In his doctoral thesis, entitled "Sketchpad," he set forth a program by which a computer could accept drawings directly from a user and help him to make and manipulate them. The concept has attracted wide attention. Sutherland writes: "Computers can store and calculate results from models of the physical world. I am excited by the prospect of being able to manipulate such models easily and observe them with great realism. Hence my work centers on human control of computers through keyboards, buttons, knobs, light pens, sound and so forth and on display of computer information through writing, pictures, sound and whatever else we are able to do."

Bibliography

Information

COMPUTERS AND THE WORLD OF THE FUTURE. Edited by Martin Greenberger. The M.I.T. Press, 1962.

CYBERNETICS: OR CONTROL AND COMMUNICATION IN THE ANIMAL AND THE MACHINE. Norbert Wiener. The M.I.T. Press, 1961.

Computer Logic and Memory

DESIGN OF TRANSISTORIZED CIRCUITS FOR DIGITAL COMPUTERS. Abraham I. Pressman. John F. Rider Publisher, Inc., 1959.

LOGICAL DESIGN OF DIGITAL COMPUTERS. Montgomery Phister. John Wiley & Sons, Inc., 1958.

SQUARE-LOOP FERRITE CIRCUITRY: STORAGE AND LOGIC TECHNIQUES. C. J. Quartly. Prentice-Hall, Inc., 1962.

SWITCHING CIRCUITS AND LOGICAL DESIGN. S. H. Caldwell. John Wiley & Sons, Inc., 1958.

THEORY AND DESIGN OF DIGITAL MACHINES. Thomas C. Bartee, Irwin L. Lebow and Irving S. Reed. McGraw-Hill Book Company, Inc., 1962.

Computer Inputs and Outputs

MACHINE PERCEPTION OF THREE-DIMENSIONAL SOLIDS. L. G. Roberts in *Lincoln Laboratory Technical Report No. 315.* Massachusetts Institute of Technology, 1963.

THE ON-LINE GRAPHICAL SPECIFICATION OF COMPUTER PROCEDURES. W. R. Sutherland in *Lincoln Laboratory Technical Report No. 405.* Massachusetts Institute of Technology, 1966.

SKETCHPAD, A MAN-MACHINE GRAPHICAL COMMUNICATION SYSTEM. I. E. Sutherland in *Lincoln Laboratory Technical Report No. 296.* Massachusetts Institute of Technology, 1963.

System Analysis and Programming

ADVANCES IN PROGRAMMING AND NON-NUMERICAL COMPUTATION. Edited by L. Fox. Pergamon Press, 1966.

A GUIDE TO FORTRAN PROGRAMMING. Daniel D. McCracken. John Wiley & Sons, Inc., 1961.

INTRODUCTION TO ALGOL. R. Baumann, M. Feliciano, F. L. Bauer and K. Samelson. Prentice-Hall, Inc., 1964.

PROGRAMMING COMPUTERS TO PLAY GAMES. Arthur L. Samuel in *Advances in Computers: Vol. I,* edited by Franz L. Alt. Academic Press Inc., 1960.

Time-Sharing on Computers

THE COMPATIBLE TIME-SHARING SYSTEM: A PROGRAMMER'S GUIDE. Edited by P. A. Crisman. The M.I.T. Press, 1965.

MAN-COMPUTER SYMBIOSIS. J. C. R. Licklider in *IRE Transactions on Human Factors in Electronics,* HFE-1, No. 1, pages 4–11; March, 1960.

SEGMENTATION AND THE DESIGN OF MULTIPROGRAMMED COMPUTER SYSTEMS. Jack B. Dennis in *Journal of the Association for Computing Machinery,* Vol. 12, No. 4, pages 589–602; October, 1965.

STRUCTURE OF THE MULTICS SUPERVISOR. F. J. Corbató, V. A. Vyssotsky and R. M. Graham in *AFIPS Conference Proceedings: Vol. 27, Part 1.* 1965 Fall Joint Computer Conference. Spartan Books, 1965.

TIME-SHARING ON A COMPUTER. Arthur L. Samuel in *New Scientist,* Vol. 26, No. 445, pages 583–587; May 27, 1965.

The Transmission of Computer Data

DATA TRANSMISSION—THE ART OF MOVING INFORMATION. Richard T. James in *IEEE Spectrum,* Vol. 2, No. 1, pages 65–83; January, 1965.

HANDBOOK OF AUTOMATION, COMPUTATION AND CONTROL. Edited by Eugene M. Grabbe, Simon Ramo and Dean E. Wooldridge. John Wiley & Sons, Inc., 1959.

MODERN COMMUNICATIONS. T. H. Crowley, G. G. Harris, S. E. Miller, J. R. Pierce and J. P. Runyon. Columbia University Press, 1962.

SYMBOLS, SIGNALS AND NOISE: THE NATURE AND PROCESS OF COMMUNICATION. J. R. Pierce. Harper & Row, Publishers, 1961.

The Uses of Computers in Science

AUTOMATIC PROCESSING OF NATURAL AND FORMAL LANGUAGES. A. G. Oettinger in *Proceedings of IFIPS Congress, 65: Vol. I,* edited by Wayne A. Kalenich. Spartan Books, 1965.

COMPUTER ANALYSIS OF NATURAL LANGUAGES. Susumo Kuno in *Mathematical Aspects of Computer Science,* edited by Jack Schwartz. American Mathematical Society [in press, 1966].

COMPUTER AUGMENTATION OF HUMAN REASONING. Edited by Margo A. Sass and William D. Wilkinson. Spartan Books, 1965.

COMPUTING PROBLEMS AND METHODS IN X-RAY CRYSTALLOGRAPHY. C. L. Coulter in *Advances in Computers: Vol. V*, edited by Franz L. Alt and M. Rubinoff. Academic Press Inc., 1964.

DATA COLLECTION AND REDUCTION FOR NUCLEAR PARTICLE TRACE DETECTORS. H. Gelernter in *Advances in Computers: Vol. VI*, edited by Franz L. Alt and M. Rubinoff. Academic Press Inc., 1965.

PLANS AND THE STRUCTURE OF BEHAVIOR. G. A. Miller, E. Galanter and K. H. Pribram. Holt, Rinehart & Winston, 1960.

A VISION OF TECHNOLOGY AND EDUCATION. A. G. Oettinger in *Communications of the ACM*, Vol. 9, No. 7, pages 487–490; July, 1966.

The Uses of Computers in Technology

AN APPROACH TO COMPUTER-AIDED PRELIMINARY SHIP DESIGN. M. L. Hamilton and A. D. Weiss in *Technical Memorandum 228*. Electronic Systems Laboratory, Massachusetts Institute of Technology, January, 1965.

AUGMENTING HUMAN INTELLECT: A CONCEPTUAL FRAMEWORK. Douglas C. Englebart. Stanford Research Institute, 1962.

THE GM DAC-1 SYSTEM, DESIGN AUGMENTED BY COMPUTERS. GMR-430 Computer Technology Department, General Motors Corporation Research Laboratories, Warren, Michigan, October 28, 1964.

SURFACES FOR COMPUTER-AIDED DESIGN OF SPACE FIGURES. Steven A. Coons in *Project MAC Technical Memorandum*. Massachusetts Institute of Technology, 1964.

The Uses of Computers in Organizations

ON-LINE COMPUTATION AND SIMULATION: THE OPS-3 SYSTEM. Martin Greenberger, Malcolm M. Jones, James H. Morris, Jr., and David N. Ness. The M.I.T. Press, 1962.

PROGRAMMING REAL-TIME COMPUTER SYSTEMS. James T. Martin. Prentice-Hall, Inc., 1965.

THE SHAPE OF AUTOMATION FOR MEN AND MANAGEMENT. Herbert A. Simon. Harper & Row, Publishers, 1965.

The Uses of Computers in Education

AUTOMATED EDUCATION HANDBOOK. Edited by E. Goodman. Automated Education Center, 1965.

THE COMPUTER IN AMERICAN EDUCATION. Edited by Donald D. Bushnell and Dwight W. Allen. John Wiley & Sons, Inc. [in press].

PROGRAMMED LEARNING AND COMPUTER-BASED INSTRUCTION. Edited by John E. Coulson. John Wiley & Sons, Inc., 1962.

Information Storage and Retrieval

INFORMATION STORAGE AND RETRIEVAL: TOOLS, ELEMENTS, THEORIES. Joseph Becker and Robert M. Hayes. John Wiley & Sons, Inc., 1963.

METHODS OF INFORMATION HANDLING. Charles P. Bourne. John Wiley & Sons, Inc., 1963.

Artificial Intelligence

COMPUTERS AND THOUGHT. Edited by Edward A. Feigenbaum and Julian Feldman. McGraw-Hill Book Company, Inc., 1963.

MATTER, MIND AND MODELS. M. L. Minsky in *Proceedings of IFIPS Congress, 65: Vol. I,* edited by W. A. Kalenich. Spartan Books, 1965.

SOME STUDIES IN MACHINE LEARNING USING THE GAME OF CHECKERS. A. L. Samuel in *IBM Journal of Research and Development,* Vol. 3, No. 3, pages 210–229; July, 1959.